British Foreign Policy and the National Interest

Also by Timothy Edmunds

OUT OF STEP: The Case for Change in the British Armed Forces (*with Anthony Forster*)

SECURITY SECTOR REFORM IN TRANSFORMING SOCIETIES: Croatia, Serbia and Montenegro

DEFENCE TRANSFORMATION IN EUROPE: Evolving Military Roles (*editor with Marjan Malešič*)

CIVIL-MILITARY RELATIONS IN POSTCOMMUNIST EUROPE: Reviewing the Transition (*editor with Andrew Cottey and Anthony Forster*)

DEFENCE REFORM IN CROATIA AND SERBIA-MONTENEGRO

TOWARDS SECURITY SECTOR REFORM IN POST-COLD WAR EUROPE: A Framework for Assessment (*editor with Wilhelm Germann*)

SOLDIERS AND SOCIETIES IN POSTCOMMUNIST EUROPE: Legitimacy and Change (*editor with Anthony Forster and Andrew Cottey*)

THE CHALLENGE OF MILITARY REFORM IN POSTCOMMUNIST EUROPE: Building Professional Armed Forces (*editor with Anthony Forster and Andrew Cottey*)

Also by Jamie Gaskarth

BRITISH FOREIGN POLICY: Crises, Conflicts and Future Challenges

BRITISH FOREIGN POLICY: The New Labour Years

Also by Robin Porter

FROM MAO TO MARKET: China Reconfigured

HONG KONG IN TRANSITION: The Handover Years (*editor with Robert Ash, Peter Ferdinand and Brian Hook*)

HONG KONG IN TRANSITION: One Country, Two Systems (*editor with Robert Ash, Peter Ferdinand and Brian Hook*)

INDUSTRIAL REFORMERS IN REPUBLICAN CHINA

MANAGEMENT ISSUES IN CHINA, Volume 1: Domestic Enterprises (*editor with David Brown*)

REPORTING THE NEWS FROM CHINA (*editor*)

THE CHINA BUSINESS GUIDE (*editor with Mandi Robinson*)

British Foreign Policy and the National Interest
Identity, Strategy and Security

Edited by

Timothy Edmunds
Professor of International Security and Director of the Global Insecurities Centre, University of Bristol, UK

Jamie Gaskarth
Associate Professor of International Relations, School of Government, Plymouth University, UK, and Head of the British Foreign Policy Working Group, British International Studies Association

Robin Porter
Visiting Professor, University of Bristol, UK; FCO retired

Editorial matter, introduction and selection © Timothy Edmunds, Jamie Gaskarth and Robin Porter 2014
Individual chapters © Respective authors 2014

All rights reserved. No reproduction, copy or transmission of this publication may be made without written permission.

No portion of this publication may be reproduced, copied or transmitted save with written permission or in accordance with the provisions of the Copyright, Designs and Patents Act 1988, or under the terms of any licence permitting limited copying issued by the Copyright Licensing Agency, Saffron House, 6–10 Kirby Street, London EC1N 8TS.

Any person who does any unauthorized act in relation to this publication may be liable to criminal prosecution and civil claims for damages.

The authors have asserted their rights to be identified as the authors of this work in accordance with the Copyright, Designs and Patents Act 1988.

First published 2014 by
PALGRAVE MACMILLAN

Palgrave Macmillan in the UK is an imprint of Macmillan Publishers Limited, registered in England, company number 785998, of Houndmills, Basingstoke, Hampshire RG21 6XS.

Palgrave Macmillan in the US is a division of St Martin's Press LLC, 175 Fifth Avenue, New York, NY 10010.

Palgrave Macmillan is the global academic imprint of the above companies and has companies and representatives throughout the world.

Palgrave® and Macmillan® are registered trademarks in the United States, the United Kingdom, Europe and other countries.

ISBN 978–1–137–39234–3

This book is printed on paper suitable for recycling and made from fully managed and sustained forest sources. Logging, pulping and manufacturing processes are expected to conform to the environmental regulations of the country of origin.

A catalogue record for this book is available from the British Library.

Library of Congress Cataloging-in-Publication Data
British foreign policy and the national interest : identity, strategy and
  security / [edited by] Timothy Edmunds (professor of International
  Security, and director of the Global Insecurities Centre, University of
  Bristol, UK), Jamie Gaskarth (associate professor, University of Plymouth,
  UK, and head, British Foreign Policy Working Group, British International
  Studies Association), Robin Porter (visiting professor, University of
  Bristol, UK).
    pages cm
Includes bibliographical references.
ISBN 978–1–137–39234–3 (hardback)
  1. Great Britain—Foreign relations—21st century. 2. National
interest—Great Britain. 3. Group identity—Political aspects—
Great Britain. 4. Strategic planning—Great Britain. 5. Strategy.
6. National security—Great Britain. 7. Great Britain—Military
policy. I. Edmunds, Timothy. II. Gaskarth, Jamie, 1976–
III. Porter, Robin.
JZ1572.B75 2014
327.41—dc23   2014025269

Contents

List of Figures	vii
Acknowledgements	viii
Notes on Contributors	ix

1 Introduction   1
Jamie Gaskarth, Robin Porter and Timothy Edmunds

Part I   Britain in the World

2 The Uncertain Merger of Values and Interests in UK Foreign Policy   23
Jonathan Gilmore

3 The National Interest and Britain's Role in the World   42
Jamie Gaskarth

4 National Interest and the Falklands War   66
Helen Parr

Part II   Whose National Interest?

5 A Citizen's View of 'National Interest'   85
Nick Ritchie

6 Critical Perspectives on the Concept of the 'National Interest': American Imperialism, British Foreign Policy and the Middle East   102
David Wearing

7 Why America?   120
Robin Porter

Part III   Strategy and Planning

8 Organising for British National Strategy   137
Alexander Evans

9   UK Nuclear Interests: Security, Resilience and Trident   155
Benoît Pelopidas and Jutta Weldes

10   Complexity, Strategy and the National Interest   171
Timothy Edmunds

11   National Interest and Strategy: An Ecologically Grounded Analysis   188
Max Taylor

12   Britain's Strategic Culture in Context: A Typology of National Security Strategies   205
Tim Oliver and Austin Knuppe

Conclusion: A Return to the National Interest?   225
Timothy Edmunds, Jamie Gaskarth and Robin Porter

Bibliography   235

Index   261

Figures

3.1	Cycle of role generation	44
3.2	Sample role orientation of 'influential actor'	47
3.3	Role orientation of isolate	51
3.4	Role orientation of regional partner	53
3.5	Role orientation of influential (rule of law state)	57
3.6	Role orientation of thought leader	59
3.7	Role orientation of opportunist-interventionist	61
3.8	Role orientation of great power	63
9.1	From 'Fact sheet 2: National security risk assessment'	159

Acknowledgements

The editors wish to acknowledge the help of all who, through their advice and assistance, have made this project possible. In particular they would like to thank Chatham House for providing the venue at which the conference on which this volume is based took place, the University of Bristol and its Global Insecurities Centre for sponsoring the project and providing financial and practical support throughout, the British International Studies Association (BISA) and its British Foreign Policy Working Group for taking the project under its wing and providing financial support, Plymouth University for its encouragement, and staff at Palgrave for the care and attention they have shown in bringing this volume to fruition.

The editors also wish to acknowledge the interest taken in this project by the Foreign and Commonwealth Office (FCO), and express their gratitude to the FCO for permission to include the chapter by Alexander Evans. The opinions expressed in this book, however, are the sole responsibility of the individual authors concerned. Acknowledgement is also gratefully made to the journal *International Affairs* for permission to use material first published in its pages, as indicated in the text. Finally, Robin Porter would like to acknowledge the role of his own mentor, the late former Vice Principal H. Noel Fieldhouse of McGill University, who as a British diplomat accompanied Harold Nicholson to Versailles in 1919; to him he owes a lifelong fascination for British diplomacy.

Contributors

Editors

Timothy Edmunds is Professor of International Security and Director of the Global Insecurities Centre at the University of Bristol. He has written extensively on issues of civil–military relations, strategy making and security policy in the post-communist region, in the Western Balkans and most recently in the UK. His work emphasises the normative and contested nature of these processes. In so doing, it highlights the ways in which externally derived, often generic, models of reform can be in tension with local political circumstance, and the manner in which local actors respond to these tensions. He is the published author of three books on these themes, alongside six co-edited volumes and numerous book chapters and articles in peer review journals.

Jamie Gaskarth is Associate Professor in the School of Government at Plymouth University, a trustee of the British International Studies Association and Convenor of the BISA British Foreign Policy Working Group. He is the author of *British Foreign Policy* (2013) and *British Foreign Policy: The New Labour Years* (2011), and has had articles published in the *European Journal of International Relations*, *International Affairs*, *Review of International Studies* and *Foreign Policy Analysis*, among other journals. He has been awarded grants from the British Academy and ESRC and has worked closely with the FCO, organising workshops on British foreign policy strategy.

Robin Porter is a China specialist and former diplomat, and currently Visiting Professor in the School of Sociology, Politics and International Studies at the University of Bristol. He is currently interested in concepts of national interest as they inform decision-making in British foreign policy, and in particular as they relate to joint action with the US. He has also recently undertaken research for the European Commission into developments in science and technology, sustainability and innovation in China and their implications for the EU. His most recent book is *From Mao to Market: China Reconfigured* (2011).

Contributors

Alexander Evans is a visiting senior research fellow at King's College London. He is a former Henry Kissinger Chair in Foreign Policy at the Library of Congress, and was a senior fellow at Yale University and a Gwilym Gibbon fellow at Nuffield College, Oxford. A senior member of the British diplomatic service, he has been posted to New Delhi, Islamabad and Washington (where he was a senior advisor to the late ambassador Richard Holbrooke at the US Department of State). In January 2013 he was appointed Coordinator of the UN Al Qaida/Taliban Monitoring Team by UN Secretary General Ban Ki-moon.

Jonathan Gilmore is Senior Lecturer in Politics and International Relations at Kingston University. His research agenda centres on the practice of cosmopolitan ethics in foreign policy, specifically in examining the ways in which militaries are adapting to undertake the new roles required in stabilisation, multidimensional peacekeeping and operations associated with the Responsibility to Protect. He recently published 'A Kinder, Gentler Counter-Terrorism: Counterinsurgency, Human Security and the War on Terror' (*Security Dialogue*, 42: 1, 2011) and is currently writing a book, *The Cosmopolitan Military: Armed Force and Armed Conflict and the Protection of Human Security in the 21st Century*.

Austin Knuppe is a postgraduate student in international relations and political methodology at Ohio State University. He has been a Robert Bosch fellow working at the German Federal Ministry of Defense in Berlin, and a visiting fellow at the Stiftung Wissenschaft und Politik. He has a master's degree from the University of Chicago and a BA from Calvin College.

Tim Oliver is a transatlantic post-doctoral fellow for International Relations and Security. He has worked at the Stiftung Wissenschaft und Politik (Berlin), the School of Advanced International Relations (SAIS) Center for Transatlantic Relations at Johns Hopkins (Washington DC), RAND Corporation (Washington DC), the House of Lords and the European parliament. He has taught at the London School of Economics (LSE), University College London and the Royal Military Academy Sandhurst. He was educated at the University of Liverpool and the LSE.

Helen Parr is Senior Lecturer in International Relations at Keele University. She has published on British and French policies towards European integration, and also nuclear weaponry in the 1960s and early 1970s. She is currently working on the politics, experiences and aftermaths of the 1982 Falklands War.

Benoît Pelopidas is Lecturer in International Relations at the Global Insecurities Centre, University of Bristol, and an affiliate of the Center for International Security and Cooperation, Stanford University. He has been awarded two international prizes, and his publications include a co-authored book, published in three languages, and scholarly articles in English and French about experts, nuclear weapons history and policy.

Nick Ritchie is Lecturer in International Security at the Department of Politics, University of York. His current research focuses on UK nuclear weapons policy and national security. He previously worked as a research fellow at the Department of Peace Studies, University of Bradford, and as a researcher on international security issues at the Oxford Research Group.

Max Taylor was until retirement Professor in International Relations at the University of St Andrews, and Director of the Centre for the Study of Terrorism and Political Violence. Prior to that, he was Professor of Applied Psychology and Head of the Department of Applied Psychology at University College Cork, Ireland. He is a legal and forensic psychologist with wide international experience of research and consultancy in the area of terrorism, terrorist behaviour and internet crime. He is currently Editor of the journal *Terrorism and Political Violence*, and Visiting Professor at the Department of Security and Crime Sciences, University College London.

David Wearing is a PhD candidate at the University of London's School of Oriental and African Studies. He is researching Britain's relationship with Saudi Arabia and the Gulf states from the end of the Cold War.

Jutta Weldes is Professor of International Relations at the University of Bristol. She currently researches everyday insecurity and everyday security practices/practitioners, US foreign policy (Cold War and after, Cuban missile crisis), and the intersections of popular culture and world politics, and gender and world politics. Her most recent publication is 'The Evolution of International Security Studies and the Everyday: Suggestions from the Buffyverse', with Christina Rowley, in *Security Dialogue* (2012).

1
Introduction

Jamie Gaskarth, Robin Porter and Timothy Edmunds

Is the idea of a 'national interest' still relevant to British foreign policymaking? If so, how should it be defined and what policies should the UK government adopt to advance it? These are questions that have achieved a new salience in contemporary debates on British foreign policy. There are a number of reasons for this. The most prominent is Britain's propensity to use force against other states in the last two decades. Interventions against the Federal Yugoslav Republic (FYR) Serbia, Iraq, Afghanistan and Libya, and the call for action over Syria's civil war, divided domestic opinion and attracted criticism (Burall, Donnelly and Weir 2006; Bailey, Iron and Strachan 2013; Reifler et al. 2014). In addition, the global financial crisis of 2007–2008 led to calls for a scaling back of UK commitments abroad, reduction of aid spending and reappraisal of Britain's place in the world (Hall 2013; Foreman 2013; Hutton 2009). The 2014 referendum on Scottish independence and the proposal to have one on British membership of the European Union (EU) have raised questions over British identity and future defence and foreign policy (Oliver 2013; Whitman 2012; Scotland Institute 2013). Meanwhile, within the policy community, there has been concern over the manner in which foreign policy is made, with numerous commentators suggesting a lack of strategic thinking at the heart of government (Strachan 2005, 2009; Cornish and Dorman 2009; Newton, Colley and Sharpe 2010; P. Porter 2010).

This call to self-consciously rationalise British foreign policy and consider whose interests it is designed to serve arguably represents a break from the trend of much of the second half of the twentieth century. Processes including interdependence, globalisation, the nuclear peace and rapidly advancing digital and computer technology seemed to render the national interest obsolete. The world was becoming far more interconnected. As a result, political communities such as states – the main institutional locus of understanding for national interest discussion – were of declining significance. It became a mantra of foreign policy speeches and texts that national interests were now global interests and vice versa (Cook 1997; Blair 2006; Hain 2001). Interstate war between great powers was now a thing of the past and the end of the Cold War removed the final state threat to the British mainland. Thus, foreign policymaking ceased to involve the kind of existential calculations associated with the national interest. Instead, the leviathan of the state was left to swat away the flies of terrorism and transnational crime, or engage in 'wars of choice' in distant lands in pursuit of diffuse goals that would supposedly advance global public goods.

However, as Britain's military operations became financially burdensome and military casualties mounted up, the public started to question their utility. How were all these uses of force in the interests of UK citizens? The government could not offer a coherent answer. In Iraq, the intervention was designed to disarm Saddam Hussein's regime of weapons, which it was soon found not to possess. Moreover, senior security personnel acknowledged that this action had increased the terrorist threat to the mainland (BBC 2010). In Afghanistan, the various interventions by UK forces had disparate and at times conflicting aims, from counter-terrorism to counter-narcotics efforts and then counter-insurgency. A discourse of humanitarianism, which had arisen in the 1990s, began to merge uneasily in government rhetoric with that of hard security imperatives. The result was a confused mix of policies advancing the goals of different communities.

Few came out of these debates with any credit. A generation of politicians with no personal experience of conflict deployed troops with negligible discussion of the political goals being sought, whether they were achievable and what strategy would be most effective at achieving them. Military chiefs seized the opportunity to highlight their continued relevance in the absence of a direct interstate threat, pushing for expensive equipment programmes and updating technology on the battlefield via urgent operational requirement orders. When their tactics failed in Basra and Helmand province, they turned on their political masters and, as generals are apt to do in instances of military failure, blamed a lack of political commitment at home (Norton-Taylor 2010). Academics contributed to this catalogue of errors, either by feeding a simplistic narrative of civilisational clashes or by offering criticism after the fact instead of constructive advice prior to action. Furthermore, far from retreating from interventionism to reconsider how effective this has been in promoting the British national interest, the coalition government has engaged in military action in Libya in 2011, assisted the French intervention in Mali in 2012 and sought parliamentary approval for strikes against the Syrian government in 2013. In each case, Britain's self-interest in acting was not articulated with any rigour.

Meanwhile, important policy dilemmas, such as Britain's relationship with the EU; the shifts in relative economic and political power in relation to rising powers, especially China; and the crises of capitalism in 1997–1999 and 2007–2008 were marginalised. In the case of the EU, a vital strategic interest has continued to be subject to tabloid distortions and immature political posturing (Daddow 2012). At the same time, the UK's relationship with the US, so long a cornerstone of Britain's strategic thinking, has led to a series of policy commitments that seem to have an increasingly tenuous link to the actual wants or needs of the British public (Wallace and Phillips 2009). Indeed, in the last decade British policymakers have often found themselves describing the US as an indispensable partner whilst pursing foreign policies, on climate change and international criminal justice (for instance), that were actively opposed by US administrations (Gaskarth 2011).

In short, avoiding hard thinking about how British foreign policy promotes national interests has, we assert, had a negative effect on the logic and quality of policy outputs. Talk of the decline of the state ignores the fact that governmental actors are still acting on behalf of political communities labelled states. In doing so, they will often justify their behaviour by invoking the national interest, albeit in an uncritical or unreflexive fashion. It is therefore imperative that such claims are subject to proper analysis. British foreign policy critics need to question these assertions so that policymakers are held accountable to the citizens they represent and policy inefficiencies or failures can be highlighted.

This book derives from a project which sought to do just that by resurrecting the idea of the national interest and demonstrating its continuing relevance to policy discussions. It brings together academics and recent practitioners to address many of the questions raised above, namely: what are the UK's national interests and how should they be prioritised? How do British values inform national interests? Are national interests and global goods always compatible? What are the best ways to achieve those interests? Whose interests does British foreign policy serve? Does it make sense to identify a unified national interest and how would this be constituted? The answers to these questions may not be uniform, indeed, the editors have deliberately assembled an eclectic mix of authors from a range of different political and theoretical viewpoints to demonstrate the breadth of ways in which it is possible to engage with the concept. Yet, all utilise it to shed light on some aspect of British foreign policy and this arguably demonstrates its continuing importance in justifying or critiquing foreign policy.

To give a context to this discussion, this introduction proceeds with a summary of the main academic and policy debates over the concept of the national interest. It does not aim to be exhaustive but instead seeks to provide a platform for the later specific analyses relating to the British case.

National interest: The academic debate

The idea that states have interests is as old as diplomacy itself. Great statesmen of the past, such as George Washington in his farewell address, or Lord Palmerston in his speech on the Polish question in 1848, would invoke the idea of abiding interests as central to rationalising policy decisions. In one of the most famous axioms of foreign policy discourse, Palmerston declared: 'We have no eternal allies, and we have no perpetual enemies. Our interests are eternal and perpetual, and those interests it is our duty to follow' (Palmerston 1848, p. 142). For interests to be 'eternal', they would have to transcend particular times and circumstances. Perhaps as a result, policymakers would often not define them in any degree of detail.

Writing a century later, realist scholars such as Hans Morgenthau tried to introduce more specificity to the idea by reducing the national interest to the fundamental goals of survival and territorial integrity (Morgenthau 1948). These constitute the 'national' interest in that most citizens of a particular state are assumed to have a desire to ensure the continuance of their community and maintain a measure of safety from external threats. Safety and survival can only be achieved through a sophisticated awareness of a state's relative power compared to other states, and capacity to exploit any advantages, and so Morgenthau defined interest in terms of power (Morgenthau 1948, 1950, 1952).

There is a curious irony in Britain's more recent failure to articulate its national interest, as many classical realists used it as a case study of a state that had ensured its survival and physical integrity by having a keen grasp of where its interests lay. Britain did so in the nineteenth century by paying close attention to the balance of power on the European continent and placing its weight with whatever faction was weaker to ensure no one state or alliance could achieve dominance. Realists often write approvingly of the 'unsentimental' manner in which British statesmen shifted alliances according to their calculation of the strategic balance in Europe in this era (Kissinger 1994, pp. 95–96). Such a policy was defended on moral grounds as it was seen as providing a basis to judge individual actions (did it further the interest of the state – and thereby the state's citizens?) and also introduced a common standard across state interactions. If all states pursued their interests defined in terms of power, then they could understand each other better and so hopefully avoid misunderstandings that might lead to conflict.

However, the realist interpretation of national interest attracted much criticism, both at the time, and subsequently. In the first place, 'survival' and 'territorial integrity' are contested concepts. It is not always clear what level of threat has to exist to constitute an existential threat; or what it is that statespeople are seeking to preserve (George 2006, pp. 9–10). Secondly, the survival of the state in its existing territorial space is not a universal goal of statespeople. Some states have voluntarily, and relatively peacefully, dissolved their political communities in recent years – the Soviet Union and Czechoslovakia being prominent examples. In each case, the statesmen who managed these changes are seen as paragons of leadership. Moreover, other states have shifted their territorial make-up and so the simple continuity of borders cannot be an irreducible aim. The willingness to grant Scotland a vote on independence, noted above, is but one recent example for the UK. Obversely, E.H. Carr suggested in *The Twenty Years Crisis* that not all statespeople wish to maintain the status quo (Carr 1939). Those with a grievance, ideological bent, or both, have been willing to risk their own state's survival, from Adolf Hitler to Fidel Castro.

A further point of critique has been over whether a unified national interest is possible or even desirable. In the view of Ernst Haas, 'the pluralistic nature of western societies' means that 'there is no unified, immutable and stable conception of the national interest'; rather, there is only 'an amalgam of varying policy motivations which tend to pass for a "national" interest as long as the groups holding these opinions continue to rule' (Haas 1953, pp. 382–383). Special interest groups within states have long been accused of working against the good of the community as a whole in the foreign policy realm. In 1858, John Bright described the pursuit of the balance of power in Europe as 'a gigantic system of out-door relief for the aristocracy of Great Britain' (Bright 1858, p. 192). More recently, a flurry of articles on the national interest in the US bemoaned the influence of 'subnational commercial interests and transnational and non-national ethnic interests' that were seen as having 'come to dominate foreign policy' (Huntington 1997, p. 29). For

Joseph Nye, 'The result is a narrow definition of the US national interest that often alienates other countries' (2002, p. 234).

Furthermore, divisions were apparent within realism over the desirability of privileging one, universalised conception of the national interest at the expense of wider ethical claims (Rice 2008, pp. 276–280). On the one hand, Morgenthau saw a moral content to the link between a statesperson, the national interest and the citizens they represent. On the other hand, Reinhold Niebuhr sought to resist the notion that self-interested actions should be imbued with moralism since this might lead to the justification of relationships of domination/subordination as divinely ordained (Niebuhr 1953; Good 1960, p. 598). Pin-Fat has noted that following Morgenthau's logic might lead us to universalise the particular values of any one state, as if they were moral laws of the universe (Pin-Fat 2005, p. 234). This is the kind of thing that totalitarian ideologies sought to do in the mid-twentieth century – with appallingly destructive results. In contrast to Morgenthau's view that 'As long as the world is politically organised into nations, the national interest is indeed the last word in world politics' (Morgenthau 1952, pp. 972–973), Niebuhr saw more of a dialectic between self-interest and global public goods, in which 'It would be fatal for the security of the nation if some loyalties beyond its interests were not operative in its moral life to prevent the national interest from being conceived in too narrow and self-defeating terms' (as cited in Good 1960, p. 605). Similarly, Arnold Wolfers saw both possession goals, of a narrowly self-interested nature, and milieu goals relating to the maintenance of a wider international society, as fundamental aspects of foreign policymaking (Wolfers 1962).

The mid-twentieth century debates on the national interest thus threw up a series of dilemmas, such as: whether the national interest can be reduced to a few criteria; how far it could represent the whole (or even a majority) of the wants and needs of a state's citizenry; the extent to which statespeople had to consider the interests of peoples outside their own community; and whether self-interest could, on its own, be a morally defensible rationale for foreign policymaking.

Following this initial flourishing of academic discussion, scholars' attention to the national interest waxed and waned in subsequent decades. For some, such as the prominent foreign policy analysts James Rosenau and Steve Smith, the term was so vague as to effectively mean whatever policymakers wanted it to mean (Weldes 1996). Any lingering importance it continued to have resided in its ability to mobilise and justify political action (Weldes 1996, p. 225). This performative aspect of national interest means that it can continue to be relevant to foreign policy analysis – since it exposes how policymakers justify their behaviour – but makes it less useful as a potential guide for policymakers trying to choose between different courses of action, given its conceptual fuzziness (Williams 2012, p. 7).

An important contribution to this discussion, which is relevant to chapters in this book by Ritchie and Wearing, emerged in a fascinating article by Friedrich Kratochwil in which he compared the concept of national interest with that of the public interest (1982). Taking issue with the tendency to essentialise national interest to one criteria (a 'platonic fallacy' according to Kratochwil), or to list certain interests supposed to constitute it, Kratochwil sees the idea's main usefulness in encouraging public deliberation over the common goods that national interest is designed to deliver. In contrast to the national interest's external focus, the notion of the public interest is used to debate and gain support for policies designed to promote the 'common weal (salus publica)' internally (Kratochwil 1982, p. 4). This is problematic since it seems to assume that a common interest can be identified that suits the community as a whole. In reality, the costs and benefits of policymaking will be unevenly distributed. Nevertheless, as Kratochwil notes: 'one needs criteria to weigh evidence offered in support of public interest claims. This might not enable us to decide once and for all the real public interest, but it provides the conditions for assessing public interest claims' (Kratochwil 1982, p. 6). In other words, the fact that the public interest cannot be defined once and for all, and is the subject of much argument, is actually its primary advantage. This process reveals the often hidden assumptions of policy in the communal interest and exposes who is gaining or losing from decisions.

Translating this to the national interest, we can see the declining attention paid to the term by academics as a retrograde step. Political scientists' love of terminological exactitude is preventing them from contributing to debates over national interest and assessing the claims made in the name of the political community of the UK. Consider how much of the academic critique of the Blair government's decision to intervene in Iraq focused on its international legality and ramifications rather than whether the assertions of acting in the national interest were credible. (For rare examples, see Strachan 2009; Doig and Phythian 2005.) This imbalance of critical attention also hampers the ability of foreign policy analysts to make a reasoned assessment of claims that states are acting primarily for 'humanitarian' reasons, or in the interest of the wider international community, rather than out of self-interest. Instead, they are left to assume that policymakers are either wholly self-interested or wholly altruistic, rather than appreciate the dialectic between these extremes. As a corollary, the question of the extent to which the 'interest' being served is genuinely national is also marginalised (for an exception, see Ritchie 2011).

Underlying a lot of the confusion about the concept of the national interest is the way it sometimes seems to refer to an overall, unifying notion of the public good and at other times a specific policy goal. This ambiguity is potentially resolved by W. David Clinton's assessment of the normative foundations of the national interest (Clinton 1991). Clinton notes that 'national interest' can be understood as the end to which policy is driving, whilst 'national interests' are 'a number of narrower goals, which serve the broader end' (Clinton 1991, p. 50). In other words, there is ultimately only one national interest – which is the abstract notion of the common good of the political community – and then lots of state interests that could be advanced to serve it, but which might also conflict with each other (Clinton 1991, p. 51). The challenge of the policymaker therefore becomes one of adjudicating between the various interest claims, some of which may have a national quality to them (i.e. serve collective goods) but which might harm the longer-term national interest if their utility is not continually reappraised. The history of British foreign policy is replete with national interests (e.g. maintaining the Indian Raj, keeping sovereignty over the Suez Canal, sovereign independence from Europe) that could be seen as having hampered the overall national interest when they outlived their original utility.

The difficulty for policymakers in weighing the merits of national interest claims lies in the extent to which these often become constitutive of the identity of the political community in their own right. Indeed, for Alexander Wendt, 'identities are the basis of interests' (Wendt 1992, p. 398). Rather than one being prior to the other in their formation, constructivists such as Wendt see interests and identities as 'intersubjectively constituted' (Wendt 1992, p. 401). Nevertheless, foreign policy analysts can trace the historical emergence of certain policy priorities, 'national interests', and note how they may either become core components of national identity conceptions or fade in salience over time. In doing so, it is possible to expose the contingent nature of these interpretations and so hopefully offer alternative descriptions – or at least compel their advocates to justify why a particular interest should continue to be considered as vital for the good of the wider community. There is a large and complex debate on the interaction between identity and interests in foreign policy – encompassing a range of theories, from constructivism to historical materialism, role theory to discourse analysis. For now, it is perhaps sufficient to note that any articulation of the national interest is, by definition, also making a claim about the identity of the political community under scrutiny.

To summarise this section, debates among academics have gone back and forth over whether the national interest can be defined objectively, or if it is a legitimising tool to hide the power of sectional interests, pursuing policies to suit their particular ends. Underpinning the arguments of those in favour of using the term is a sense that there is a collective good that policymakers should seek to advance. Furthermore, even if the costs and benefits of policy choices are not distributed evenly, the concept of the national interest does provide a framework for questioning the utility of policies in terms of the broader political community. If we are going to take governments seriously as actors pursuing notional collective goods, the concept of the national interest provides a descriptive term and a mechanism for appraising whether officials and policymakers are genuinely acting in the interests of the political community as a whole.

However, as Niebuhr and others have cautioned, the idea that self-interest is imbued with a moral force of its own can lead to policy that is actively harmful, both for international society as a whole, and the community whose interests are supposedly being served. This is because the cloak of moralism could be used to hide the baser motive of securing short-term advantage which might undermine the fabric of law and norms that keep that society functioning in the long term. For that reason, as Gilmore hints in this volume, claims that national self-interests and the interests of international society are one and the same should be continually questioned.

National interest: The policy debate

If academics have questioned the possibility of arriving at any consensus as to what a 'national interest' might be, policy debates among those charged with the actual practice of our diplomacy have been equally inconclusive. Whilst 'national interest' has been referenced periodically in various reports and official statements over the years, and continues to be, there can be few terms so widely used but so inadequately or infrequently defined.

From the end of the Second World War, apart from specific concerns related to the dissolution of the British Empire, British foreign policy was dominated by the defence and security considerations of the Cold War. The alliances, obligations and actions of the UK were understood through the prism of this overriding strategic framework and as a result interests were often defined and prioritised according to international factors. Indeed, as Parr argues in this volume, even the military action to recover the Falklands was not primarily explained or justified in national interest terms. Rather, it was policy decisions that advanced the interests of 'the West' in their competition with the Soviet Union that were deemed to be 'in the national interest'. This was certainly the case during the Thatcher years, and to a degree the momentum generated has meant that international security concerns have continued to 'lead' our foreign policy to this day. In this period, the lack of public articulation of the strategic direction and purpose of foreign policy – separable from alliance politics – was arguably a defining characteristic of British foreign policy.

The introduction of a mission statement for the Foreign and Commonwealth Office in 1997 was therefore a novel development and seemed to buck the trend by actually setting out a framework for understanding the government's view of the national interest (Wheeler and Dunne 1998). In his first speech as foreign secretary, Cook declared that 'security, prosperity and quality of life are all clear national interests' and that the UK had 'a clear national interest in the promotion of our values and confidence in our identity' (Cook 1997). Thus, the subtext was that, for New Labour, values and interests should be 'merged' in the making of UK foreign policy.

As noted above, the conflation of morality with national interests can be problematic and in New Labour's second term of office, particularly after the terrorist attacks of 9/11, this conflation of interests (often defined in physical security terms) and values (the normative aspirations of the UK for the international community as a whole) proved difficult to sustain. Cook himself was an early casualty of the tensions between these imperatives, as he was reshuffled after the 2001 election and then resigned over Iraq in March 2003. So too was the international development secretary, Claire Short, who belatedly followed him to the back benches over Iraq in May 2003. Meanwhile, Tony Blair strained credulity with his often repeated arguments that there was no tension between the UK's values, its security needs and wider international norms. Blair's efforts to globalise his own world view into a universal aspiration for all humankind meant that fundamental questions about the *strategic* direction of Britain's foreign policy, and what Britain's particular national interest might be, were effectively postponed. The difficulties in adopting such an expansive view of national interest are directly addressed by Gilmore in this volume.

During Gordon Brown's premiership, more effort was made to articulate a sense of national purpose in British foreign policy. For example, in 2008, the cabinet office published its *National Security Strategy of the UK*. Yet, this 64-page document used the term 'national interest' only once, and in doing so failed to define it. Indeed, its use of the term appeared to conflate 'national interest' with 'national security'. As one critic argued: 'The use of the word "strategy" here is meaningless as it does not address choices. Instead, it lists threats, many (indeed the majority) of which are not defence-related, and most of which are global' (Strachan 2009, p. 67). Two years later, it appeared that this neglect might be addressed with the publication of the 2010 *National Security Strategy* (NSS) and the 2010 *Strategic Defence and Security Review* (SDSR). References to 'national interest' were more frequent in these texts, but the contested nature of the term was still apparent. As academic observers remarked at the time, the NSS and SDSR, together with the *Spending Review* of that year, collectively sought to 'lay down the bounds of Britain's future role in the world, to articulate Britain's national interests, establish the goals of policy and set the means by which to achieve them' (LSE Ideas, October 2010).

Yet in spite of this, there was still no clear indication of what the UK's national interests might be, or how they might relate to the task of formulating our longer-term strategy in foreign and defence policy. The Parliamentary Committee for Public Administration concluded that the government had lost the art of making national strategy in relation to defence and security, with the Conservative chairman, Bernard Jenkin, protesting that an inability to 'think strategically' had fundamentally undermined the process of reviewing the UK's national strategy (PASC 2011, p. 5; Kitchen 2010).

The difficulty of introducing rigorous strategic thinking to British foreign policy is one that has been identified by policymakers themselves (Coles 2000). We take it up here in the chapter by Evans, who offers insights from the US experience; arguing that the emphasis should be on people rather than systems, on innovative thinking rather than grandly worded but vague documents. Countering the pessimistic account given above of the UK's capacity for strategy-making, Edmunds in his chapter suggests that this ignores the many innovations in thinking and practice that have been implemented in recent years. Similarly, Oliver and Knuppe, through their typology of strategic approaches, hint that there are actually a number of ways to formulate a strategy. Those that criticise the government for lacking strategic thinking may actually only be criticising the lack of a particular type.

Interwoven with these debates over the ethical content of foreign policy and the strategic policymaking process have been questions over British identity. Commentators have asked whether a militaristic identity is one that the UK wishes to project (Goodhart 2009), if our alliances are appropriate to the values Britain professes to advance (Milne 2013) and what the UK's place in the world might be, now and in the future (Morris 2011). As our discussion of Wendt above suggested, discussion of the national interest is implicitly also one of national identity. Whilst many policymakers will seek to rationalise their foreign policy in terms of shared historical memories and collective identity positions (Daddow 2011), there is little acknowledgement that the domestic make-up of the UK has changed substantially in recent decades, not just ethnically, but also in terms of religious and social attitudes. The multicultural nature of British society has real but often underexplored implications for national interest (Hill 2013). Moreover, the UK has an identity abroad that shapes how it sees itself and the scope of its interests. Gaskarth, in his chapter, addresses the debate over Britain's role in the world to consider how it might pursue a sense of a collective national interest that accords both with domestic ideas about British identity and the expectations of the other members of international society. Meanwhile, Porter asks if the US–UK alliance is still, as is often claimed, in the UK national interest.

To summarise our discussion so far, the policy arena has thrown up a number of similar themes to that of the academic debate outlined earlier. Commentators deliberate over how far national self-interest is separable from international ethical claims; attempts have been made to reduce the national interest to a specific objective (such as security); discussion of the national interest leads to reflection on identity and how far foreign policy is in the collective public interest; and there is disagreement over how the national interest, or national interests, should be pursued (i.e. over national strategy). In the policy world, there is a sense that the discourse is designed to try and close down debate. The nineteenth-century view that interests are eternal and so self-evident that they need little elaboration has shifted into a contemporary view that the world is so complex that any attempt to fix a sense of national interest is out of step with the need to be flexible to meet the challenges of a newly 'globalized' world (Williams 2012, p. 8). However, this move is continually challenged by a public desire for policymakers to justify their policies and explain how they are acting in their interest. As such, the term continues to have resonance in contemporary British foreign policymaking.

We now turn to an explanation of the structure of the book to outline how each chapter seeks to contribute to this discussion and address the questions laid out above.

The structure of the book

The first part of this book, 'Britain in the World', seeks to address how questions of identity and values have influenced Britain's foreign policymaking over recent decades – and how they may continue to do so in the future.

Jonathan Gilmore, in his opening chapter on the uncertain merger of values and interests in Britain's foreign policy, explores how ethics and values relate to the British national interest. The idea that ethical commitments to distant non-citizens should occupy a position within British foreign policy was a controversial element of New Labour's foreign policy during its first term in office. Rather than undermining traditional national interest concerns, one of the defining themes within New Labour's foreign policy was that values and national interests were becoming increasingly *merged* in a globalised world. Although the post-2010 coalition government has crafted a more pragmatic and national-interest-based foreign policy approach, significant continuities with their predecessor's 'ethical dimension' are evident. Moreover, the suggestion that British values and interests are interrelated and mutually reinforcing has been reasserted, with renewed vigour, by coalition policymakers.

Gilmore's chapter traces the ways in which values and interests have become increasingly merged in the language of recent British foreign policy and the implications for our understanding of the UK's national interest. He argues that the idea of an almost symbiotic relationship between values and interests is fundamentally unhelpful and makes the case for greater disaggregation of the two. Using the examples of failed state stabilisation and UK arms trade regulation, the article demonstrates how uncritical acceptance of the values–interests merger masks the choices being made and the politics underlying policy direction.

In his chapter, **Jamie Gaskarth** observes that both the New Labour governments and the current coalition government have been criticised for lacking strategic thinking. Academics describe a 'strategy gap' and note that old ideas about Britain's role in the world, such as Churchill's 1948 reference to 'three circles', continue to be recycled.

14 *Introduction*

Parliamentarians bemoan the 'uncritical acceptance of these assumptions', which has led to 'a waning of our interests in, and ability to make, national strategy'. Gaskarth argues that a primary problem has been the lack of consideration of how identity, strategy and action interrelate in foreign policy.

Using the insights of role theory, he seeks to address this by outlining six 'ideal type' role orientations that the UK might adopt in world politics, namely: isolate, influential (rule of law state), regional partner, thought leader, opportunist–interventionist power and great power. By addressing how variations in a state's disposition towards the external environment may translate into different policy directions, the author aims both to highlight the range of roles available to policymakers, and to emphasise that policymaking often involves making a choice between those roles. Failure to recognise this has resulted in role conflicts and policy confusion, he maintains. In setting out a variety of different role orientations, Gaskarth aims to offer a means of introducing a genuine strategic sensibility to policymaking, one that links identity with policy goals and outcomes.

In the concluding chapter of this section, **Helen Parr** adopts a historical approach to see how ideas about the national interest have motivated military action in the recent past. Her analysis takes us back to the Falklands conflict. The recent release of documents in the National Archives facilitates reconsideration of the reasons why Britain responded by sending a task force, and the reasons why the government resorted to war. Study of these decisions, she maintains, enables examination of the ways in which the British government perceived Britain's national interests in the aftermath of the invasion, and the ways in which they articulated those interests both domestically and internationally in order to legitimate the course of action they took. Parr concludes that the government was prepared to make compromises over the self-determination of the Falkland islanders, at least to an extent, but that the primary sticking point was that Argentine aggression should not pay. Hence, Britain's interests were defined in terms of preventing the consolidation of gains made by force, thereby protecting Britain's international prestige and, to an extent, international public goods such as sovereignty and peaceful settlement of disputes that underpin international society as a whole.

Whose national interest?

In the second section of the book, 'Whose National Interest?', there are several contributions which explore the validity of the concept of a 'national interest' and the implied communities that British foreign policy ultimately serves. As noted above, the costs and benefits of national interest calculations have disproportionate impacts among the different interest groups, classes and actors within the UK. In addition, a raft of different transnational communities, state actors and international networks intersect in the construction of foreign policy. These chapters explore different facets of the policy process to see how different understandings of what the national interest is, and how it should be pursued, often mask the fact that some actors are gaining and others losing from the choices being made. In exposing the implications of British foreign policymaking in this way, the authors ask: whose interest is served by the way the national interest is promoted?

For instance, **Nick Ritchie**, focusing on the role and needs of the individual citizen, challenges the idea of objectively knowable, axiomatic interests belonging to an ideologically unified state. Instead, he encourages us to place people at the centre of our collective interpretations of national interests and apply the concept of *human security* to the British citizenry. The result, it is argued, would be that the referent object of interest/security becomes the individual and community rather than the state. This exploratory analysis draws on the dissonance between a Whitehall narrative of national interest as the defence and promotion of a collective 'way of life', on the one hand, with state actions that have undermined the way of life of many people, on the other. In particular, Ritchie examines the case studies of the British state's response to the 'war on terror' (including its involvement in the military invasions of Iraq and Afghanistan in this period) and the government's response to the 2008 financial crisis, to question how far the goals sought, and the policies adopted to pursue them, can be seen as furthering the collective good.

David Wearing takes this theme further, employing the critical perspective of historical materialism to examine British foreign policy. In an insightful analysis, Wearing posits that the resources of the British state are usually not committed to the service of the national interest, as often portrayed by successive governments, but are instead employed to further the interests of a ruling class through the maintenance of a capitalist international political economy, managed by a global state and corporate elite, under the leadership of the US. This approach is supported by an analysis of British foreign policy in the Middle East. The Middle East, as a key energy-producing region, is seen as a major strategic prize, highly valued by the system of power of which the British state is a part. Britain's economic interests in the region are regularly cited by officials as the reason why the UK has a stake in maintaining 'stability' and 'order' in this area. However, the extent to which these interests are primarily elite ones, whilst the costs are disproportionately borne by ordinary citizens in the Arab world and at home in the UK, is downplayed, Wearing maintains.

In his chapter, **Robin Porter**, a former diplomat, questions whether Britain's 'special relationship' with the US in defence and foreign policy has served, or will continue to serve, the country's national interests. Referring to the UK's recent history, geographical location, economic circumstances, commercial aspirations and its distinct views on scientific and environmental matters, justice and human rights, Porter believes that the UK may not automatically be presumed to share foreign policy goals with the US. As a superpower operating in the context of its own particular domestic and international circumstances, the US quite legitimately has its own national interests to protect.

Porter contends that policymakers in the US seem far more comfortable appraising the UK–US relationship in hard, self-interested terms than their British counterparts. Through an examination of the UK's stated global objectives, this chapter suggests that a reconsideration of the 'special relationship' in terms of the British national interest may be overdue. In contrast to the naturalised, unquestioning belief in mutual interests, the author advances a more nuanced posture, one that respects the US's important and positive contribution to international diplomacy, whilst also acknowledging that at times Britain may have diverging interests.

Strategy and planning

In the third and final part of the book, a number of authors try and get to grips with how foreign policymakers might introduce a greater degree of strategic awareness and rigour to their conception of the national interest. As the world becomes increasingly complex, with a greater volume of interactions and information confronting policymakers in a digital age, there is a fear that officials and policymakers alike are losing a sense of the collective good that foreign policy is designed to pursue. Competing sectional interests threaten to obscure the sense of national purpose that is supposed to underpin government actions. Meanwhile, the desire to keep on top of day-to-day issues risks leaving officials chasing headlines and reacting to events rather than anticipating developments and galvanising public support by articulating the rationale for policy decisions. Thus, these chapters intend to contribute to policy understanding by showing how long-term strategy and planning can be enabled with reference to the national interest.

In his piece on organising government for strategy and policy planning, former practitioner **Alexander Evans** argues that the challenge of long-term strategy persists: how should government be organised to support it, how can the right people be found to staff it and how can political leaders have time for strategy given the weight of immediate policy decisions? Within the British Foreign and Commonwealth Office, he notes, thinking about strategy was partly handed to the policy planning staff. This small group of diplomats – later leavened by externals from the media, NGOs and the private sector – was meant to generate longer-term thinking on British interests and policy.

In both Britain and the US, efforts to utilise these 'long-headed' staffers to provide greater strategic depth to foreign policy have been mixed. One former British planner said he felt like 'a spare part rattling around in a tin'. Former American planners have written about the difficulty of injecting strategic thinking when semi-detached from high decision-making. Policy planning could be intellectually rich but often failed to become the source of actionable strategic thinking about the long-term national interest. Other planners were dragged into operational work or speech-writing. Many planners nonetheless enjoyed the opportunity to think more broadly. This chapter suggests that a greater focus on people rather than systems might help foster more strategic, anticipatory and innovative thinking about the national interest.

In their study, **Benoit Pelopidas** and **Jutta Weldes** examine the security and nuclear dimensions of the UK national interest in relation to Trident, and the recent putative shift in conceptions of UK national interests from a discourse of 'security' to one of 'resilience'. This change in language marks a fundamental reappraisal in security policymaking and how policy is presented to the public. Security providers have in the past tended to portray their efforts as seeking to avoid disasters and ensure people are 'safe'. By contrast, the idea of resilience recognises that people are vulnerable, that disasters will happen, and so aims to enable the population to endure and cope when emergencies arise. The authors reflect on this move and its implications for security policy. They then assess the practice of UK nuclear weapons policy, and Trident in particular, in relation to the requirements with which a resilient nuclear weapons policy would need to comply. They conclude that completing the move to resilience as the overriding framework for understanding security is complicated by the perceived requirements of deterrence. As a result, the government has arguably failed to properly acknowledge the risks of a nuclear accident occurring, and has not put in place sufficient preparedness to ensure the public could be resilient in the face of this threat.

Timothy Edmunds, in his chapter on complexity, strategy and the national interest, begins by observing that British strategy-making has been subject to a sustained critique in recent years, from parliamentarians, retired members of the armed forces and scholars of strategic studies. In his contribution he examines the nature of this critique, and the evolving character of strategic practice in Britain. He argues that the criticisms of British strategy-making are often misplaced, for two main reasons. First, many of them base their critique on a reductionist notion of unitary 'national interest' that fails to capture systemic patterns of complexity and contestation in the wider security environment and at home. Second, they underestimate or ignore the extent to which the UK strategic community is itself innovating in response to these themes, particularly since the 2010 Strategic Defence and Security Review.

This is not to argue that considerable challenges do not remain for strategy-making in Britain. Chief among these, Edmunds suggests, are: how to translate strategic innovation in departments and elsewhere into a coherent national strategic agenda; how to do this whilst maintaining institutional coordination and a shared sense of strategic purpose across government (and beyond); how to sustain and consolidate institutional expertise and experience in a rapidly changing civil service and at a time of continuing public austerity; and how to articulate and legitimate security policy decisions amongst a general public that is both disengaged from elite strategic discourse and sceptical of the efficacy of military force. Despite these challenges, the chapter concludes, it is possible to see the outline of an emergent and distinctive theory of action in contemporary British strategic practice, characterised by principles of adaptivity, anticipation, self-organisation and nascent cross-governmentalism.

From a creative, alternative perspective, **Max Taylor** offers an analysis of national interest and strategy drawn from the discipline of psychology. Taylor argues that if the UK's national interest lies in maximising the social and economic benefits to the UK of a globalising and changing world, this seems to imply a need for openness to the possibility of change. As a corollary of this, policymakers and foreign policy analysts will need to make the effort to develop useful new lenses through which to view the world, befitting the shifting patterns of actors and behaviours with which they are confronted. What Taylor proposes is the need for a holistic approach to policymaking, drawing on not just official structures, but civil society agencies and commercial organisations to identify priorities and opportunities.

The structures that might be put in place to do this follow, he says, from an understanding of the structure of the environment, particularly its physical, ecological, psychological and social affordance qualities. Ways must be explored that will allow flexibility to emerge; this will not necessarily come from governments or politics, but from an understanding of the accelerating ecological and evolutionary context in which we live. Thus, the analysis notes the need for a more challenging investigation into what constitutes the national interest than the conventional governmental approach, one that notes the limits to the capacity of the UK state to adapt to a changing world environment, but also identifies opportunities for beneficial change. A further implication of this analysis is that whilst ecological and evolutionary psychology insights may identify an alternative 'lens' through which we might view national interest, the critical issue is the sense of how the wider environment defines the scope of what is possible in this policy field.

In a final contribution, **Tim Oliver** and **Austin Knuppe** examine initiatives taken in recent years in the attempt to develop a British national security strategy and find differing agendas and aims across the various policy documents and public statements. As part of a project to compare the UK's 2010 approach with several other recently published strategies from other states and international organisations, they set out a typology of national security strategies, basing their research on an analysis of the policy planning documents of the US, Britain, the EU, Germany, France and NATO. The typology divides national security strategies into: foreign policy-led, threat-oriented, capabilities-driven, budget-constrained and risk-based. The authors explain the typology, its background and purpose, and then set out their case study of the UK's national security strategy, focusing on the 2010 strategy and subsequent updates. The UK strategy is located within the typology, and a final section compares the UK's approach with those of the US, the EU, Germany, France and NATO. In the process, the authors aim to put the challenge of introducing strategic thinking and rigour to conceptions of the UK national interest in its wider context. Many officials and policymakers are grappling with this problem in states across the world. Their endeavours offer useful lessons to British policymakers about the errors that can be made and successes that are achievable.

We conclude by drawing these various chapters and their insights together to justify our focus on the national interest. Key points of inquiry are over the *contestation* of the national interest, which has been shown to be a battleground for various groups to claim policies as advancing the good of the community as whole; *legitimacy*, which is a central function of national interest since it professes to fulfil a wider public good – something we argue cannot only be conferred by debate among elites but must also involve civil society and the general public; and *utility*, since the national interest implies a rational calculation of how means can be deployed to achieve certain ends. Wrapped up in all of these facets is the question of who benefits from foreign policies supposedly in the collective interest and whether the costs are distributed in a just manner. Whilst sometimes conveyed as a conservative and reactionary concept, the fact that the national interest allows us to consider such an array of questions suggests it retains significant analytical force.

Part I
Britain in the World

2
The Uncertain Merger of Values and Interests in UK Foreign Policy[1]

Jonathan Gilmore

Introduction

What is good for Britain is also good for the rest of the world. The increasingly consistent, and surprisingly unchallenged, claims that Britain's national interest and its moral responsibilities to international society and to vulnerable non-citizens are merging seem to lean towards this controversial sentiment. Accompanying Labour's foreign policy with an ethical dimension, the idea that values and Britain's national interests were merging was a central plank in Tony Blair's 'Doctrine of the International Community' (Cook 1997a; Blair 1999). Despite claims of a return to national interest and a more 'pragmatic' foreign policy, suggestion of a values–interests merger has been maintained in the foreign policy of the Conservative–Liberal Democrat coalition. Analysing speeches and documents, this article explores the implications of this claim. Although ethical reflection in British foreign policy is not necessarily new, the idea that concern for non-citizens should be manifested in overt commitments, to which governments are held accountable, represents an innovation that has endured beyond Labour's tenure. Understandably, the coalition has made concerted attempts to depart from the more controversial and hubristic aspects of Labour's internationalism. The coalition claims a foreign policy with a more pragmatic approach, more measured and modest ambition and closer attention paid to national interest. However, its foreign policy draws simultaneously on ethical commitments to non-citizens, in maintaining the initiatives associated with the previous government's 'ethical dimension'; now re-framed as the projection of 'British' values internationally.

So what might this mean for a conception of British national interest? The process of identifying national interest inherently involves allocating an elevated sense of importance to proposed courses of action or existing policy commitments. Moving away from the idea of an objective or static national interest, Weldes (1996, p. 280) argues that 'national interests emerge out of the representations... out of situation descriptions and problem definitions through which state officials make sense of the world around them'. In this view, national interest is a social construct, one in which state policymakers have an instrumental role. The values–interests merger, with which this article is concerned, represents a relatively recent construction of national interests and 'values' as almost symbiotic, in an increasingly globalised or 'networked' world. However, whilst not suggesting national interests are static, it seems important that the objectives and commitments with which they are associated have a tangible link to the wellbeing of a specific national community, if they are to be useful in guiding policy development.[2] Overly expanding conceptions of national interest beyond this or drawing misleading connections with other foreign policy initiatives would thus appear problematic. The presence of such a tangible link is central to the understanding of national interest within this article.

It is here that the construction of the values–interests merger in UK foreign policy runs into trouble. Although a convenient rhetorical crutch, the suggestion of a values–interests merger obscures how different areas of ethical responsibility often conflict. Although these realms of responsibility are certainly interrelated, assuming an intrinsic coherence serves to obscure, rather than shed light on the relationship between them. Failing to acknowledge this problem will likely result in increasingly unstable policy formulations, which succeed neither in promoting traditional conceptions of national interest or the wellbeing of vulnerable non-citizens overseas. A way forward might be to reject the idea of 'enlightened' UK national interest, which assumes an intrinsic coherence between values and interests. More helpful might be the disaggregation of national interest from responsibilities to international order, and overseas ethical commitments. In this way, overseas ethical responsibilities might be privileged as important ends in themselves, rather than subsumed within an incoherent, catch-all conception of British national interest.

The first section of the article explores the 'ethical dimension' in the foreign policy of the 1997–2010 Labour government and the suggestion that values and interests were becoming increasingly merged. The second section examines continuities in the coalition's foreign policy, the retained focus on values-based commitments, and a renewed effort to suggest a mutually supportive relationship between values and interests.

Using the examples of fragile-state stabilisation and UK arms exports, the final section highlights the instability of the values–interests merger in practice, and the emerging tensions and contradictions.

Embedded ethics in New Labour's foreign policy

The idea that the UK's foreign policy should contain an ethical dimension was a prominent feature of Labour's early foreign policy, following their election victory in May 1997. Closely associated with the foreign secretary, Robin Cook, the new agenda was characterised by expressions of trans-border moral solidarity and an appeal to the universal values of an international community. The 'mission statement' outlining this agenda, committed the Foreign and Commonwealth Office (FCO) to 'promote the national interests of the UK and to contribute to a strong world community', with an explicit focus on promoting human rights, civil liberties and democracy (FCO 1997). There was an explicit commitment to the wellbeing of vulnerable non-citizens, suggesting that 'the right to enjoy our freedoms comes with the obligation to support the human rights of others. It is not acceptable to try to evade that obligation by pleading that there is too much evil in the world for us to put it right' (Cook 1997b). This responsibility was later echoed in the more explicit context of armed humanitarian intervention, by Tony Blair's 'Doctrine of the International Community'. These overseas ethical commitments manifested themselves in the foundation of the Department for International Development, a pledge not to sell arms to states where they might be used for internal repression and the production of an annual report documenting the UK's human rights work (Cook 1997b). More controversially, overseas ethical obligations provided a key rationale for Britain's involvement in the 1999 Kosovo intervention and for operations associated with the 'war on terror'.

As Williams (2010, p. 18) notes, the idea of ethical reflection in foreign policy decision-making was not necessarily new. Indeed, senior policy-makers have, for many years, wrestled with ideas of ethical obligation when formulating foreign policy. Former Foreign Secretary David Owen suggested that 'ethical foreign policy has been around way before me. Canning could be argued to do it, Castlereagh, Gladstone himself as Prime Minister' (Cited in Gaskarth 2013, p. 196). Similarly, Frost (1999, p. 81) argues that ultimately 'it is not possible to understand the international arena, or to act in it, without an ethical position about right or wrong'. Therefore, all foreign policy is 'ethical'. A policy limited to defending the narrowest interests of the UK and its citizens is itself based around specific ideas of ethical responsibility.

The significance of Labour's foreign policy was not necessarily ethical reflection per se, but the idea that ethical responsibilities to non-citizens deserved overt consideration. Additionally, there was the suggestion of an almost symbiotic link between values and interests. This was evident in Blair's (1999) argument that,

> Now our actions are guided by a more subtle blend of mutual self-interest and moral purpose.... In the end values and interests merge. If we can establish and spread the values of liberty, the rule of law, human rights and an open society then that is in our national interests too. The spread of our values makes us safer.

In a world of inescapable interdependence, moral concern for non-citizens, the expansion of the liberal world order and British national interest were now inseparable. This sentiment was later reinforced by Cook's successor, Jack Straw (2003), who noted that not acting to overthrow Saddam Hussein 'would not only be a betrayal of British national interests, but of our internationalist values and beliefs too'.

The merger of values and interests within Labour's foreign policy mirrored the earlier concept of the 'Good International Citizen', advanced by then Australian Foreign Minister Gareth Evans. Evans (1990) similarly highlighted the crossover between national interest and the projection of values, resulting in a form of 'enlightened self interest'. He was notably unspecific about which values might be considered Australian and which were more authentically universal. This discursive slippage was also a common feature within the language of Labour's foreign policy, with frequent appeals both to universal values – reflected in Cook's (1997b) suggestion that 'we are not seeking to impose some particularly British concept' – alongside references to 'our' (British) values. Just as the boundary between values and interests became blurred, the distinction between universal and culturally situated values was also ambiguous.

Whatever the precise source of values to be promoted, the practical themes with which they were linked – human rights, democracy, development – were in the end very similar. However, the distinction between advancing universal values as an end in themselves, and promoting 'our' liberal values is significant. It indicates the roots of a divide between a cosmopolitan view on ethical foreign policy, and what might be defined as an 'offensive liberal' outlook. Although cosmopolitanism is a broad church, what is common across its spectrum is a concern with authentically universal values, trans-border moral solidarity and ethical responsibilities to non-citizens as ends in themselves. Alternatively, offensive liberalism, although similarly concerned with the role of values, works from a different standpoint, advocating the aggressive universalisation of specifically liberal democratic values – a faith in democratisation as a means of achieving long-term peace and a preference for hard power in promoting regime change in authoritarian states (Miller 2010). The robust agenda promoted by the Henry Jackson Society, whereby Western states would be committed to using hard and soft power in the assertive promotion of liberal democracy, provides the clearest UK example of offensive liberalism.[3]

Coinciding with the apogee of sectarian violence in post-invasion Iraq, Blair's speeches in 2006 drew heavily on the offensive liberal idea of a conflict between the progressive forces of democracy and those of extremism (Kettel 2013). Arguing that democratic values 'do not belong to any race, religion or nation, but are universal', and that the UK was engaged in 'not a clash of civilizations but a clash about civilization', Blair (2006) implicitly characterised those who reject liberal values as barbaric or uncivilised, rather than as adhering to a different worldview. However, the construction of a dichotomy between a supposedly universal, civilised international order and a barbaric, illiberal Other, suggests that the values promoted by UK foreign policy were not in actuality those of a universal 'international community'. Labour's turn towards a more offensive liberal vision in the post-9/11 context has important ramifications when conceptualising national interest. When the values–interests merger is situated within an offensive liberal outlook, the extension of liberal values becomes a weapon in a global existential fight against authoritarianism and extremism. Overseas ethical commitments become framed as instruments in support of the UK's security interests, rather than independent ends in themselves.

Some criticisms of Labour's foreign policy during the party's 1997–2010 tenure are closely related to the increasingly blurred boundaries between values and interests. Chandler (2002, p. 63) frames Labour's ethical turn as a means of shoring up domestic legitimacy, in a world that now lacked the ideological rivalries once associated with the Cold War. He argues that ethical foreign policy has come to represent 'rhetoric without responsibility' and a departure from the 'traditional lines of accountability in a modern democracy, where the government was seen to have a duty to reflect the desires and priorities of its citizens in its policy making' (Chandler 2002, p. 70). Alongside this departure from accountability to a more grounded sense of national interests, the government is similarly unaccountable to the intended beneficiaries of overseas ethical commitments. This results in policies that are increasingly symbolic, divorced from long-term consequences and demonstrating only abstract concern for the wellbeing of non-citizens (Chandler 2002, p. 78). The Labour government's failure to acknowledge their share of responsibility for the catastrophic impact of the pre-2003 sanctions regime on the Iraqi population could be taken as an example of failure to acknowledge the consequences of ethical foreign policy on the intended beneficiaries (see Herring 2002). The breakdown of accountability for the results of aggressively promoted liberal values in UK foreign policy also flowed into responses to forms of domestic extremism that might be considered as direct threats to Britain's national security interests. Brighton (2007, p. 3) notes the downplaying of potential causal links between intervention in Afghanistan and Iraq and the increased threat from home-grown Islamic fundamentalist terrorism. Mirroring the merger of values and interests and the aggressive promotion of liberalism overseas, Labour's response to this domestic security threat, apparently situated within minority communities, was the reassertion of liberal values and the moral legitimacy of UK foreign policy (Brighton 2007, pp. 9–11).

Labour's foreign policy thus provided a blurred vision of national interest, as inseparable from the promotion and defence of liberal values in a world seemingly divided between freedom and authoritarianism/extremism. Significant here is the way foreign policy simultaneously became disconnected from an ethical commitment to a narrower conception of national interest – defending state sovereignty, territorial integrity and vital economic interests – but also from a fuller regard for the wellbeing of non-citizens.

British values, national interest and the coalition's foreign policy

The incoming coalition government of 2010 faced the challenge of how to manage Labour's foreign policy legacy, in particular the overt inclusion of overseas ethical commitments. Conservative policymakers were also presented with the question of where to position themselves in relation to the decaying, more sceptical conservative tradition in foreign policy (see Hall and Rengger 2005). The formulation eventually adopted by the coalition appears an attempt to reconcile these two divergent paths.

Returning to the national interest?

More modest foreign policy aspirations appear perhaps a logical antidote to the perception of overstretch and excessive normative ambition associated with Labour's vision. Economic contraction and the UK's national deficit have led to criticisms of the notion that 'the UK can be simultaneously Europeanist and Atlanticist, pro-sovereignty and pro-human rights, an upholder of "rules", yet a spreader of values', without consideration of the capacity needed to achieve this (P. Porter 2010, pp. 6–11). Moreover, the British public's appetite for ethically minded foreign policy, if ever particularly great, currently appears limited. When members of the public, surveyed by Chatham House/YouGov in 2012, were asked to choose the three issues they felt should be the main focus of UK foreign policies, the promotion of democracy, the rule of law and human rights were selected by only 10 per cent of respondents as a key priority. Similarly, 47 per cent of those surveyed felt that British foreign policy should support the national interest at all times, even if it meant doing things that might be regarded as unethical.[4] Whilst not representing the outright rejection of foreign policy commitments to vulnerable non-citizens, it provides some indicators of the ambivalent public opinion landscape within which the coalition have crafted their policy.

The coalition has responded to these circumstances with a foreign policy narrative that highlights the centrality of national interest and a return to a more 'pragmatic' foreign policy. The Conservatives' election manifesto commitments were to a foreign policy that was 'hard headed and practical, dealing with the world as it is and not as we wish it were' (Conservative Party 2010, p. 109). Incoming Foreign Secretary William Hague (2010) later suggested that 'we are determined to do better and to be more realistic. We will replace the sweeping generalisations of "ethical foreign policy" with a clear, practical and principled approach, persistently applied. We understand that idealism in foreign policy always needs to be tempered with realism'. Particular emphasis is placed on the contrast between the coalition's commitment to Britain's national interest, and Labour's more hubristic internationalism. A specific manifestation of this has been the sharpening of the FCO's focus on international engagement to enhance the UK security, and its contribution to domestic economic growth by enhancing market access for British companies (FCO written evidence in Foreign Affairs Committee 2011, Ev. 77–91). The centrality of national interest even permeates the seemingly unrelated 2011 FCO *Human Rights and Democracy* report, with human rights protection overseas linked to its role in creating an environment more conducive to UK security, stable investment and the safety of British citizens abroad. A distinct effort has thus been made to differentiate the coalition's foreign policy, by re-articulating the tangible links between different policy instruments and the benefits sought for the UK and its citizenry.

This supposed refocusing onto national interest must, however, be viewed against potentially contradictory references to a 'values-based approach' and a commitment to 'enlightened national interest' (Conservative Party 2010, p. 109). Although coalition policymakers are cautious to avoid referring to 'ethics' directly, elements of Labour's 'ethical-dimension' remain in evidence. In particular, the focus on human rights and the wellbeing of non-citizens is retained. This was emphasised by Hague's (2012) suggestion that human rights and development are 'part of our (the UK's) national DNA and will be woven deeply into the decision-making processes of our foreign policy at every stage'. The coalition's 'liberal conservative' agenda has maintained overseas aid at 0.7 per cent of GDP in the face of wide-ranging spending cutbacks, continues to produce annual human rights reports and supports humanitarian intervention and the 'stabilisation' of fragile states (see Conservative Party 2010, p. 109; FCO 2013; HM Government 2011). The coalition has also maintained the prohibition, in principle at least, on supplying weapons to states where they might be used for internal repression, and lent its support to the 2013 Arms Trade Treaty (Hague 2013). Overseas ethical commitments thus continue to play a significant role in coalition foreign policy. Just as successive Labour foreign secretaries were unable to return the 'cosmopolitan genie'[5] to its lamp, the coalition has similarly had to find a place for these forms of ethical foreign policy.

Merging values and interests in the 'liberal conservative' foreign policy agenda

The coalition has attempted to fuse the promotion of 'values' with a national-interest-based approach, in their construction of a 'liberal conservative' foreign policy. However, in doing so, the ambiguous relationship between values and interests emerges once again. Cameron's (2012) reflections on his foreign affairs position reveal this incorporation of two competing strands:

> So, I describe myself – which for an American audience, I know, is very tough – as a liberal Conservative. What that means in British

terms is a 'liberal' foreign policy because I think we should be actively engaged in the world; we should be trying to spread human rights and democracy; we should be working with those that want to achieve those goals. But the Conservative bit of me is that we should be sceptical, we should be careful, we should be cautious; we should be asking questions about the grand plans and schemes to remake the world, because it's no good in international affairs to do something, or to start to do something, unless you know how you're going to finish it.

The application of a conservative sensibility to international affairs is coupled with an increased willingness to accept moral diversity and the limitations of universal values. Cameron (2012) has also argued that 'I am not naive in believing that democracy alone has some magical healing power. I am a Liberal Conservative, not a Neo-Conservative. I respect the different histories and traditions that each country has'. Likewise, when discussing possible UK responses to the Arab Spring, Hague stated that 'it is important not to generalise too much...if we want them to work with us in our interest and to develop more of our values. We mustn't push them down their throats, we have to be careful about that' (Hague, oral evidence in Foreign Affairs Committee 2012a, Ev. 13).

The coalition's 'active and activist foreign policy' involves the promotion of values that are 'democratic, progressive and liberal' and 'strengthening the rules-based international system in support of British values' (FCO 2011, p. 28; FCO written evidence in Foreign Affairs Committee 2011, Ev. 77–79). Confusingly, the values that the coalition seeks to re-frame as 'British' – human rights, democracy, the rule of law – are little different from those often suggested by Labour to be the universal values of the international community. There is also striking similarity between Blair's suggestion of a values–interests merger in an increasingly globalised world, and the coalition's suggestion of a harmony between values promotion and national interest in a 'networked world'. For Hague (2010),

> We have a strategic interest in promoting our values, which form the essential framework for the pursuit of our security and prosperity. In a networked world we cannot thrive alone. Our security is weakened when others lack the conditions for safety and where the absence of law creates fertile ground for future conflict or terrorism.

The role overseas ethical commitments are seen to play in supporting national interest is also evident in Cameron's (2010) reflections on the use of development aid as a form of soft power:

> When you sit round the table at the G8 or G20 discussing Haiti, Pakistan or Yemen, often the modern equivalent of a battleship is the C17 loaded with aid and the brilliant Oxfam team that is going to go in and help deliver water or whatever. They are real tools of foreign policy and influence and heft in the world. We should be quite frank about that, and not be embarrassed about it.

In addition to supporting the wellbeing of vulnerable non-citizens, aid is thus conceived as a functional tool in expressing British power and influence.

The suggestion of a mutually reinforcing relationship between overseas ethical commitments and national interest indicates further continuities with Labour's foreign policy. However, coalition foreign policy moves a step beyond this. Presenting the values to be promoted as explicitly 'British', rather than universal norms, combined with the idea that these values can serve immediate UK interests, bears more than a passing resemblance to the neo-conservative agenda recently influential on US foreign policy. For neo-conservatives Kristol and Kagan (1996, p. 27), 'American foreign policy should be informed with a clear moral purpose, based on the understanding that its moral goals and its fundamental national interests are almost always in harmony'. The influential Project for a New American Century (1997), similarly drew clear links between promoting 'the cause of political and economic freedom abroad' and 'preserving and extending an international order friendly to our security, our prosperity, and our principles'.

There are, of course, significant differences between US neo-conservativism and the coalition's policies. US neo-conservatism is concerned primarily with the maintenance of American global leadership and assumes that the projection of US values will be supported by overwhelming military capacity. The similarity is the role of values as a key tool in promoting the state's national interest. Although the coalition formulation suggests that these values might be promoted through soft power, the 2010 Strategic Defence and Security Review (SDSR), also highlights the need for British forces to remain configured for expeditionary warfighting in support of UK interests. Most likely as a result of the perceived overstretch in Iraq and Afghanistan, the SDSR is very clear that the coalition will be 'more selective in our use of the Armed

Forces, deploying them decisively at the right time but only where key UK national interests are at stake' (Ministry of Defence 2010a, p. 17). However, if the promotion of British values is seen by policymakers as intrinsically linked to the pursuit of national interest, the circumstances under which hard power might be used appear somewhat more broadly defined.

Albeit on a smaller scale to Iraq and Afghanistan, the deployment of UK forces as part of the Libya intervention in 2011 suggests that the overlay of values and interests in coalition foreign policy has the continued potential to be expressed in the use of force. Similarly, the connections drawn between values, interests and force were again evident in August 2013, with the coalition's push for more robust action, including the possible use of force, in response to the use of chemical weapons during the Syrian civil war. The coalition's case was grounded primarily on an emotive appeal to halt human suffering and to uphold international humanitarian law.[6] However, Cameron also made a direct link to national interest, suggesting that 'a stable Middle East is in the national interest, but there is a specific national interest relating to the use of chemical weapons and preventing its escalation'.[7] Notably, there is little further elaboration on the nature of this relationship. Although the Commons debate on Syria revealed a range of different arguments against the government's proposal, challenges to its compatibility with UK national interest, and the potential of military strikes to undermine regional stability and further endanger the safety of Syrian civilians were all raised.[8] As the defeat of the proposal on 29 August 2013 suggests, the argument that values and interests might be merged in a coherent UK foreign policy response to the Syrian civil war appeared unconvincing to the majority of MPs on this occasion.

Merging values and interests in practice: Stabilisation policy and arms exports

The coalition's foreign policy reveals distinct commonalities with Labour in the prominence afforded to ethical commitments to vulnerable non-citizens, whilst also attempting to create room for a more sceptical, cautious and pragmatic foreign policy approach. However, this new strategy remains centred on assumed harmony between UK national interests and the promotion of values. It internalises many of the tensions evident in the previous government's approach and doubts have already been expressed in parliament as to whether values and interests can be aligned in UK foreign policy (Foreign Affairs Committee

2012b, p. 39). Despite continued emphasis on the mutually reinforcing nature of values and interests, the emergence of what Kettel (2013) refers to as 'plausibility gaps' – the point at which a discursive strategy becomes untenable in the face of the real life events it attempts to narrate – appear increasingly likely.

The stabilisation of fragile states and UK arms exports are two policy areas where continuities in the approach of Labour and the coalition are evident. Moreover, these are also areas where syntheses between national interest and overseas ethical commitments are said to be located and, more importantly, where this claim begins to unravel.

'Stabilising' fragile states

Foreign policy that simultaneously serves UK interests, whilst providing a net benefit to vulnerable non-citizens, finds a particular expression in fragile state stabilisation. Stabilisation policy represents an area of continuity between Labour and the coalition, and borrows a range of concepts from existing peace operations doctrine and from historic experiences of British counter-insurgency. It is aimed at helping to address the problem of fragile states and to 'prevent – or contain – violent conflict', 'protect people and key people and key assets and institutions', 'promote political processes which lead to greater stability' and 'prepare for long-term development' (UK Stabilisation Unit 2008, p. 13).

The concept draws directly on ethical commitments to non-citizens. In seeking to help resolve violent conflicts, improve security within fragile states and build foundations for longer-term development, a role for stabilisation could be found in the pursuit of human security. Indeed, direct reference is made to infrastructure development and state capacity building in realising both national and human security in fragile states (Ministry of Defence 2010b). Moreover, stabilisation techniques could also play a role in the protection of vulnerable civilians from mass atrocity crimes, in the 'responsibility to react' and 'responsibility to re-build' phases of the Responsibility to Protect, a concept currently gaining traction in UK foreign policy (FCO 2010).

In the thinking of the coalition, stabilisation approaches have a dual function, one which plays into the apparent merger of values and interests. The practice of stabilisation is conceived as a means of addressing the threat posed to the UK by failed states. The 2010 UK National Security Strategy argues that 'fragile, failing and failed states around the world provide the environment for terrorists to operate as they look to exploit ungoverned or ill-governed space' (HM Government 2010). Advocating stabilisation as a logical and coherent response to the problem of failed states, the coalition argues that the practice simultaneously defends UK security interests, whilst also supporting the wellbeing of vulnerable non-citizens (Ministry of Defence 2010a, pp. 44–46; HM Government 2011, pp. 7–8). This would seem an ideal practical manifestation of the values–interests merger. However, closer analysis of this straightforward claim begins to reveal an unstable and unconvincing policy formulation.

Stabilisation approaches, if executed correctly, could help discharge ethical commitments to vulnerable non-citizens. The relationship between conflict, security and (under)development in fragile state environments poses significant threats to the wellbeing of their inhabitant populations. Fragile states are frequently characterised by entrenched corruption, ethnic stratification and very limited capacity to manage borders, provide security and administer natural resources. For Collier (2008, pp. 17–74) this produces a range of interrelated 'traps', which prevent positive economic development, foster chronic poverty and place fragile state populations in ongoing conditions of vulnerability. In addition to vulnerability created by poverty and economic exclusion, the societal stresses experienced within the fragile state also provide a fertile environment for forms of criminal and political violence that have often resulted in large-scale abuses of human rights (World Bank 2011, pp. 74–89).

Although there is a compelling case to suggest that greater UK foreign policy engagement in fragile states could help satisfy ethical responsibilities to vulnerable non-citizens, the tangible links between stabilisation and the UK's core security and economic interests are less clear. The argument that the ungoverned space emerging within failed states provides a breeding ground for terrorism and insurgent activity threatening the UK remains difficult to substantiate. Hehir (2007) highlights the poor empirical basis for the supposed link and questions why, in a heavily interconnected information age, terrorists would choose to train somewhere with invariably poor infrastructure, communication and transport links. Whilst ungoverned space can provide a fertile environment for terrorists training for operations within the host country or its immediate neighbours, it does not automatically follow that these groups threaten the security, sovereignty or territorial integrity of the UK. Hague's difficulty in explaining the precise links between national interest, values and the wellbeing of the Afghan population to a parliamentary committee appears indicative of the lack of clear reflection on this purported relationship (Foreign Affairs Committee 2012a, Ev. 4–5).

Secondly, given the problem of overstretch identified in the SDSR, combined with the large-scale projected cutbacks in armed forces personnel, it is questionable whether these kinds of mission may actually be feasible in the future. The original guidance by the Stabilisation Unit (2008, p. 15), acknowledges that 'stabilisation can have no predetermined duration, and some countries require active military engagement complementing peace-building efforts for many years'. However, the coalition's *Building Stability Overseas Strategy* subsequently re-drew the commitment envisaged for stabilisation operations in vaguer terms, with more ambiguous references to 'upstream prevention' and 'expeditionary diplomacy', rather than more immersive military interventions (HM Government 2011). The issue of (under)capacity poses significant questions for the attempted merger of values and interests. With respect to national interest, entering into long-term and complex stabilisation operations without adequate resources risks the lives of British citizens for objectives that might not be attainable. For the inhabitants of fragile states that might be subject to UK stabilisation operations, the lack of resources, combined with the vaguer way in which stabilisation is conceived, risks reducing stabilisation to limited tokenistic initiatives which promise much but have little capacity to uphold these commitments. Whilst ostensibly uniting values and interests, when subject to closer scrutiny, stabilisation appears an unstable formulation that risks serving neither and undermining both.

Arms exports and commercial interests

One of the first challenges to Labour's foreign policy with an ethical dimension was the difficulty in reconciling the promotion of human rights with the clear national economic interests associated with Britain's successful arms industry. Labour's initial pledge not to sell arms to countries where they might be used for internal repression was later expanded in light of the 1998 EU Code of Conduct on Arms Exports, to produce the 'Consolidated EU and National Arms Export Criteria', effective since 2000 (HM Government 2013, pp. 38–48). Several additional criteria expand the regulatory regime, including a prohibition on exporting arms to areas where they may 'provoke or prolong armed conflicts or aggravate existing tensions or conflicts in the country of final destination' (HM Government 2013, p. 47). Labour's moves to regulate the UK arms industry received immediate criticism in light of continued arms exports to Indonesia during the period of internal turmoil and violence prior to East Timor's independence. When questioned about the 22 arms export licenses to Indonesia approved between May and

November 1997 and the potential conflict with Labour's 'ethical dimension', Cook (1998) argued that 'we made a very clear distinction between legitimate defence exports for self-defence, which could not be used for internal repression, and equipment such as that sold by the last government, like the water cannons, which can be'. Cook's response here disregards the obvious potential for military equipment, designed for national self-defence, to have a secondary role in internal repression. Whether the weapons were for internal repression or not, the broader moral question of whether Britain should be engaged in an arms trading relationship with a regime notorious for human rights abuse appears to come secondary to UK economic interests. This prioritisation of arms trading relationships indicates a conflict, rather than a merger, between the 'ethical dimension' and national interest was occurring.

Running parallel to the continued focus on overseas ethical commitments, the coalition's re-engagement with national interest has manifested itself in the renewed pursuit of economic prosperity. One recent priority has been to 'increase exports and investment, open markets, ensure access to resources and promote sustainable global growth in a rules-based international trading system' (FCO 2012a, p. 2). Renewed economic prosperity has tangible links to British national interest – enhancing the material wellbeing of UK citizens, alongside providing a source of funding for Britain's hard and soft power capabilities. In keeping with the continued commitment to human rights, the coalition emphasises economic interests as being compatible with human rights' promotion. The FCO (2012b, p. 109) states: 'Human rights are intrinsic to our foreign policy and we will not promote trade at the expense of human rights. We see trade promotion and human rights work as mutually supportive'. Hague is similarly clear in suggesting that 'at no stage in the conduct policy do we reduce emphasis on human rights for any commercial reason' (Hague, oral evidence in Foreign Affairs Committee 2011, Ev. 70). Again, that which is seen as conducive to the UK's national interest is presented as supportive of overseas ethical commitments.

This 'mutually supportive' link between human rights and UK economic interests is envisaged partially as a form of constructive engagement, an opportunity where soft power might be exercised and human rights concerns introduced into trade relationships with authoritarian states. The FCO (2013, p. 109) affirms that

> The UK is prepared to engage with all states on the links between business and human rights, including those whose record on human rights is poor. We will continue to raise our concerns about human

rights wherever and whenever they arise, including those countries with which we are seeking closer commercial ties.

The effectiveness of this strategy is unclear and it remains difficult to isolate specific examples of successful leverage on human rights issues being exerted when developing new trading relationships. An activist foreign policy strategy could mean concerted efforts to include human rights conditions within trade agreements. However, it could also be reduced to little more than a gentle mention of underlying human rights concerns, with little further pressure applied. Much depends on the weight afforded to human rights concerns in comparison to commercial interests. Given the clear electoral benefits of improved UK economic performance and the relatively ambivalent public attitude to ethical foreign policy, it can be imagined that commercial interests would be prioritised. The relationship between economic interests and human rights need not always be a zero-sum game. However, the coalition's discourse glosses over the conflict that sometimes exists between the two by again reasserting the notion of a values and interests merger.

Reminiscent of Labour, the coalition's suggestion of a supportive relationship between human rights and British economic prosperity has come under increasing scrutiny in relation to arms exports. In July 2013, the parliamentary Committees on Arms Export Controls (2013, p. 29) levelled an explicit challenge to the idea of a values and interests merger, arguing that

> The Government would do well to acknowledge that there is an inherent conflict between strongly promoting arms exports to authoritarian regimes, whilst strongly criticising their lack of human rights at the same time, rather than claiming, as the Government continues to do, that these two policies are 'mutually reinforcing'.

Their report highlights that, at the time of publication, there were 3,074 Standard Individual Export Licences, for military goods worth £12.3 billion, approved for the 27 countries identified by the FCO as 'of human rights concern' (Committees on Arms Export Controls 2013, p. 32; FCO 2012b). Indeed, two of these, Libya and Saudi Arabia, have also been identified as 'priority markets' for defence exports (Committees on Arms Export Controls 2013, p. 21). The use of British-made armoured vehicles, supplied to Saudi Arabia, in suppressing the 2011 Bahrain uprising was also noted as a problematic example of UK exports being used in internal repression (Committees on Arms Export Controls 2013, pp. 36–37). The FCO (2013, p. 78) responded by arguing: 'While we do export licensable equipment to countries of concern... commercial relationships do not prevent us from speaking frankly and openly to the governments of these countries about issues of concern'. Again, the implication is that commercial relationships feed into the promotion of human rights as a form of constructive engagement with authoritarian states.

Empowering authoritarian states by supplying military equipment appears inconsistent with ethical concerns for the populations of these same states. The pledge to only sell weapons for legitimate self-defence, and not where they might be used for internal repression, deliberately ignores the dual-use capability of many pieces of military equipment to be used to suppress internal dissent. As the Arab Spring uprisings indicate, even if it does not occur at the time of export, this does not guarantee that it will not happen in future. British economic interests, in particular arms exports, have thus come to display a problematic relationship with the promotion of human rights in both Labour's and the coalition's foreign policy. This tension is arguably unavoidable, and largely reflects conflicting realms of ethical responsibility. Whilst Britain's economic interests and overseas ethical responsibilities may not be fundamentally incompatible, the suggestion of a 'mutually reinforcing' relationship between them appears disingenuous as currently conceived, and obscures, rather than resolves, the tension between the two.

Conclusion

The 1997–2010 Labour government made considerable efforts to craft a foreign policy that pursued the traditional objectives of national interest alongside an 'ethical dimension' that attempted to improve the wellbeing of vulnerable non-citizens. One principal claim during this period was that, in an increasingly interconnected and globalised world, concerns for the 'Other' and national self-interest could not be viewed in isolation. Moreover, it was argued that, in this new global context, they had merged. The infusion of concerns for the human rights, security and material wellbeing of non-citizens was controversial, and the difficult relationship between ethical claims and interventionist foreign policy in Afghanistan and Iraq has done little to ameliorate this. Labour became associated with a highly moralistic and militarised foreign policy that, when combined with the polarising rhetoric of the war on terror, left little room for ethical diversity in international relations.

Given the controversy of the previous decade, it seems predictable that, following the change of government in 2010, the incoming Conservative–Liberal Democrat coalition would seek to differentiate themselves from Labour. Indeed, a central claim of their foreign policy has been a rejection of hubristic 'doctrines' of foreign policy. However, what appears evident, both in policy and ministerial discourse, is that the ethical agenda has become embedded in UK foreign policy. Although emphasising their commitment to the primacy of national interest, the ethics/values-based agenda of the coalition is similar to that promoted by Labour, and the idea of values–interests harmonisation in an increasingly globalised/networked world has been maintained.

This policy continuity has significant ramifications for what might be conceived as the UK's national interest. As the examples of stabilisation and arms exports illustrate, the plausibility of claims about the merger of values and national interests remains questionable. The tendency to repeat the idea of a merger, in speeches and policy discourse, is rarely paired with explication of actual connections or a mutually supportive relationship. The suggestion of a harmony of values and interests is ultimately an unhelpful way of thinking about either of these. It represents a convenient means of packaging British foreign policy to appeal to a wide range of constituencies, by making ethical responsibilities to non-citizens appear beneficial to the national interest, or by creating the appearance of narrow national interests simultaneously benefitting a wider human community. The discourse associated with the ethical foreign policies of both Labour and the coalition has a tendency to obscure the tensions that might exist between values and interests, and the processes by which some commitments are prioritised over others, and the ways in which they may ultimately compromise one another.

A more helpful conceptualisation of British national interest might be found by disaggregating values and interest. This would not involve rejecting overseas ethical commitments, nor should it suggest that different realms of ethical responsibility exist in isolation. However, it would require the acceptance that overseas ethical commitments are important ends in themselves, rather than a sub-component of an 'enlightened national interest'. An 'enlightened foreign policy', which disaggregates national interest from ethical responsibilities to non-citizens, would provide a means through which the requirements and objectives of each might be more clearly delineated. The process of disaggregation would help expose both the tensions that might exist between values and interests, and the ways in which they could complement one another. The broader risk of maintaining the current trajectory of UK foreign policy is that the policy instability resulting from the assumed harmony of values and interest may eventually lead to a 'worst of all worlds' outcome; one where neither national interest nor the wellbeing of vulnerable non-citizens is supported effectively.

Notes

1. This is a revised and updated version of an article that first appeared in *International Affairs*, London, vol. 90, no. 3, May 2014, pp. 541–557, and is reproduced with permission.
2. Traditional national interest objectives of protecting a specific population from harm or supporting their economic wellbeing would seem to demonstrate this tangible link.
3. See: http://henryjacksonsociety.org/about-the-society/statement-of-principles/
4. Survey conducted 13–15 June 2012. Sample size 2,078.
5. I have appropriated this term from Williams (2010, p. 31).
6. HC Deb 29 August 2013, cols. 1431–1438.
7. Cameron, HC Deb 29 August 2013, col. 1437.
8. See HC Deb 29 August 2012, cols. 1425–1556.

3
The National Interest and Britain's Role in the World[1]

Jamie Gaskarth

If ever there was a contested concept in politics, it is the 'national interest'. The term has been used to mean an expression of the 'general will' of the political community, the aggregation of individual citizens' needs, commitment to longstanding policies and state secrecy, as well as a state's relative power in the international system (Kratochwil 1982; Morgenthau 1993; Clinton 1991; Weldes 1996; Nye 1999). In a recent reformulation of the idea, Alexander George argues that it is reducible to three core components: the security and physical survival of the state, its independence and liberty, and the economic prosperity of the populace (George 2006, pp. 9–10). However, as he goes on to note, the term 'national interest' when applied to such goals is a misnomer. In reality, these are 'irreducible national values' rather than interests (George 2006, p. 10). Values can remain constant over time (in the abstract) whereas interests involve more specific and historically contingent ways of preserving these values.

Thus, if interests are ways to achieve the ends of national values, then discussion of national interest is really about strategy (Jermyn 2001, p. 18). The question is: how are these national values best advanced? Is Britain more secure because the UK intervenes militarily abroad? How can some measure of independence be maintained in a globalised world? Can Britain uphold its values of democracy and liberty at home if it is supporting undemocratic regimes abroad? Is Britain's prosperity advanced by its financial sector or undermined by it? A number of recent parliamentary reports have sought to examine questions of strategy at the national level (House of Lords 2012; PASC 2011; Hill 2010). What they have found is that the answers rely heavily upon the identity we ascribe to the UK as a global actor. As the Public Administration Select Committee (PASC) argues: 'strategic aims cannot be set or adjudicated without an articulated account of who "we" are and what we believe, both about ourselves and the world' (PASC 2011, para. 7). The UK policymaking community has historically resisted frank consideration of Britain's identity (Coles 2000, p. 11; Mangold 2001, pp. 5, 68). The PASC suggests that this needs to change and unstated assumptions 'need to be exposed so that they may be tested and, if necessary, altered' (PASC 2007, para.7).

A primary driver of this reflection has been the economic impact of the 2008 financial crisis. It soon became apparent that this would affect key components of British foreign policy activity, especially its defence spending and commitments (Cornish and Dorman 2011; McGuire and Werth 2009). In a report by the Institute for Public Policy Research (IPPR) in 2009, the authors asserted: 'Most serious commentators now believe the situation cannot continue as it is...fundamental choices are necessary. The attempt to maintain the full spectrum of conventional combat capabilities at current scale has produced acute strains on resources and, increasingly, on operational effectiveness' (IPPR 2009, p. 47). Similarly, a joint House of Lords/House of Commons committee on the national security strategy argued in 2010 that: 'Given the UK's low economic growth rate compared with those of the world's emerging economies, we believe it is wholly unrealistic not to expect any diminution in the UK's power and influence in the medium and long term' (House of Lords 2010).

The latter quotation hints at another motivating force for reconsidering the UK's identity position in world politics: the rise of new poles of power in the shape of Brazil, China and India. Futurologists predict a 'historic shift of relative wealth and economic power from West to East' in coming decades (NIC 2008, p. 1). Longstanding assumptions about Britain's status and leadership in global forums, alliance patterns and policy behaviour are under scrutiny. In response, parliamentarians have asserted that national strategy 'should be based on a realistic vision of the UK's future place in the world, which will both shape, and be shaped by, the UK's interests and objectives' (House of Lords 2010, pp. 18–19).

In short, the new reality of economic austerity and diminished influence requires some hard thinking about how Britain should be expected to act in future. This in turn requires consideration of how identity shapes strategic thinking. In this chapter, I argue that role theory provides a practical framework for understanding the relationship between identity, strategy and action in foreign policymaking. Discussion of Britain's 'role in the world' is arguably the nearest policymakers have come to a genuine engagement with identity issues. However, the term has been used loosely and rarely led to a genuine appraisal of the range of identity positions available to Britain's policymakers (Hill 1979). This chapter will continue by outlining role theory and its contribution to foreign policy analysis before suggesting a number of 'role orientations' that could be possible for British foreign policy. In doing so, it aims to fulfil the critical function of demonstrating that alternatives to current policies do exist, as well as exploring the challenges making such choices would present.

Role theory

References to national roles are commonplace in foreign policy rhetoric (Cantir and Kaarbo 2012, p. 18; Thies 2009). However, the concept is used to describe a range of behaviours, identities and status positions (Le Pestre 1997, p. 4). The term derives from sociology and its core assumption is that participants in a social system adopt roles, rather like actors in a play, according to a script based on certain prescribed identities and behaviours (Aggestam 2006, p. 12). This could give the impression that policy is structurally determined. It is a view seemingly reinforced on a material basis by Naomi Wish's suggestion that: 'a nation's foreign policy behaviour is in large measure a product of its national capabilities or attributes' (Wish 1987, p. 96). Yet, Wish actually intends to convey a more circular process. Material attributes feed into conceptions of the national role, in a way that then shapes behaviour; but a state's behaviour then affects national attributes in turn. Thus, the cycle Wish outlines goes as follows (Figure 3.1):

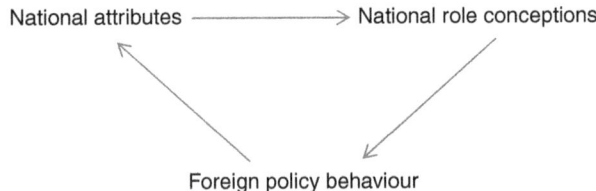

Figure 3.1 Cycle of role generation

Indeed, one of the primary benefits of a role-based approach to foreign policy analysis is that it gives a more nuanced and dynamic account of identity formation and policy behaviour than purely individualist or structuralist accounts. Roles come with expectations about behaviour that do shape actions. These role expectations or 'role prescriptions' derive from a state's membership of institutions, interactions with external actors, and domestic audiences, and condition what policies are deemed appropriate and how they are received (Aggestam 2006, pp. 14–18). For instance, at the institutional level, membership of NATO prescribes the role of 'reliable ally' when a fellow NATO member is attacked; interactions with other states may lead to the role of 'bridge' or 'mediator'; whilst domestic political groups might call for either withdrawal from global commitments, towards the role of 'isolate', or for the state to be a more active 'defender of the faith' or 'liberator' in support of domestic values (Holsti 1970). Governments that deviate from the 'script' can face punishment or at the very least confusion from domestic audiences or other international actors. Yet, there is also scope for policymakers to be creative in their choice of roles and how they interpret or enact them (Elgstrom and Smith 2006, p. 5). Consequently, role theory provides for agency in foreign policy, even as it recognises it is bounded by social expectations.

As role theory has developed, analysts have developed a complex understanding of how this concept can be used to trace the policymaking process. At the broadest level of a state's disposition towards its external environment, Hermann describes 'role orientations' that provide an overarching rationale and pattern to how states interact with others. The examples offered are: expansionist, active independent, influential, mediator/integrator, opportunist, developmental (Hermann 1987, p. 134).[2] To this list might be added the role of isolate. Underlying each is a different primary goal or driver, these are (respectively): power; autonomy; influence in the international system; solutions to problems; public support; the development of the state; and isolation (Hermann 1987, p. 134). With the above role orientations, status plays an important underlying role – either as the ultimate goal of these role adoptions (states might crave power or influence to achieve or maintain a high status) or as a source of social expectation (great powers might see being influential or a mediator as their duty because of their elevated status in international society) (Clark 2009, p. 212; Macleod 1997, p. 162).

The concept of role orientation is vital to our discussion since it represents the highest order of strategic thinking in foreign policy. It begs the question: what role orientation does the UK want to adopt, given the economic pressures it faces and the emergence of rival powers in the international system? Since role orientation is closely linked to social structures, and is the ultimate expression of how a state interacts with the system, it would seem to be a particularly difficult level at which an actor could exercise agency. Material constraints (i.e.

national capabilities and relative power) as well as social structures (i.e. status and social interactions) combine to narrow the available choices. Switzerland cannot simply choose an expansionist role orientation. The US would struggle to be an isolate given the volume of its trade and interactions abroad. Nevertheless, role theorists have noted that policymakers do have the opportunity to alter their role orientation provided social and material constraints allow it (Shih 1998, pp. 602–603).

The way governments pursue role orientations is by making choices from a range of more specific national role conceptions. By describing this as a choice, the author does not wish to imply this is always a deliberative process. The choice may at times be made for the policymaker by social expectations. In his 1954 Reith lecture, Oliver Franks confidently predicted that Britain would continue to be a great power, not as a result of 'reflection' and a 'conscious decision'; rather, he suggests that 'It is part of the habit and furniture of our minds: a principle so much one with our outlook and character that it determines the way we act' (Franks 1954). Examples of national role conceptions include 'balancer', 'defender of the faith', 'leader' or 'reliable ally', among others (Holsti 1970, pp. 296–297). Role orientations may imply particular 'role sets' or groups of such identities that enable a role to be fulfilled (Walker and Simon 1987). Yet, no single role orientation will encompass all national role conceptions. That means there is always scope for reorientation if the pattern of conceptions shifts.

The fact that role conceptions might point to different identities or policies also raises the prospect of role conflict. Rather than a purely negative process, role conflict can actually provide a mechanism for change in foreign policy and so is seen as a useful means of ensuring policy evolves and is appropriate to the specific policy environment (Rosenau 1984, p. 270). However, conflicts can have damaging consequences for policy and reputations if either internal or external actors reject one role in favour of another against the grain of public opinion. This highlights the importance of role performance or 'role enactment' (Thies 2012). Narrowing the analysis still further from the abstract to the empirical, role theorists examine how these conceptions are performed through particular policy choices and outputs – and how these are received. This process represents a powerful feedback loop, shaping the expectations of others in a way that could have an impact on future role orientations or national role conceptions.

For illustrative purposes, I explore the role orientation of Britain being an influential actor in the international system in Figure 3.2 below.

The list of national role conceptions is not exhaustive and many others might have been added (e.g. regional protector, example to others, liberator). Each could in some way be expected to afford the UK influence over other international actors but none automatically translate into favourable outcomes. For example, being a generous aid donor could enhance the UK's identity as a positive influence on global development; but, if British policymakers sought to exploit this for political or economic advantage then others may object to that role as neo-colonialism or cynical self-interest.[3] In other words, this list of role conceptions and performances also contains within it the seeds of potential role conflict (Figure 3.2).

As such, this is not a closed system but a dynamic process of interpretation, interaction and contestation that does not automatically relate roles to outcomes in a linear way. Nevertheless, in outlining a role orientation, as well as the role conceptions and performances that flow from it, we begin to understand policy identities and behaviour in a more strategic manner. The next step for this chapter is to ask whether policymakers could make a strategic choice as to which role orientation they adopt in order to further their national values.

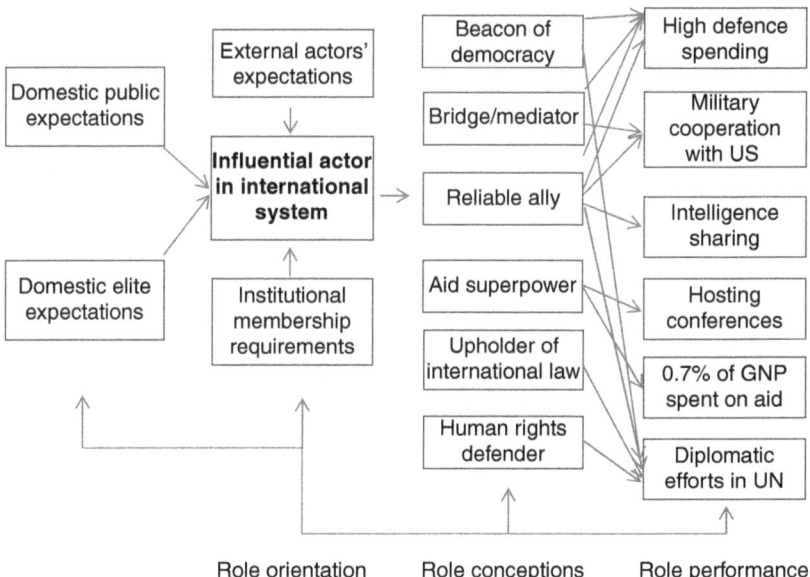

Figure 3.2 Sample role orientation of 'influential actor'[4]

Role theorists have tended to be cautious about the level of deliberate agency policymakers can exercise when it comes to role making and role taking (Harnisch 2012). Lisbeth Aggestam asserts that acknowledging scope for agency 'does not mean that we consider roles to simply be like hats that you can take on and off' (2006, p. 18). Nevertheless, as stated above, role orientations do change and policymakers, as key interpretive actors, can contribute to shifts in understanding. As Martin Hollis and Steve Smith note, foreign policymakers are sometimes able to achieve a level of 'role distance' – meaning finding space to reflect on and interpret what roles are available and how they should be performed (Hollis and Smith 1986).[5] Therefore, it does not seem unreasonable to suggest that there exists the scope for British foreign policymakers to examine the range of potential role orientations available to a state such as the UK and explore the likely benefits and costs of each.

What follows is a preliminary investigation into six such role orientations that feature prominently in recent debates over British foreign policy. These are: isolate, regional partner, influential (rule of law state), thought leader, opportunist-interventionist and great power. In providing a preliminary sketch of each, the author aims to offer a more useful platform for debates on role orientation than the sterile debate on whether the UK should align itself with the US or Europe. In the process, I also aim to give a sense of the different policy directions that result from choices about role orientation.

Isolate

The role orientation of isolate is inward looking and the state will expend as little energy and resources externally as necessary to allow it to focus on domestic concerns (Wish 1987, p. 538). In the British context, this image is usually evoked and then summarily dismissed. For example, Franks noted: 'There are some who suggest that the...thing to do is to withdraw from world affairs and lead a quiet life on our island, democratic, contented, and reasonably industrious', a position which he described as 'impossible' (Franks 1954). Similarly, the 1998 Strategic Defence Review acknowledged that: 'We could of course as a country, choose to take a narrow view of our role and responsibilities which did not require a significant military capability.... This is indeed a real choice'. But in the same paragraph, without elaboration, it decided this was 'not one the Government could recommend for Britain' (MOD 1998, p. 1).

Throughout Britain's history, there have been voices calling for the country to adopt a more circumspect, non-interventionist stance on particular regional or global issues. This 'dissenting tradition' in British foreign policy commonly saw foreign policy as a conspiracy run by the aristocratic class (Taylor 1957). However, it was more often military intervention rather than involvement in international affairs per se which raised objections.[6] In the mid-nineteenth century, non-intervention was championed by the Manchester school of John Bright and Richard Cobden, two members of the British parliament. Bright protested against alliances with foreign powers as leading to 'a system which binds us in all these net-works and complications, from which it is impossible we gain one single atom of advantage' (Bright 1858, p. 194). Bright's fellow radical MP, Richard Cobden, launched a 'no foreign politics' campaign, which he asserted would 'comprise every representative of our manufacturing and commercial districts' (Cobden 1886, p. 34). This was designed to subvert the conduct of foreign policymaking by elites and argued for 'as little intercourse as possible between governments' (Cobden 1886, p. 34). This is perhaps the nearest that British politics has come in the last two centuries to a movement advocating a non-internationalist role for the UK.

More recently, a growing public scepticism about the UK's international duties is apparent in the fallout from the 2003 Iraq war and the 2008 financial crisis. In a 2009 poll, 51 per cent of the public disapproved of the UK's military involvement in Afghanistan and 57 per cent felt that the UK would not benefit from their actions there (Reifler et al. 2014). In April 2011, 50 per cent of the British public polled disapproved of intervention in Libya, with only 23 per cent approving – despite the limited nature of the operation (Reifler et al. 2014). Opinion polling on intervention in the last two decades suggests that public support for military action can wane dramatically when it comes to talk of casualties (Gaskarth 2013, p. 78). Similarly, support for development aid has declined as government budgets have been tightened, with those favouring an increase falling from 49 per cent to 35 per cent between 2008 and 2010, and 66 per cent believing the UK gave too much aid (Gaskarth 2013, p. 118). This could hint at an emerging discourse in favour of isolation. In sum, a policy of reduced global commitment, particularly when it came to military action, would seem to be garnering public approval.

In its favour would be the immense financial savings to be had. Keith Hartley has estimated that Britain's role as a global military actor costs around 1 per cent of GDP, equivalent to an annual cost of £15 billion (2010, p. 5). The UK's involvement in Iraq between 2001 and 2010 is reckoned to have cost £9.24 billion (BBC 2011) and its Afghanistan campaign, £25 billion to May 2013 (Norton-Taylor 2013). At a time when public debt is at unprecedented levels and major cuts are being implemented to public services, this is an unusually propitious time to argue for a more isolated role orientation for the UK in the international arena. A focus on economic prosperity and more productive non-military industrial activity would be likely to attract public support.

However, the national role conceptions that might support a shift like this are sparse. The UK has been a prominent international actor for such a long time that there are few 'scripts' of the UK as an isolate available for policymakers to enact. By contrast, the national role conceptions of the UK as 'influential' by being a 'reliable ally' and 'upholder of international law' are recurrent themes (Strachan 2009, p. 51; Kitchen and Vickers 2013). Cutting the defence budget substantially would imperil the UK's relationship with the US – a cornerstone of British strategic thinking since the Second World War. It would also cause friction with European neighbours, since it might threaten the future of NATO, as well as European defence initiatives that have been led by the UK and through which the UK has been able to express the national role conceptions of 'regional leader' and 'positive European partner'. Although successive defence reviews, from the 1998 Strategic Defence Review to the 2008 National Security Strategy (NSS) and 2010 Strategic Defence and Security Review (SDSR) and NSS, have suggested that: 'there is today no direct military threat to the United Kingdom or Western Europe' (Ministry of Defence 1998, p. 9; Cabinet Office 2008, p. 3), the US pivot to Asia, combined with a UK adoption of the role of isolate, might lead to a revival of regional security threats (Rühle 2013). Russia's actions in Georgia and the Ukraine remind us that some states see military force as a viable tool for achieving foreign policy aims.

Moreover, even those discourses that at first glance seem to imply isolationism often in reality support an internationalist orientation. Cobden may have been critical of government-to-government interaction but he also called for 'as much connexion as possible between the nations of the world' (Cobden 1886, p. 34). In doing so, he was not advocating isolation, but rather the development of people-to-people networks on an informal and hence non-governmental basis. Underlying this attitude was a belief that trade and human contact would spread peace (Cobden 1886, p. 36). Similarly, more recent dissent over Britain's membership of the EU is usually framed not as a desire for isolation but rather to withdraw from a role orientation of 'regional power' towards a more internationally influential role via trade with the wider world.[7]

In other words, despite appearances, advocating a role orientation of isolate is unlikely to accord with the traditions and beliefs of the British public, or their elites.[8] There is also the practicality of pursuing a policy of isolation when the UK is a member of so many international organisations and treaty arrangements.[9] The fallout from Britain reversing its involvement in NATO, the UN, the EU or, to a lesser extent, the Commonwealth would be severe. Overall, any effort to pursue a truly radical non-interventionist stance would face challenges not only from the militarist groups in British society but also those in favour of regional integration and/or international organisations and human rights and global civil society activists, as well as multinational firms pursuing a globalist agenda. In short, there is unlikely to be enough political or social force to carry it through. Despite this, it is worth raising as a potential role orientation, if only to highlight the limits to policymakers' choices given the existence of longstanding alternative orientations premised on the idea of the UK as an active participant in international affairs (Figure 3.3).

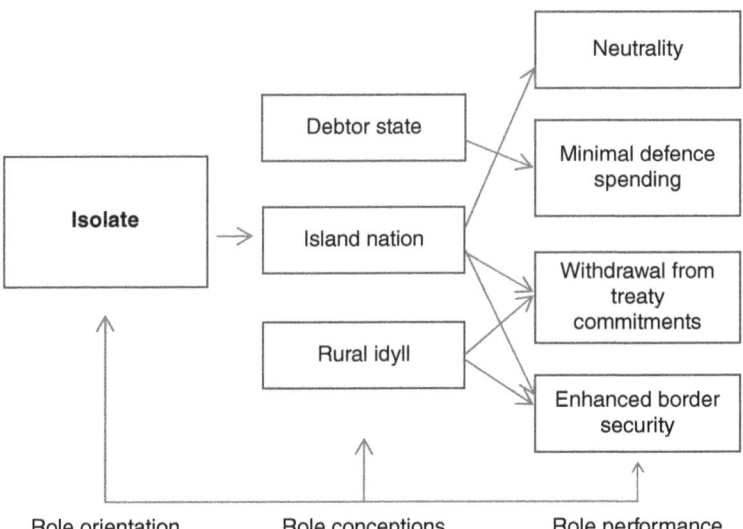

Figure 3.3 Role orientation of isolate

Regional partner

Given the economic crises that have affected the eurozone in recent years, combined with the political tensions in the EU over how to respond, it may seem strange to consider a role orientation that aligns the UK closer to Europe. The rhetoric on all sides of the political divide in the UK is about renegotiation of Britain's relationship with the EU to repatriate powers. Politicians want to reassert the UK's autonomy from the forces of European integration and even arrange a referendum to decide whether Britain's membership of the union should continue. Nevertheless, a role orientation that posits the UK as a regional rather than a global power has to be considered in the light of the rise of alternative centres of power in Asia and South America. With the end of the Cold War, a number of commentators rejected the idea of Britain as a great power with an international role and advocated an acceptance that the UK's power had declined (Wallace 1992; Young 1999; Hutton 1992). Rather than cling to the coat tails of the US, an often capricious ally, Britain was urged to embrace its historical European identity and play a fuller leadership role in Europe. As a result, Britain would be able to have a more meaningful influence on events than it could in isolation or as a transatlantic groupie of the US.

British foreign policymakers have periodically made efforts to put forward a national role conception of the UK as a longstanding European state. Jack Straw, when foreign secretary, asserted: 'We are a European nation, and always have been. Our monarchy was Danish, then Norman, then Dutch, then German' (Straw 2001). For Straw, it was engagement with Europe that led to the UK's international role in the first place. This narrative can be seen as flowing from a wider revisionist effort in academic circles during the 1990s to reconnect British history with its European past (Garton Ash 2000). But, as Timothy Garton Ash has noted, even though the material exists to create a European identity for Britain, 'it cannot be the identity.... The other identities are too strong' (Garton Ash 2000, p. 13). In particular, the UK populace continue to associate themselves more with English speaking countries, especially Australia, Canada and New Zealand, than their European neighbours (Gaskarth 2013, p. 69). Resistance to a regional orientation, and a national role conception of Britain as European, is powerfully reinforced in public discourse by media images of the continent as a source of 'un-British' systems of government and laws as well as security threats from immigration (Daddow 2004; Forster 2002). Despite the potential advantages in terms of regional and global influence that could

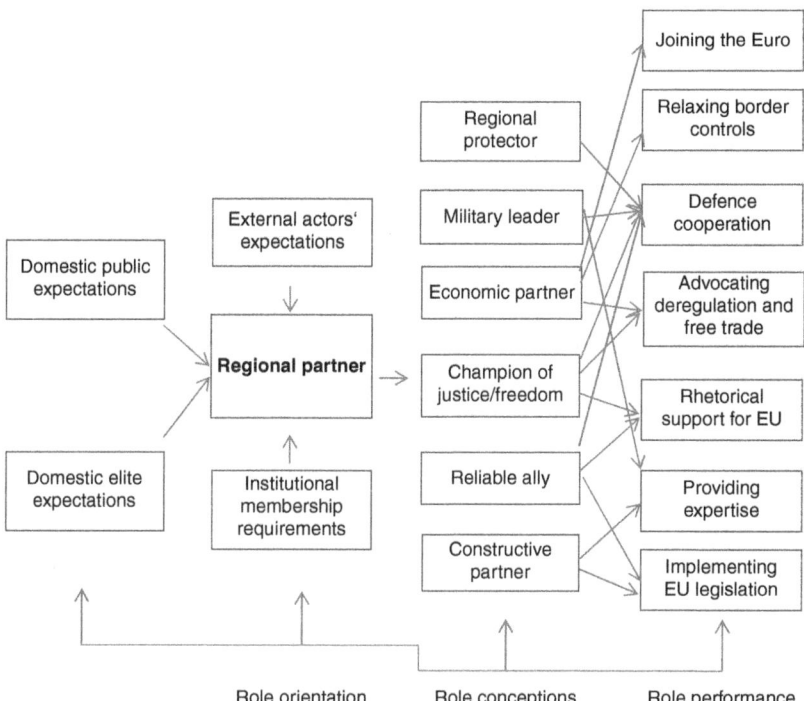

Figure 3.4 Role orientation of regional partner

flow from the UK embracing an orientation towards Europe, and the potential 'role resources' available to policymakers as outlined below, these seem counteracted by stronger role orientations and national role conceptions that wish to emphasise separation and distance (Figure 3.4).

Influential – Rule of law state

The next role orientation the UK might pursue is that of being an influential power, with an emphasis on the national role conception of being an upholder of international law. Since the UK already has a high status in global politics, via its institutional memberships and relative prosperity, it clearly benefits from the existing arrangement of international society. It could therefore carve out a niche for itself as a constructive member of that society that wishes to preserve the status quo. The role of being a status quo power has been at the core of Britain's self-identity for centuries. The nineteenth century German chancellor, Otto Von Bismarck, described Britain as one of 'les satisfaits' (Platt 1968, p. 354), a state that was happy with its position in world affairs and so would not seek radical reform of the prevailing international order. In his famous 1907 memorandum Sir Eyre Crowe asserted that 'England, more than any other non-insular Power, has a direct and positive interest in the maintenance of the independence of nations' (Crowe 1907). Other states could justifiably critique the idea of Britain as a longstanding and unequivocal supporter of the norms of sovereignty and non-intervention that are so central to international law (and order). However, this role conception proved useful in providing the ultimate rationale for the UK's involvement in both world wars, the Korean war in 1950 and the Falklands war in 1982 (McCourt 2011).

In addition, the idea of upholding international law and preserving the essential character of the states system is likely to be attractive to other actors, such as the rising powers of Brazil, China and India. These states are very protective of the norms of sovereignty and non-intervention, particularly when it comes to their own national values and interests. UK support for liberal interventionism and preventive war after 1998 has caused concern in these quarters. This reminds us that choosing among role orientations, and their underlying national role conceptions, should involve consideration of how these will be received by the wider international community. If Britain is to exert influence in the coming decades, it will increasingly have to co-opt the rising powers into accepting British assumptions about policy priorities and appropriate forms of action. Emphasising national role conceptions for the UK that accord with their values, such as 'status quo power', 'upholder of international law', and so on, would help to facilitate these relationships.

The kinds of role performances that might flow from these positions include doing the basics of international diplomacy: drafting papers and legal treaties, hosting conferences, conducting observer missions, verifying commitments and offering expertise. These are already acknowledged as being particular strengths of British foreign policy. Lord Malloch-Brown has suggested that despite the furore over its involvement in the 2003 Iraq invasion, Britain was still seen in the UN as 'in all other ways, very active – with all the first-class ambassadors and first-class staff in New York, sending some of our best diplomats, you know just working the UN with a seriousness that, say, the US didn't do'.[10] It is also one that fits with Britain's self-identity of being a constructive member of international society. A commitment to multilateral institutions has been a mainstay of a number of strategy documents in the last decade (FCO 2003, p. 24; Cabinet Office 2008, pp. 9, 47; HM Government 2010, p. 10). In its 2012 annual report, the FCO boasts that: 'The UK continues to believe that a rules-based system is the best way to promote British interests.... The FCO has been active in ensuring that international institutions are effective'. (FCO 2012, p. 4).[11] One could imagine the UK playing a useful part in international society by providing diplomatic expertise and financial support for the institutions of global governance; in the process, moving away from the more militaristic role performances of recent decades.

However, maintaining the existing institutions of international law and society in aspic is not sustainable in the long term. For one thing, there are continuing calls for reform of key international organisations such as the WTO, World Bank/IMF and the UN Security Council. Thus, being a status quo power and upholder of international law means, in practice, managing the continual pressures for change. There is also the thorny question of when intervention is required to uphold the law. When Nicholas Wheeler and Tim Dunne (1998) advocated Britain taking the role of 'good international citizen' in the 1990s, they left open the possibility of transgressing international law to promote human rights. One could see this as a straightforward role conflict between the role conceptions of 'human rights defender' and 'upholder of international law'; but, it might also be interpreted as a conflict internal to the latter role, over whether international criminal law and human rights conventions should be upheld over legal norms of sovereignty and non-intervention.

In the last decade, there has been a great deal of controversy over what kinds of action are required to maintain the status quo of a rules-based international system. The UK's involvement in the Iraq conflict in 2003 was justified by Tony Blair on the basis that Saddam Hussein had breached 17 UN Security Council Resolutions and the credibility of international law and the UN system was at stake (Blair 2003). Opposing this view among the permanent members of the Security Council were China, Russia and France, who felt that Iraq had been contained and did not pose an imminent threat to international peace and security. The political fallout from these conflicting interpretations of the role of 'upholder of international law' was considerable.

The coalition government seemed to have resolved this tension over Britain's use of military force via David Cameron's assertion of the importance of consent in the international community at large for action. Discussing intervention in Libya in 2011, Cameron defined his three essential criteria used to decide action as: 'Demonstrable need.

Regional Support. And a clear legal basis' (Cameron 2011). The inclusion of regional support and a 'clear' legal position as vital factors was designed to distinguish this situation from that of Iraq in 2003. Through substantial diplomatic effort, the UK and its allies had been able to gain the support of all the permanent members of the UN Security Council, as well as that of the African Union and Arab League, for military action to halt the abuses of the Gaddafi regime. Yet, in August 2013, the UK was again contemplating military action against the wishes of Russia, China and some regional actors, this time over Syria's use of chemical weapons. When the two motions were opposed in the House of Commons, a brief flurry of debate emerged about what this would mean for Britain's influence in the world, with some seeing this as symptomatic of a retreat from the role orientation of 'influential' and national role conception of 'reliable ally' of the US (Osborne 2013; Ashdown 2013).[12]

Despite this, polls suggested the general public was not in favour of military action without a clear legal mandate. When the subsequent deal was brokered between Russia and the US encouraging Syria to relinquish its chemical weapons, the UK was sidelined by both parties as neither a likely military belligerent nor a mediator for peace. Therefore, we can see that trying to fulfil a role orientation that does not accord with the views of the British public or key actors in the global arena has profoundly negative consequences. If the UK government had stuck to its original formulation of the need for a clear legal basis and regional support, this role conflict might have been avoided. It would also have provided greater clarity for allies in predicting when they could rely on UK support (Figure 3.5).

Thought leader[13]

A more recent role to be suggested for the UK is that of 'thought leader'. In light of Britain's declining influence, a number of commentators have suggested that the country's capacity to respond to risks and shape outcomes in global politics will depend on its ability to persuade other states and transnational actors to take action. As Alex Evans and David Steven put it, the UK will need to: 'adopt and excel in the role of thought leader, recognizing that it will often have greater comparative advantage in this area than in the "endgame" on key risks, where larger powers will tend to dominate' (2010, p. 14). In addition to providing creative thinking and actively promoting innovations in world politics, the authors also see a role for the UK in supporting the thought leadership of others,

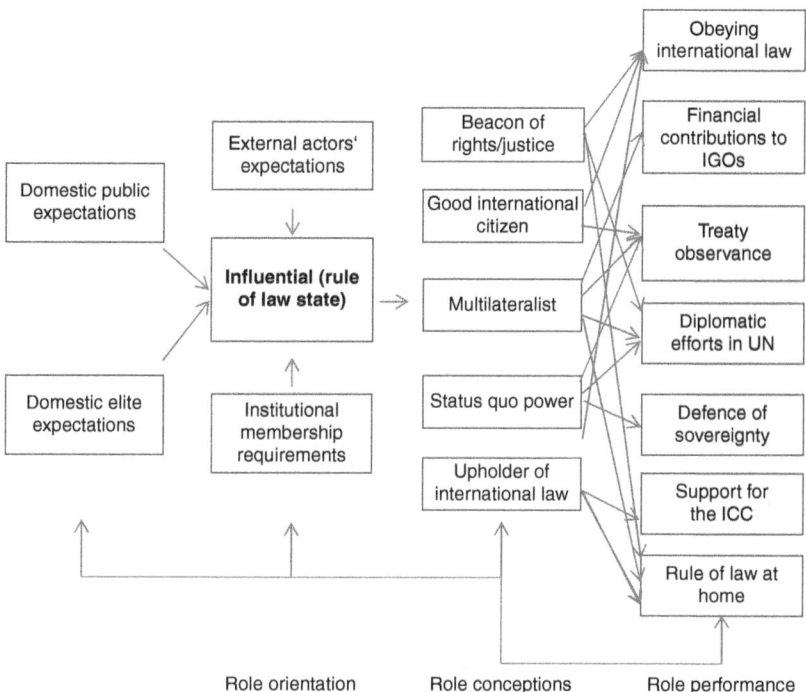

Figure 3.5 Role orientation of influential (rule of law state)

'acting as a convenor for debate, discussion and dialogue' (Evans and Steven 2010, p. 14). On a practical level, the role of thought leader would involve creating shared awareness of risks, as well as shared platforms and operating systems to campaign for change and manage the risks identified.

In a discussion on the concept at Chatham House, one of the contributors asserted that thought leadership should be seen as 'part of a systematic shift in an approach to global affairs, not a tactical way to deliver in the national interest, because then you are instrumentalising again, and you can't align your forces around a kind of narrow definition of an interest. These are just bigger coalitions' (Mabey 2010, p. 10). This implies that acting as a thought leader is about identifying risks and solutions that affect the international community as a whole. Whilst the UK would derive some kudos from drawing attention to such problems and coordinating responses, the subsequent action would need to be in the group interest. As a result, it is hard to see how this could be a defining identity for the UK as, at times, self-interest would have to prevail.

That said, being a thought leader would seem to fit naturally with aspects of Britain's self-identity in world politics. The UK is often a prominent advocate for pursuing global normative initiatives. It was instrumental in creating an International Criminal Court in 1998 and supported a ban on landmines under the auspices of the Ottawa Treaty. It provided a platform for discussion on African development and debt relief via its presidency of the G8 in 2005 and has been at the forefront of promoting climate change as a major security issue (Evans 2010, p. 18).

Although this has afforded the UK a prominent position in global debates, it is not clear whether such a role is sustainable as a guiding identity for the state. In essence, this is a form of 'activist' diplomacy. Indeed, the 2012 FCO annual report states 'Our aim is to pursue an active and activist foreign policy' (FCO 2012, p. 3). Perhaps one of the most overt examples of this approach has been the FCO's campaign to prevent conflict zone rape and sexual violence. William Hague launched this initiative in May 2012 with the UNHCR special envoy, Angelina Jolie, and the two travelled to the Democratic Republic of the Congo (DRC) in March 2013 to raise awareness of this phenomenon prior to the G8 meeting, at which Hague argued for a new international protocol to fight impunity for this crime (FCO 2013a). The result was the prominent endorsement of a 'Declaration on Preventing Sexual Violence in Conflict' by G8 foreign ministers on 11 April 2013 (FCO 2013b).

Such an initiative is comparatively uncontroversial since it is unlikely to impinge on the core national interests of other states and is clearly to the advantage of weaker members of society. Where an activist foreign policy could be more problematic is if it seemed to be promoting sectional interests over those of the wider community of the UK. An NGO can argue for action over human rights violations in Syria, for example, on the basis that their purpose is to encourage global action against such crimes. The focus of their interest is on the individuals being abused. However, the policymaker has to consider the interest of his or her own community first. Should they risk the lives of British soldiers to intervene in a civil war? What would be the wider implications of British involvement and how might this affect the security of British citizens and its economic assets in the region? An activist foreign policy might also run the risk of losing sight of 'grand strategy' or broader interests in favour of short-term initiatives. Being a 'thought leader' is an interesting notion but it doesn't really provide much in the way of

Jamie Gaskarth 59

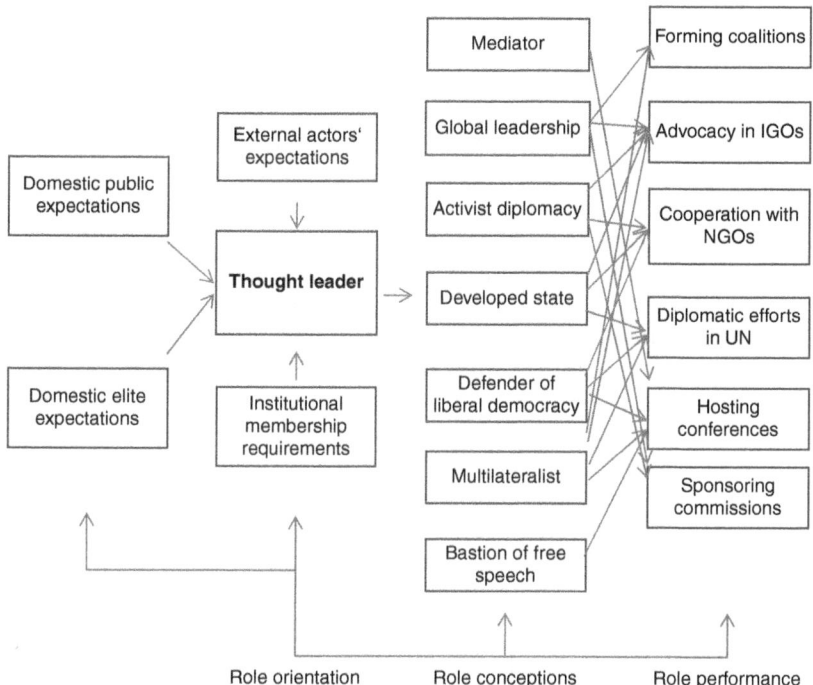

Figure 3.6 Role orientation of thought leader

guiding principles as to what the UK should be prioritising. Instead, it provides a sense of 'how' (Figure 3.6).

Opportunist – Interventionist power

The role orientation of opportunist was originally intended by role theorists to describe those statespeople and governments that seek public support and acclaim in international affairs (Hermann 1987, pp. 138–139). For the purposes of this chapter, I would like to adapt the term to refer to those who seek to exploit current disruptions in the international system to advance liberal ideas about human rights, democracy and good governance, even at the expense of existing frameworks of international law. The New Labour governments of Tony Blair were exemplary in this regard.

From 1997, the UK enacted the role of opportunist-interventionist power extensively, engaging in military action in Iraq twice, Kosovo,

Sierra Leone and Libya.[14] This role orientation was, I would argue, a radical change from previous role-taking behaviour. New Labour's foreign policy predecessors such as Douglas Hurd may have implied that intervention in Kosovo was a natural progression from lessons learned after the Bosnian war (Hurd 1997, p. 211); however, the use of military force to promote human rights represented a major development in the Kosovan case since it involved wide-scale bombing of a sovereign state and effective annexation of its territory. It is worth contrasting the 1991 Gulf War, which had the limited objective of restoring the sovereignty of Kuwait following aggression by its neighbour, with the preventive war of 2003 against Iraq to eradicate a threat that hadn't yet materialised. The extent of public anger over the latter intervention is perhaps a strong indication that it broke with the expectations of behaviour the public held on how the UK should act abroad (Cook 2003; Burall, Donnelly and Weir 2006).

Critical scholars could argue that the UK violated the sovereignty of many states during the Cold War (Curtis 2003). However, what have come to be dubbed 'Blair's wars' were justified according to a rationale that sought to explicitly challenge prevailing ideas of sovereignty and non-intervention that were core components of the UN Charter and international law. Between 1998 and 2003, the UK arguably moved from being a status quo oriented power to a revisionist one (Buzan 2010). Its self-identity was transformed from a self-declared upholder of international law to one that wished to subvert existing rules to create a new order based on 'sovereignty as responsibility'. Whether this was to the benefit of the UK is contestable.

On the one hand, this role orientation did bring some measure of increased status to the UK, since it seemed to be shaping the agenda of global politics. It also reinforced the alliance with the US. On the other hand, the opportunist-interventionist stance had a number of negative consequences. The UK was derided as the 'poodle' of the US and arguably lost a sense of its own autonomy of action. Public support for military action wavered and there is a sense that the British people may be tired of sacrificing money, effort and lives on crises that are remote from core British interests. In a 2010 Chatham House-YouGov survey the public appeared to favour Britain remaining a 'great power with a large army' but one that would 'cut the overseas aid budget and use foreign policy solely to defend Britain's national interest' (Chatham House-YouGov 2010).[15] In other words, they wished to retreat from the role of an interventionist power. The sense that policymakers were acting opportunistically rather than as a measured response to external threats has also impacted on trust in the

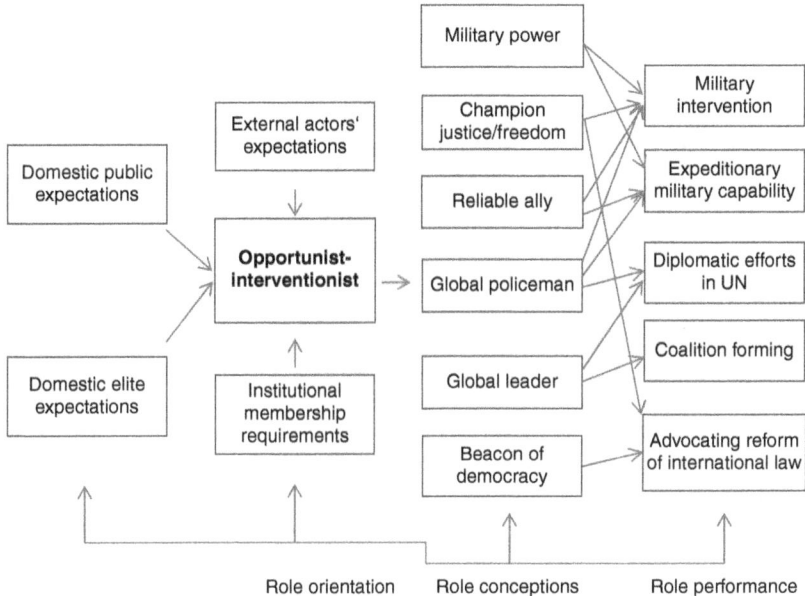

Figure 3.7 Role orientation of opportunist-interventionist

intelligence services – something that could have important long-term repercussions.

Moreover, it is a role that has had a poor reception from rising powers such as China, Brazil and India. Whilst these states may have benefitted from the UK's willingness to support action in places such as Libya and Mali, they are also acutely sensitive to Western powers transgressing sovereignty and seeming to reprise their past roles as imperial powers. It is arguable that Britain's role as an interventionist in Libya has allowed these states to 'free ride' on the back of Western efforts to maintain regional security whilst at the same time benefitting from their own enactment of the roles of anti-imperialists or peaceful traders. A role orientation that comes with a high financial and reputational cost and at the same time benefits rival states would not seem to be advantageous to a state such as the UK, which must make hard choices about how to fulfil its immediate national interests (Figure 3.7).

Great power

The last role orientation, one that is perhaps only worth mentioning to underline how far it has faded from resonance in the UK's self-identity, is that of great power (Morris 2011). Franks was accurate in his prediction that the UK would try and continue to perform this role despite the end of Empire. However, it has arguably proven unsustainable in the twenty-first century. Traditional great power behaviour involved alliances and rivalries with other states in the pursuit of relative gains. It also implied the maintenance of a preponderance of power in key military or industrial sectors to afford a state competitive advantage in the event of war. The end of the Cold War brought an end to power blocs and made redundant European fears of major conflict. Interstate rivalry still exists but it is for the most part economic rather than military power that counts in a world of dense multilateral institutionalisation. That is not to say that such behaviour might not return. However, the population size and material resources of the rising powers is such that the UK could not compete with them even if it wished to do so.

The recent SDSR is viewable as a final recognition that the UK could no longer play a great power role. According to Anthony King, retaining the capacity to deploy a division-sized force overseas was vital to a state continuing to belong to the 'elite club of great powers' (King 2011). The SDSR has reduced Britain's capacity to intervene abroad to that of a brigade and as such effectively ended the UK's ability to deploy the sort of force used in the Gulf wars in 1991 and 2003. The fact that these commitments were justified as part of Britain's obligations as a major power to uphold international law indicates that this is not a role which policymakers wish to fulfil in the future. The SDSR suggests that from now on operations will only be conducted with allies and so force levels can be reduced without a loss of influence. However, a key part of the assessment of a great power is its capacity to act independently (Mearsheimer 2003). Even if the UK tends to act in concert with others, its contribution has historically been large and this was attributable to its desire to play the part of a 'great power' in world politics. Financial constraints seem to have finally compelled a retreat from this role (Figure 3.8).

Conclusion

The above selection of role orientations is designed to show the range of possible strategic alignments the UK might adopt towards the international system. Outlining national role conceptions, and the role performances that flow from each stance, gives a fuller sense of the costs and benefits of each choice. Pursuing a particular role orientation carries with it advantages. It might result in a stronger narrative about British identity that could galvanise public support at home for British

Jamie Gaskarth 63

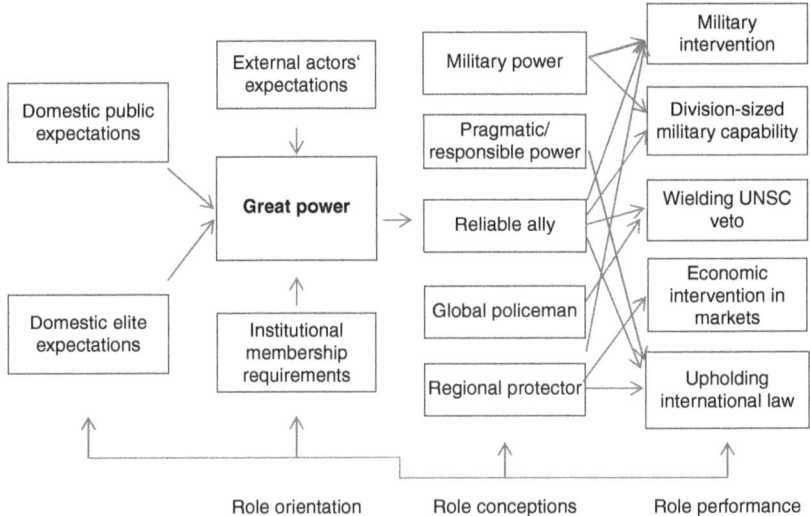

Figure 3.8 Role orientation of great power

foreign policy. Behaving in a consistent fashion according to a reasonably defined script also allows foreign policymakers to shape how Britain is viewed by others and to build trust in the UK's interactions abroad (Harnisch 2012, p. 54). Moreover, identifying the links between identity, strategy and action gives a clearer framework for devising policies. In the process, it may be possible to deploy resources more strategically in the service of policy goals.

Of course, strategic thinking needs to continually reflect upon and challenge assumptions, responding to the test of practical experience. Policymakers should not be distracted from immediate priorities in the dogmatic pursuit of an abstract role; rather role theory offers a means of interpreting current events in light of their long-term implications. Nor should role conflict be avoided at all times if the result is that policy choice loses pragmatic flexibility, is out of touch with system changes, or leaves the state open to the exploitation of rivals. That said, if policymakers are to harness the potential benefits of strategising and committing to roles, they may have to eschew immediate self-gratification for the sake of the broader interests roles embody.

Policymakers might be tempted to assume that the UK can adopt all or most of these role orientations at any one time. However, this fails to take into account the way in which role conflict can hamper the success of policy efforts. One cannot be an influential/rule of law state and at the same time seek to transgress international law in an opportunist-interventionist fashion. Attempts to be an 'honest broker' and mediator, in the thought leader mould, could be hampered by either of these other roles if the UK is overly associated with the existing order; or, self-interested policymaking. Tensions over British foreign policy towards Iraq, Afghanistan and Syria arguably demonstrate the importance of strategising Britain's role in the world in a more systematic fashion. Becoming aware of role orientations, and the role conflicts that can arise within them, provides a good starting point.

Notes

1. This is a revised and updated version of an article that first appeared in *International Affairs*, London, vol. 90, no. 3, May 2014, pp. 559–581, and is reproduced with permission.
2. In the original framework, Hermann is discussing how individual statespeople orient themselves to the international realm; however, since many of the subjects were autocratic leaders, their personal orientations were, by extension, those of the state. This chapter transfers the concept from individuals to the UK as a state actor, encompassing both individuals and the governments to which they belong.
3. A recent example of this might be the attempt by Andrew Mitchell, development secretary from 2010–2012, to portray aid to India as useful in securing defence contracts. Similarly being a reliable ally of the US, through intelligence sharing and military cooperation, is often perceived to bring influence, see Blair (2010, p. 410); Straw, (2012, p. 371). But, being aligned so closely with a state alleged to have broken international law and violated human rights has also led to charges of British complicity that have had negative impacts on the UK's influence, particularly in Islamic countries, e.g. Gaskarth (2011); Blakeley (2009).
4. In devising this chart, the author has combined the formulation in Aggestam (2006) with insights from the various authors in Walker (1987).
5. This is not to assume policymakers can adopt an 'objective' position. As Hollis and Smith put it: 'role-distance can be thought of not as standing outside the play but as detached judgement within it' (1986, p. 277).
6. Yet, this did not stop them from advocating intervention abroad on occasion; see Taylor (1957, pp. 33, 189).
7. In his 2013 conference speech, Nigel Farage, the UK Independence Party (UKIP) leader, asserted: 'only by leaving the union can we regain ... our ability to trade freely with the fastest-growing economies in the world', and described party members as: 'Open to the world. The opposite of insular', available at: http://blogs.spectator.co.uk/coffeehouse/2013/09/nigel-farages-speech-full-text-and-audio/.
8. Both Cobden and Bright lost their parliamentary seats in 1857 as a result of their anti-war stance, see Hurd, D. and Young, E. (2010) *Choose Your Weapons* (London: Weidenfeld & Nicolson).

9. According to the FCO website, the UK is involved in over 14,000 treaty arrangements, https://www.gov.uk/uk-treaties.
10. Interview with the author 2010.
11. FCO, *Annual Report and Accounts 2011–12*, 4. Evans and Steven (2010, p. 15) assert: 'Britain already excels at the nuts and bolts of foreign policy. Few governments are better at coordinating a UN Security Council Resolution or a summit communiqué, at getting candidates into senior international jobs, or at the day-to-day work of managing bilateral relationships or administering aid spending'.
12. See http://www.telegraph.co.uk/news/politics/georgeosborne/10275655/Syria-crisis-Britain-shouldnt-turn-its-back-on-world-says-Osborne.html; http://www.theguardian.com/world/poll/2013/aug/30/paddy-ashdown-syria-comments-poll.
13. This role is similar to that of mediator-integrator in Hermann's typology, an orientation in which policymakers are 'genuinely interested in seeing that problems are solved' (1987, p. 138).
14. Intervention in Afghanistan was represented for the most part as in self-defence and so I exclude it from this category of role performance.
15. Meanwhile, elite respondents to the survey wanted 'Britain to give up the attempt to remain a great power and instead to seek influence in today's world by setting a good example – with an ethical foreign policy and large overseas aid budget' (Chatham House-YouGov 2010, p. 4).

4
National Interest and the Falklands War

Helen Parr

Was Britain's decision to use military action in the 1982 Falklands/ Malvinas War guided by concerns for Britain's 'national interest'? This chapter seeks to answer this question by surveying the events of the crisis and exploring the reasons British policymakers gave for their actions. To recap the conflict in brief, the Argentines invaded East Falkland on 2 April 1982, forced a small group of British Royal Marines to surrender, raised the Argentine flag over Government House and occupied Port Stanley. On 3 April, the House of Commons unequivocally backed the despatch of a task force from Britain. On 26 April, British special forces retook the British Antarctic Survey base at South Georgia. On 2 May, the British submarine HMS *Conqueror* hit and sank the Argentine cruiser *General Belgrano* and an Argentine Exocet missile torpedoed HMS *Sheffield* on 4 May. British troops landed on East Falkland on 21 May. On 14 June the Argentine forces surrendered and British administration was restored.

Debate about the Falklands has tended to revolve around the extent to which Margaret Thatcher willed a war to save herself and her government (Hobsbawm 1983, pp. 257–270). It has been commonly argued that she agreed to sink the *Belgrano* in order to jeopardise new peace proposals forwarded by the Peruvian president, and thus to fight for her own and her government's popularity (Dalyell 1983; Rodgers 2007, pp. 25–31). Others have agreed on the primacy of domestic politics, but add the importance of identity. It was a war to save Britain's face, and to enable Thatcher to present herself as Churchillian. She harnessed old ideas of 1940, when Britain stood alone against fascist aggression, and reasserted through achievement in war a new sense of British pride (Barnett 1983; Monaghan 1992).

Lawrence Freedman's *Official History*, based on exhaustive study of diplomatic documents, offers a different perspective. He explained Thatcher's actions in terms of values. Thatcher went to war because it was the right thing to do. There were international principles at stake. Britain had to underscore the principle of sovereignty, demonstrate that aggression should not be permitted to gain the upper hand and protect the rights of people to determine their own allegiances (Freedman 2005). McCourt suggests that Britain acted from an expectation that as a 'status quo' power in the Western international system, it must demonstrate that it could use force to repel aggression. Britain's sense of identity came not from domestic politics, but from Britain's 'role' in the international system (McCourt 2011, pp. 1599–1662).

This chapter seeks to examine the development of events in order to assess why Britain resorted to military force to take back the islands. It argues that the international and the domestic have to be brought together. The British government was not of one mind as to whether to employ the military it had sent to the South Atlantic. Thatcher's position within her cabinet and the Conservative Party were vital in explaining why events developed in the way they did. Moreover, international opinion was wary about Britain applying force to resolve its dispute with Argentina. British diplomats could forcefully argue that British actions were legitimate in international law, and this position was accepted by the EEC, the US and the UN. Britain's domestic and international roles were not pre-set, but were recreated by the actions Britain took.

Background

At the beginning of the 1980s, the Falkland Islands remained a British Crown Colony. Britain and Spain had asserted conflicting claims to the islands in the late 1700s and early 1800s, and a Spanish settlement had been abandoned in 1811. The islands had then been in Britain's continuous possession from 1833 (Beck 1992, pp. 12–46; Charlton 1989, pp. 4–5). Argentina inherited the title from Spain and maintained that Britain had evicted an Argentine garrison when it took the islands over. This claim is disputed, but the Argentines continued to regard Britain's sovereignty over the islands as outdated European colonialism. The idea that the 'Malvinas' were part of greater Argentina had emotional resonance in Argentina, and was important to Argentine geopolitical ambitions in Antarctica. In December 1981 General Galtieri took power in Argentina, forming a military government which rapidly became unpopular because of the prevailing economic crisis, but also because the regime caused tens of thousands of people to 'disappear' (Freedman and Gamba-Stonehouse 1990, pp. 3–7).

The economy of the Falklands was managed from London by the Falkland Islands Company. Agricultural workers were generally reliant on itinerant seasonal work, often had few rights and depended on their employer for accommodation. Islanders sometimes moved away in anticipation of being handed over to Argentina and many were also accustomed to travelling to Argentina for health care. However, the islanders did not want the status quo to be disturbed, nor did they want sovereignty to be ceded to Argentina, and the Falkland Islands lobby actively campaigned to prevent this from happening (Ellerby 1992, pp. 85–108).

As early as 1967 however, the British government had been seeking ways to yield sovereignty of the islands while safeguarding the islanders (Charlton 1989, p. 13). By 1977, British ideas centred on 'lease-back', in which the Argentines would take sovereignty of the islands but the islanders would remain under British jurisdiction, although this was unlikely to be popular with all of the islanders. The 1974–1979 Labour government also worked to deter potential Argentine attack.

Coming to power in 1979, Margaret Thatcher was determined that the islanders' wishes should be safeguarded; but HMS *Endurance* was removed from patrol in the area and the islanders were excluded from the 1981 Nationality Act. These actions were taken by the Argentines to be an indication of a lack of British interest in protecting the islanders (Charlton 1989, pp. 52–75; Freedman and Gamba-Stonehouse 1990, pp. 10–11). Thus diplomacy had reached an impasse by the time the Argentine force was sent.

Consensus: Despatching the task force, 3 April 1982

Once it was obvious that Argentina had invaded, it did not prove difficult to decide to despatch the task force. Freedman wrote, of the full cabinet meeting at 19h30 on 2 April,

> this decision was assumed as much as taken, a reflection of genuine indignation at the Argentine act of aggression and a determination to demonstrate that the government was not completely helpless. Once it was apparent that a task force could be sent, there was never any doubt that it would be sent.
>
> (Freedman 2005, loc. 1051)

The British government did not see itself as a colonial power, and felt it necessary to protect Britain's reputation against incursion made by aggression, and to assert the Falkland Islanders' right to live as they wished.

Though their action was not without criticism, the House of Commons fully endorsed the government's decision. While the Labour Party and Social Democratic Party (SDP) oppositions saw an opportunity to capitalise on the government's weakness, the debates illustrated consensus about the need to respond to the Argentine invasion. Michael Foot, leader of the Labour Party, argued that the people of the Falklands wanted to be British, that the Argentine regime was repugnant, and that aggression could not be permitted to bring gains. He also made a broader point,

> there is the longer-term interest to ensure that foul and brutal aggression does not succeed in our world. If it does, there will be a danger not merely to the Falkland Islands, but to people all over this dangerous planet.
> (House of Commons Debates, 3 April 1982, cols. 639–642)

Domestically, the course of British action was set. Internationally, opinion was more uncertain. In the UN, in line with the view of US Ambassador to the UN Jeanne Kirkpatrick, many believed that Argentina's claim to the sovereignty of the islands was sound, and that it had nothing to do with the wishes of the islanders. In America some, like Defence Secretary Caspar Weinberger, thought that the Americans should back Britain as a NATO ally and the US did provide Britain with critical military support (Bluth 1992, pp. 203–223). But President Reagan wanted to avoid war and was mindful of the importance of Argentina to America's southern strategy. Soviet expansion into the third world in the 1970s highlighted the importance of access to the South Atlantic's shipping lanes, and led to fears that the region was becoming a 'Soviet lake'. Argentina, as well as Brazil and South Africa, were essential in resisting communism in the region (Hurrell 1983, pp. 188–191). The European Community consented to sanctions against Argentina, and France immediately declared support for Britain, but Italy and Ireland later distanced themselves from sanctions. As British forces landed on East Falkland, Ireland proposed new negotiations in the UN (Stavridis and Hill 1996, pp. 52, 62, 114, 146–148).

Thus, British diplomatic activity was vital in urging international opinion to support Britain's response. On 2 April, Britain's ambassador to the UN, Sir Anthony Parsons, was authorised to push for Resolution 502. It needed nine votes in the Security Council to pass, and with the communist countries certain not to support, Panama's opposition clear, Spain unlikely and Ireland uncertain, everything depended on Togo, Uganda, Jordan and Zaire (Parsons 1983, pp. 170–172). These countries favoured Argentina's sovereignty claim, but also appreciated that aggression should not be allowed to gain the upper hand.

Parsons proceeded with great care. He called for an adjournment in order to insert the words 'Islas Malvinas' into the resolution, and used the delay to get London to phone the king of Jordan to pressure him to support the resolution rather than abstain. On 3 April, Resolution 502 passed with ten votes in favour. Only Panama voted against, and the USSR, China, Poland and Spain abstained. The resolution urged restraint on both sides, but cast Argentina as the aggressor and demanded Argentine withdrawal and compliance with the UN Charter (Freedman 2005, loc. 1751).

The American secretary of state, Alexander Haig, embarked on a 'mediation' mission. Thatcher was not keen on this, but Haig judged that only the US was powerful enough to mediate, and that mediation would be weaker if the US appeared as Britain's agent. The mediation was difficult. The Argentines desperately wanted assurance on the eventual transfer of sovereignty; whereas Britain's opening position was that the Argentines should withdraw from the islands, British administration should be restored, talks could only open following withdrawal and the wishes of the islanders had to be taken into account (Freedman 2005, loc. 3434). Negotiations were also hard because all the issues were connected (Bluth 1992, p. 212). Self-determination for the islanders was linked to eventual sovereignty, because the composition of any interim administration, and regulations as to who could travel to the islands during the interim period, would have a bearing on the interpretation of self-determination, and so on eventual sovereignty. Both self-determination and sovereignty were also linked to whether Argentina could make any gains by the use of force.

Concessions? 12–29 April 1982

Britain would have made concessions in early April. On 12 April, Haig returned from Argentina with a seven-point plan. Had it been implemented, it would have permitted Argentine representation in an interim administration and committed both parties to open-ended negotiations to be concluded by the end of 1982 (Freedman 2005, loc. 3861).

On 13 April, the proposal was modified, as Argentine Foreign Minister Nicanor Costa Méndez insisted to Haig that Argentine sovereignty must be recognised, but agreed that there could be local self-determination in the context of the 1964 UN resolution on decolonisation (Freedman 2005, loc. 3995). Haig pushed Britain towards this significant concession, saying that Britain's position on sovereignty had been eroded over the years.

In full cabinet on 14 April, the view was put that: 'the aggressor must not be permitted to benefit from his aggression. The wider principle was even more important than the fate of the islanders. If aggression was shown to pay, it would be a disastrous precedent for the world as a whole'. Thatcher prodded colleagues towards compromise. She said,

> a diplomatic solution on the lines outlined would be a considerable prize. The withdrawal of Argentine forces would have been secured without military action. Argentina would gain representation on the interim Commission and on the local Councils; and a commitment to negotiation to decide the definitive status of the Islands by the end of the year, although without any commitment to a transfer of sovereignty. Repugnant as it was that the aggressor should gain anything from his aggression, this seemed an acceptable price to pay. But it would be crucial to secure against a second invasion and the best way of achieving this appeared to be to involve the US government in the enforcement of the interim agreement and the security of the Islands thereafter.
>
> (National Archives, CAB128/75, CC(82) 17th, 14 April 1982)

British concessions were not met with similar compromises by Argentina. At the airport in Buenos Aires, Costa Méndez handed Haig a note saying that the negotiations must conclude with Argentine sovereignty (Freedman 2005, loc. 4255).

A further draft paper reached Britain on 19 April, a paper that Haig admitted was disappointing (Freedman 2005, loc. 4264). The British war cabinet set up to manage the crisis were losing patience with what they saw as his even-handedness, 'there seemed to be a danger that he [Haig] had been persuaded by the Argentines to make concessions unacceptable to Britain, who would then be blamed if negotiations broke down' (NA CAB148/211, Defence and Overseas Policy Committee, Sub-Committee on the South Atlantic and the Falkland Islands [henceforward OD(SA)](82) 9th, 19 April, 11.15am). Thatcher told the war cabinet that the most important principle was that the wishes of the islanders should be paramount. In response to Haig, she said, Britain should emphasise that: 'Argentina was intransigently seeking to retain what she had taken by force'. Haig should not come to London but should return to Washington. At the same meeting, Thatcher indicated that Operation Paraquet, the operation to retake South Georgia was preparing to go ahead, subject to confirmation the following day (NA CAB148/211, OD(SA)(82) 10th, 19 April, 10pm; NA CAB148/211, OD(SA)(82) 11th and 12th, 20 April, 12pm and 6.30pm).

On 20 April, Haig suggested that Foreign Secretary Francis Pym go to Washington, and the war cabinet saw this as an opportunity to press counter-proposals (Freedman 2005, loc. 4321). Pym returned to London with a text that he wanted to endorse. He wrote that while it fell short of British demands in key respects, it offered 'the best chance of a peaceful solution, was clearly preferable to a military solution and should be accepted'. Haig's idea was that Britain would agree and then he would put it to Argentina, as an American, not an Anglo-American text. He did not think that Argentina would embrace it, but if the junta refused, it would be entirely clear where lay the blame for breakdown (NA CAB148/212, OD(SA)(82)25, Falkland Islands: Washington Discussions with Mr Haig, Memorandum by the Foreign Secretary, 24 April 1982).

The proposals required withdrawal by both sides, an interim arrangement based on local administration but including a special executive with Argentine representation, no restriction on trade or travel and negotiations on the 'removal of the islands from the list of non-self governing territories'. Essentially, there could be no return to the status quo ante (Freedman, loc. 4399). There was no formal American guarantee, but Haig assured Britain that if Argentina did not comply with withdrawal then 'it would be looking down the barrel of a US gun', and America would maintain a presence on the islands during the interim and would propose a settlement if none were reached by the end of the negotiating period (NA CAB148/212, OD(SA)(82)25, Falkland Islands: Washington Discussions with Mr Haig, Memorandum by the Foreign Secretary, 24 April 1982).

In her memoirs, Thatcher made it clear why she wholly rejected this agreement: 'I could not have stayed as Prime Minister had the War Cabinet accepted Francis Pym's proposals. I would have resigned' (Thatcher 1992, pp. 205–209). She thought the proposals conceded far too much to the Argentines. They did not protect the wishes of the islanders and virtually guaranteed that sovereignty would be transferred. As Moore says, there was more to her distaste than just the fact that the proposals did not meet her preferences. Moore claims she did not like the fact that Pym had negotiated it on his own (Moore 2013, p. 703). There is perhaps also some self-justification after the fact in Thatcher's account. Her published memoirs were based on a private diary written in 1983, after she knew that her judgement had been vindicated (Moore 2013, p. 679). The war cabinet records simply note the outcome and do not show disagreement, but certainly there were differences of view. Pym canvassed for support. In his memoirs, John Nott claimed that the division was between the 'Foreign Office representatives' who wanted to accept, and the rest, who did not (Nott 2002, pp. 292–293). Later he recalled that cabinet and parliament could have been brought to endorse the agreement (Institute of Contemporary British History 2005). In the end, it was Nott who came up with the formula that they should make no comment on the draft, but put it first to the Argentines. It was a gamble; the junta might accept. If they did not, however, it would show that the blame for breakdown lay with them and not Britain.

South Georgia was recaptured on 26 April. Haig put the proposals to the junta on 27 April and on 29 April, the full cabinet decided it must push America a little in order to demonstrate that it was the junta's intransigence that had brought negotiations to a halt. The junta argued that they could only be flexible on a provisional administration if they were confident about an eventual transfer of sovereignty (Freedman 2005, loc. 4536). On 29 April, Reagan wrote to Thatcher to confirm that America would 'tilt' to Britain and the Haig mediation was over (Moore 2013, p. 708). On 30 April, Haig made a public statement: 'we had reason to hope that the UK would consider a settlement along the lines of our proposal, but Argentina informed us yesterday that it could not accept it' (Freedman 2005, loc. 4545).

What did this mean? The April negotiations showed that Thatcher was pragmatic about the extent she could go to illustrate that aggression did not pay, because international opinion expected a considerable effort to avoid war. The British agreed to compromise on 14 April. British concessions would have allowed Argentine representation on an interim administration and, while not conceding sovereignty, would have certainly opened the possibility that, during negotiations, sovereignty would be returned to Argentina. On 24 April, it was evident that Thatcher was not prepared to go as far as Pym in making concessions in order to avert military action. It is difficult to say what the outcome would have been if Britain had accepted Pym and Haig's paper at this juncture. Had the junta then agreed to the proposals in the paper, Britain would almost certainly have had to yield sovereignty of the islands, and it would have been difficult to guarantee the wishes of the existing islanders. There was a good chance that even though the text was favourable to Argentina, the junta would still decline. Had that been the case, some of the difficulties Britain had in the coming weeks in persuading international opinion of the rightness of their cause might have been alleviated.

Diplomacy and the use of force, May 1982

The decision to sink the Argentine cruiser the *General Belgrano* generated much subsequent controversy, but at the time, for the British government, it was a tense but uncontroversial decision. The *Belgrano* posed a threat to the British task force. The British had intercepted an order at 22h13 local time on 1 May that appeared to authorise an attack on the British fleet (Freedman 2005, loc. 6826). The submarine HMS *Conqueror* was shadowing the *Belgrano* (Wreford Brown 2012). There was an opportunity to attack it which they could subsequently lose. Although the *Belgrano* subsequently changed course, as poor weather conditions meant the Argentine air attacks could not be carried out, this did not make a difference to the judgement that the *Belgrano* was a serious danger to British ships.

The *Belgrano* was not sunk to up the ante, to bring a close to mediation now being attempted by the Peruvian president. Military action was not a good way to terminate diplomacy. In fact, after it was sunk, and despite Argentina's retaliation against the HMS *Sheffield* on 4 May, the diplomatic tide turned against Britain. Haig suggested a joint Peruvian–American initiative which each side would have 48 hours to accept (Freedman 2005, loc. 7599). On 5 May, at cabinet, Thatcher recognised that she had no choice, if she were to keep international opinion on side, but to accept Haig's paper. The paper was ambiguous about a local administration to administer the islands in the interim period, but Britain now had to ensure that blame for collapse of the negotiations lay with Argentina. (NA CAB128/75, CC(82)23rd, 5 May 1982, 11.45am). To make things more difficult for Britain, on 10 May, an Argentine paper did appear to indicate that the outcome of negotiations would not be prejudged (Freedman 2005, loc. 8183, 8194). Parsons reported that opinion at the UN was 'stunned' that Britain had not offered any concessions; consequently, he suggested moving towards acceptance of a UN interim administration (Freedman 2005, loc. 8307).

On 13 May, the war cabinet met. The Joint Intelligence Committee's assessment of Argentina's aims underlined the importance the junta attached to preventing the return of a basically British administration. Therefore the point of view was put forward that Britain should secure termination of the New York negotiations in circumstances which left the Argentines with most of the blame. On the other hand, the point was also made that 'it was beginning to be understood that the wishes of a community as small as the Falkland Islanders could not in all circumstances be the decisive factor'. Thatcher attempted to steer a middle course: 'the Government's aim should be to keep the New York negotiations going for the time being, without making major concessions and to ensure that if they did subsequently collapse, the fault was seen to be Argentina's' (NA CAB148/211, OD SA (82)33rd, 13 May 1982, 9.30am).

On 14 May, the war cabinet convened again. It noted that,

> parliamentary debates the previous day had made clear that any concession on South Georgia [Argentina wanted to include South Georgia and other dependencies in the region in any discussion, while Britain did not], or on the interim administration, would not be acceptable to the Government's supporters. The end of the road therefore seemed to be reached in the New York negotiations.

The war cabinet saw how important it was that Argentina be regarded as responsible for breakdown: 'the issue over the interim administration was essentially one of democracy; the issue over South Georgia was one of law'. More generally, it was Argentina who had flouted Resolution 502 and invaded. In order to buy time, London would recall Parsons and work on counter-proposals (NA CAB148/211, OD SA (82)34th, 14 May 1982, 10am).

The war cabinet's reference to the opinion of the 'government's supporters' was notable. Debate in the House had been strong, but MPs were not unanimous that the wishes of the islanders had to be paramount. There was unequivocal support for 'minimum force' and for force as a backing for diplomacy, but there was not unanimous agreement for force to be used to protect Britain's negotiating stance. Denis Healey, Labour's defence spokesman, argued that the government was right to make concessions (House of Commons Debates [HCDeb] 13 May 1982, col. 961). Former Prime Minister Edward Heath made the longest intervention against the use of military force, arguing that,

> Therefore, in continuing these negotiations, the Foreign Secretary is right to say that the wishes of those in the Falkland Islands must be given full consideration but not to resume our previous position,

which was certainly adopted by the Government of 1970 to 1974, that they could veto any solution that was put forward. I have said that publicly before, but I think that it is right.

(HCDeb 13 May 1982, col. 966)

The SDP's Foreign Affairs Spokesman David Owen disagreed. He said that ideology mattered and that, like Hitler, Galtieri's regime was evil. This was a principle in the international system and they could not give way. Other Conservative members agreed with Owen. Bill Benyon, formerly of the Royal Navy and MP for Buckingham, said:

> To me there is no more pernicious doctrine than that which says that because there are only 1,800 Falkland Islanders this principle should not apply. Where does it end? Does it end with Gibraltar, with whatever its population is – 20,000? Does it end with Ulster, with a population of 1 1/2 million? Does it end, indeed, with Afghanistan and Poland?

(HCDeb 13 May 1982, col. 990)

Former soldier Stephen Hastings (MP for mid-Befordshire) added:

> If the Government should be prevailed upon to surrender now on any essential principle, when victory is within our grasp, we should all be aware of the potential consequences, and in my opinion they are these: it would break the confidence and trust of this nation – how could anyone who watched the QE2 sail yesterday doubt that? – it would destroy the special relationship with the United States and do perhaps irreparable harm to the Western Alliance, because people would come to know exactly what happened and they would never trust the United States again; it would betray this Government and all that they stand for and have stood for with such courage and consistency till now; lastly, it would mean that those who have died have died in vain.

(HCDeb 13 May 1982, col. 1018)

It was significant, therefore, that on 14 May the war cabinet accepted that its political allies would not agree to further concessions. While the mood in the House was mixed – there could have been consent for a deal with Argentina, even at the cost of ceding sovereignty of the Falkland Islands eventually, and even at the cost of losing self-determination for the islanders – Thatcher's strongest champions would not have supported her backing down. Thatcher almost certainly would have fallen had she yielded further in negotiations.

After 14 May, Parsons was brought back to London for instruction. The British government persuaded UN Secretary-General Javier Pérez de Cuéllar that otherwise his mediation initiative would collapse, and they would have to go to the Security Council. Thatcher also telephoned de Cuéllar and emphasised to him her anxieties about 'her boys' and the potential loss of life. He later remarked: 'I sensed that this was the woman and the mother who was speaking to me... I was certain that Margaret Thatcher was not... hell-bent on war' (de Cuéllar 1997, p. 376).

On 16 May, the war cabinet had a long debate at Chequers. Here, on the advice of Parsons and Britain's ambassador to Washington, Sir Nicholas Henderson, and to combat the pressure for decolonisation from the UN, they agreed to emphasise that the Falkland Islanders should have more control of the interim administration (thus diluting 'colonial' rule); there was to be a verification regime, including the US, to supervise withdrawal; South Georgia was no longer to be part of the negotiations; and the issue of the final outcome of sovereignty over the islands could not be prejudged (NA CAB148/211, OD SA(82)35th, 16 May). The UK also put a 48 hour limit on a decision. The agreement steered towards taking account only of the islanders' interests, rather than their wishes. However, Henderson recorded that 'the PM veered the whole time towards being uncompromising.... She would never abandon the Falkland Islands.... Did other countries not realise that we were doing their work for them in resisting aggression?' (Henderson 1995, pp. 461–462).

De Cuéllar recalled later that he wished he had challenged the deadline more insistently, as he had suspected at the time that Argentina would not accept if it looked like an ultimatum. The British, he felt, had not taken account of Argentine pride (de Cuéllar 1997, p. 380). On 19 May, the Argentine text arrived. It returned to Argentina's original position, asking the UN General Assembly to decide the terms of the final settlement. When de Cuéllar spoke to him, Galtieri was apparently incoherent with drink (Freedman 2005, loc. 8674). De Cuéllar suggested new proposals. Thatcher reluctantly agreed, but this led to a new lease of life for the negotiations, which had not been her intention. On 18 May, Pym wanted to accept de Cuéllar's initiative as a new step forward, but Thatcher did not.

On 18 May, the war cabinet weighed up whether it could 'authorise the military repossession of the Falkland Islands', and decided that it could, if there was no alternative. The chief of general staff, Field Marshall Sir Edwin Bramall, in military terms no hawk, said that there were risks. Britain did not have air superiority. He continued that if they won, 'Britain's status in the world, the respect shown to her and the strength and credibility of her own deterrent strategy would be that much more enhanced for years to come'. He emphasised that 'in the circumstances, and in the absence of alternatives, those risks would have to be taken and any resulting casualties to troops and ships accepted' (NA CAB148/211, OD SA (82) 37th, 18 May 1982).

On 20 May, Pym wanted to consider new proposals from the UN, but Thatcher insisted that 'there can be no question of holding up the military timetable' (NA CAB148/211, OD SA (82)39th, 20 May 1982). By the 27th, as the Second Battalion, Parachute Regiment moved towards Goose Green, the lack of forward movement was causing concern; by this point, London did not want pressure to build for a ceasefire (NA CAB148/211, OD SA (82)45th, 27 May 1982). Even after the recapture of Goose Green, Reagan called Thatcher to urge her to accept further talks. Thatcher was able to convince him that she could not now turn back. (http://www.margaretthatcher.org/document/110526, Ian Glover James, 'Reagan phone call to Thatcher, 31 May 1982', *Sunday Times*, 8 March 1992; Moore 2013, p. 738).

Why did Britain move to a position of repossessing the islands by force? Partly, it was because Thatcher believed that the use of military force to repel an invader and to protect the wishes of people to determine their allegiance was the right thing for Britain to do. Her actions were certainly guided by her beliefs, and her beliefs were different to those of other senior Conservatives and to many in the diplomatic service. She was not, however, determined to have a war. She did not sink the *Belgrano* to get war, and she agreed concessions in April that would, had the junta accepted them, have averted armed conflict. By May, and after British life had been lost – 'we've lost a lot of blood, and it's the best blood' – (Moore 2013, p. 738) she felt that the concessions Britain would have to make were too great to be credible; partly because of her views, but also because she knew that if she conceded, her cabinet colleagues would probably take the opportunity to turn against her, and her parliamentary support would be lost.

Domestic politics thus plays a decisive role in explaining Britain's course of action. It mattered a great deal that Thatcher was in a weak position. In a general sense, she had not proved herself by the spring of 1982. Thatcher had been desperately unpopular in 1981. The 1981 budget was challenged by 364 economists, and cabinet ministers resisted further public spending cuts in July 1981 (Vinen 2009, p. 115). Although the economy was beginning to recover, Thatcher's economic policy was far from proven by the spring of 1982. More specifically, it had been a catastrophic oversight that the Argentines had been permitted to invade the Falkland Islands in the first place. Lord Carrington took responsibility for it, but with Carrington gone, Pym was the only senior Conservative Thatcher could realistically appoint as foreign secretary.

Thatcher's relations with Pym go some way to explaining the weakness of her position. Pym was the kind of Tory she had spent her career battling against. He was an old Etonian, his forefathers had been Conservative MPs, he was the son of a landowner. He supported one-nation Conservatism and consensus politics. She did not trust him, and she knew that if she shifted to accept a negotiated settlement that would result in the handing of sovereignty to the Argentines, or a dramatic change in the status of the islanders, it was extremely likely that she would have to go and he would replace her. Nor could she fully trust Nott, whose judgement was thought to be dithering; and who, over time, has distanced himself from the decisions that were taken. William Whitelaw was an ally, but a man who was loyal to successive leaders, and Cecil Parkinson, on whom she could probably count, was the most junior of the war cabinet members (Moore 2013, p. 697). In the cabinet, she could not depend upon senior members like Chancellor of the Exchequer Geoffrey Howe. He may have supported her economic ideas, but he was not a political friend (Vinen 2009, pp. 79–80).

Thatcher was therefore bolstered by the support of parliamentarians, such as Edward du Cann, the chair of the 1922 Committee, Private Secretary Ian Gow and Stephen Hastings, whom she stayed with while the operation at South Georgia was underway. Her defenders in parliament believed that Britain should be prepared to use force to urge the principle that aggression should not pay, and the islanders had a right to remain British. They also believed Britain's reputation had to be saved. Patrick Cormack, MP for South Staffordshire, illustrated just how perilous Thatcher's position would be if she were not able to rise to the occasion: 'We are talking about restoring credibility. That is restoring the credibility not merely of a set of politicians and of a Government, but of our nation.... This is one of the most critical moments in the history of our country since the war...' (cited in Barnett 1983, p. 39).

The lack of depth to Thatcher's cabinet support also perhaps augmented her reliance upon military advice. She had exceptionally good relations with Chief of Defence Staff Admiral Lord Lewin and First Sea Lord Admiral Sir Henry Leach (Young 1989, pp. 272–275). Her style suited them. She was able to express clearly what she wanted to happen, but did not interfere with the process (Vinen 2009, p. 149). This correlation of style reflected her awareness of her own military inexperience. Unlike Pym, Nott, Heath, Healey, Anthony Parsons or Alexander Haig, she had never worn uniform and served her country. She had never had a foreign brief, nor even shown excessive interest in international affairs. At the same time, Thatcher was acutely concerned about putting British forces at risk. From early May, there was a strong fear that delay would disadvantage Britain militarily, because the weather meant there was only a small window of opportunity for landing on the islands, and because any solution such as halting the task force would involve wear and tear on the ships. A military disaster would be the worst outcome of all for Thatcher: 'an awareness of the possibility of her political destruction was never far away' (Young 1989, p. 278).

In many ways, Thatcher was a very unlikely war leader and this only increased the distance she had to climb in order not to fail. She was female, she was not upper class nor even upper middle class. Pym once said, before the Falklands, 'we've got a corporal at the top not a cavalry officer' (Evans 2013, p. 48). The war boosted her personal approval ratings by 30 per cent (Price and Sanders 1993, pp. 327–328) and the vindication of her judgement meant that her power in the Conservative Party was now unquestionable in the short to medium term. The war was popular in Britain partly because of the recreation of an idea of 1940. Britain was a great power, a military power, a stand-alone power, capable of heroism and bravery (Noakes 1998, pp. 103–133). The boost to Thatcher's popularity also reveals much about the country and the establishment's expectations of the component parts of leadership: decisiveness, fortitude, courage and observable, unequivocally successful outcomes.

Conclusion

This chapter has attempted to understand the development of Britain's policy, and thus to explain why British policy took the course that it did. It shows that Thatcher authorised the use of force to retake the Falkland Islands primarily because her political weakness meant that she knew she would fall if she did not. It may seem, therefore, as if 'interest', in a very narrow sense of political survival of the prime minister, does explain why Britain went to war over the Falkland Islands. But 'interest' did not precede people's perceptions of how best to preserve it, nor did it precede the prime minister's ability to carry British policy out. In both the domestic and the international arena, British policies depended partly upon pre-existing expectations of appropriate action, and also on the legitimacy that Thatcher at home and Britain abroad could engender (Boyce 2005). Domestic and international opinion called for an appropriate response. A significant section of domestic opinion called for the use of force, but nevertheless, Thatcher still had convincingly to justify the action she chose. Internationally, British diplomats had to work to confer legitimacy onto British policies.

The furore over the sinking of the *Belgrano* illustrates the point. Domestic opinion challenged the idea that in opting to torpedo the cruiser, Thatcher was using reasonable force. The incident appeared unprovoked, it appeared to have contravened the rules of engagement, it appeared designed to scupper a peace plan and the government appeared to be covering up its true motives, or details about the *Belgrano*'s coordinates. The sinking was uncomfortable for Britain because it was a display of violence (Connelly 2002, p. 14). *The Sun* had to retract their initially gung-ho headline of Gotcha! Hence, although it clearly was a military interest to attack the ship at that time, it did not meet with unquestioning approval as it challenged ideas of legitimacy, both in terms of the proper conduct of British democracy, and the idea of minimum or proportionate force.

Aside from the *Belgrano*, there was acceptance of the identity Thatcher forged for Britain in response to the crisis. The Commons sitting on 3 April demonstrated consensus for the despatch of the task force, because Britain had betrayed the Falkland Islanders, and British sovereign territory had been invaded. As a formerly great power, Britain had to send a fleet, because this would save or indeed remake Britain's reputation and would illustrate the principle that aggression should not pay. The Commons debates showed expectation about what Britain must do, but as the crisis developed Thatcher created her own and Britain's role and, *Belgrano* excepting, managed to avoid the condemnation of those who would have chosen a different route. The narratives employed domestically and internationally were slightly different. At home, Thatcher legitimised British action by showing that Britain was doing what it reasonably could to avert conflict and by arguing that resisting aggression and defending the self-determination of people was part of a long tradition of British foreign relations. She also re-imagined the period in 1940 when Britain had held out alone against fascism, and she evoked tropes of gender, whiteness and of 'deep' England contained within defending a remote island (Barnett 1982; Noakes 1998;

Monaghan 1992). History and identity, not interest, was the arc within which military force was justified.

In the international sphere, even though there may have been ideas of what a 'status quo' power would do, the role Britain played during the Falklands was not a given. British actions were made possible by an explanation not that Britain was defending its interest, but that Britain's interests were coterminous with the interests of the UN, the US and therefore the international system in the West (Sharp 1997, p. 78). Parsons and Henderson worked exhaustively to demonstrate that there was an international benefit in upholding the right of sovereign territories not to be invaded by others, and an international benefit in maintaining sovereign territorial integrity. On this basis, the UN endorsed British policy, first with Resolution 502 that cast Argentina as the aggressor, and secondly by permitting the repossession of the islands under self-defence as set out in Article 51. Similarly, the US supported the British military endeavour, despite Reagan's personal ambivalence.

This analysis emphasises the importance of agency. Individuals carried out policy and enacted the roles. They did so in response to events, guided by expectations of domestic leadership and international posture, permitted by the persuasion of the legitimising arguments they used. Those legitimising arguments depended upon others' understandings of Britain, and British history; and others' understandings of international law, and the vulnerabilities of the international system in the Cold War West. Thatcher was defending her interest, but she had to defend it to parliamentarians who anticipated force and believed in a British identity that could use force in the right circumstances. Thatcher recreated an idea of Britain based on a reading of Britain's 'finest hour', when Britain stood alone; and internationally, British diplomats recreated a sense of Britain as acting for the international body. National interest by itself does not explain, nor justify, nor legitimise Britain's recourse to military force in the 1982 Falklands War.

Part II
Whose National Interest?

5
A Citizen's View of 'National Interest'

Nick Ritchie

There is no 'national interest', at least not in a singular and objective sense. Instead, there are multiple interpretations of national interest based on different positions (Ritchie 2011). Four positions can be discerned. First, perceptions of national interest by virtue of being an individual member of the national community; second, by virtue of being a modern urban-industrial island state; third, by virtue of ascribing to our collective self a particular national identity or role conception; and fourth, by virtue of being part of a global human community and society of states in terms of a collective vision of a preferable global order.

National interest is broadly about national-level objectives, or ends. Generic ends can be described in relation to these four positions as:

- development of a cohesive national society, particularly in terms of how policies justified by reference to a national interest affect our own individual, family and community lives;
- reproduction of a functioning state over time in terms of assured access to resources vital to a functioning economy such as energy, food, water, commodities and finance, the state's continued monopoly of legitimate violence within its borders, and protection from external armed attack;
- reproduction of a particular national identity based on elite conceptions of a unified national role that tells us who we are and therefore how we should act as a national community; and
- development of an amenable global order based on a set of long-term capitalist and cosmopolitan global governance objectives.[1]

These ends are contested, interconnected and can often sit in tension, as do understandings of the means by which these broad interests-as-ends can and should be met. The problem here is that the idea of a national interest is very difficult to quantify.[2] Discourse on national interest is often subjective and aspirational, except perhaps in terms of practical requirements for a functioning state, for example sufficient levels of energy supply. Defining the national interest is therefore a deeply political debate, one in which appropriation of the 'national interest' label is routinely used to denounce or legitimise specific policies and the exercise of executive power.

Government often uses the phrase 'way of life' in relation to the idea of a national interest. From the perspective of the state the ultimate objective and purpose of government is to protect the population and its way of life in terms of territorial integrity, core values and national wellbeing. This implies a single and accepted way of life whose protection constitutes a single, unified national interest. The notion of protection links to the equally amorphous idea of national security. The two are intimately linked in that actions justified in the name of national security are by definition in the national interest. In fact, the terms 'national interest' and 'national security interest' are often interchangeable (Wolfers 1952). The 2010 National Security Strategy, for example, defines national interest in the broadest of terms as comprising 'our security, prosperity and freedom' (Cabinet Office 2010b, p. 10). But defining national security, just like defining national interest, is a politicised process shaped by competing discourses of values, threats, interests and identities (Burke 2007; Smith 2005; Baldwin 1997). There is no single, objective national interest, there is no single, objective definition of national security, there is no single, objective national identity, and there is no single, objective way of life to be protected.

Nevertheless, when we talk about the national interest and whether this or that policy is in the national interest we tend to do a number of things. First, we tend to focus on the state, specifically the idea of a unified state accumulating and exercising material power for the collective benefit of the national community. Second, and related, we tend to project the idea of national interest outwards in terms of external threats and risks to the functioning of the state and society. National interest has traditionally been associated with foreign and defence policy, although the discursive line between domestic/public and foreign/national interests has blurred.[3] Nevertheless, we don't tend to turn discussion of national interests inwards and speak about domestic social policy in these terms. Third, we tend to relate the idea of national interest to national identity – an ideologically unified conception of the role the UK can and should play in global politics and constructing global and regional order. In fact, we're a little obsessed with defining a national role against which we might define a more concrete set of national interests. Fourth, we tend to adopt an empiricist epistemology that implies we can unproblematically deduce or discover an objective and rational national interest or set of interests from the world around us. Such an approach sidelines the role of interpretation and the political power of the concept of national interest in legitimising government actions and framing particular policies as essential (Weldes 1996, p. 276).

The Conservatives' 2010 *A Resilient Nation* policy green paper on national security, for example, defined a 'liberal conservative' and 'enlightened' set of state-centric national interests as

> maintaining the UK's territorial integrity and interests and ensuring the safety of British citizens; the security of international trade, investment and resource flows; a stable, just and rules-based international system and, within it, the continued primacy of the ordered nation state; and effective Alliances and institutions of international governance.
>
> (Conservative Party 2010, p. 5)

In this chapter I want to move the collective 'us' as members of the national community towards the centre of a discussion of national interest. In some aspects it is a move that parallels the shift over the past two decades from national security to human security, a shift in the referent object of security from the state to the person in ways that have challenged how we think about security and insecurity. Why? Because, as Ken Booth (2009, p. 103) so forcefully argues, 'ordinary insecurities determine lives'. The democratic requirement of government accountability and legitimate expectations of the state by the citizen are reason enough to move the everyday experience of UK citizens and communities closer to the centre of any discussion of national interest. This raises questions about the extent to which public opinion and public, as opposed to state, interests are, or should be, at the centre of national interest discourse. As the House of Commons Public Administration Select Committee (PASC) noted in 2012, 'We have little confidence that Government policies are informed by a clear, coherent strategic approach, itself informed by a coherent assessment of the public's aspirations and their perceptions of the national interest' (PASC 2012, p. 3).

Interestingly, however, the most recent formal elaboration of national interest *did* focus more specifically on the UK citizenry. It was formulated for the House of Commons PASC inquiry cited above in December 2011. It defined national interest as

> promoting the welfare of our citizens, through the advancement of six strategic aims: 1) a free and democratic society, properly protected from its enemies; 2) a strong, sustainable and growing economy; 3) a healthy, active, secure, socially cohesive, socially mobile, socially responsible and well educated population; 4) a fair deal for those who are poor or vulnerable; 5) a vibrant culture; and 6) a beautiful and sustainable built and natural environment.
> (PASC 2012, Ev. 73)

The PASC criticised this iteration as well-meaning but

> too meaningless to serve any useful purpose, because they provide no indication of what policies the Government might pursue as a consequence. They do not define how UK national character, assets, capabilities, interests and values are distinctive in any way whatsoever, or define the particular risks and challenges we face. Nor do they define what sort of country we aspire to be beyond the most general terms.
> (PASC 2012, p. 13)

The difficulty, as noted above, is that moving beyond general requirements for the reproduction of a functioning state and general aspirations for society quickly gets you into political, subjective and contested territory.

The terms of any discussion of national interest are therefore fluid and definitions and understandings are contestable. With that in mind, I want to challenge some of the more orthodox ways in which the idea of national interest is discussed by looking from the bottom up, as it were, at national responses to two defining issues of the past decade or so: the global financial crisis and the war on terror. In doing so the chapter is asking two critical questions about how 'national interest' is constructed:

- whether permanent war as a tool for managing global security risk is in fact in the 'national interest';
- how 'national interest' relates to the wellbeing of the national community.

Selective austerity[4]

The UK has faced a very serious financial and economic crisis following the collapse of the sub-prime mortgage market in the US, the bankruptcy of Lehman Brothers and the 2007–2009 international banking crisis that precipitated an unprecedented bailout of the UK banking sector. This flowed into a deep recession from which the country is barely recovering with the 'green shoots' of recovery set to remain hindered by the sovereign debt crisis engulfing the eurozone and a US economy only recently showing signs of improvement. The state was complicit in this crisis through its facilitation of unfettered financialisation of the economy and subsequent corruption of the banking sector (though it did act decisively in October 2008 under Prime Minister Gordon Brown to stave off complete collapse of the banking system by taking a controlling interest in three major UK banks).

The Conservative–Liberal Democrat coalition government forged after the 2010 general election sought to assure the electorate and mollify party spoilers by invoking the national interest. The coalition agreement stated 'After the election, of course, there was the option of minority government – but we were uninspired by it. Instead, there was the option of a coalition in the national interest – and we seized it' (Cabinet Office 2010a, p. 8). The coalition defined the core national interest for the current parliament (2010–2015) as a radical reduction in the structural deficit through severe constraints on public spending. David Cameron labelled this the 'age of austerity' in a speech to the Conservative Party Forum in April 2009, a year before becoming prime minister (Cameron 2009). Government plans in 2010 involved eliminating the bulk of the UK's structural deficit through deep and rapid public expenditure cuts of £40 billion per year from 2010–2011 through 2014–2015 (HM Treasury 2010, p. 4). This was extended to 2017–2018 by Chancellor George Osborne in his autumn statement in December 2012 as the economy continued to malfunction. The coalition has consistently declared that deficit reduction is *the* primary national interest of our time. We must all accept the burdens of a long austerity programme as members of the national community. This will involve 'tough choices' and 'rebalancing the economy'. It is framed as choosing 'to do what is right over what is easy or popular; what is in our country's long-term interest over our parties' short-term interest' (Cabinet Office 2013, p. 5).

The impact of deep cuts in government spending has been severe, notably for the most vulnerable in our society – the national community in whose name the austerity programme is being conducted.

A fifth of our society lived in poverty before the financial crisis and economic recession despite the UK being the world's sixth richest country. By 2008–2009, for example, 13 million people in the UK were in poverty, with 5.8 million of these in 'deep poverty' with household income at least one-third below the poverty line, and 1.6 million children living in poverty in workless families (Parekh et al. 2010). As Oxfam noted in its *Perfect Storm* report in 2012: 'The UK is one of the most unequal rich countries in the world, with the poorest tenth of people receiving only 1 per cent of total income, while the richest tenth take home 31 per cent.'

This has been compounded by austerity measures that have had a profound impact on families on low incomes. Save the Children estimated in 2012 that there were 3.5 million children living in poverty in the UK out of a total of 13.3 million (27 per cent). The number of children living in poverty is expected to increase by 400,000 over the coming years in the 'perfect storm' of a lack of jobs, stagnating wages, a housing crisis, increased living costs and spending cuts. A report in 2012 by the NSPCC, Action for Children and the Children's Society estimated that the number of vulnerable children and families is set to increase under austerity, with vulnerability defined by criteria used in the Families and Children Study data set and adopted by the Cabinet Office in 2007. They conclude that 'By 2015 there will be significantly more children living within vulnerable families than there were in 2008; they will be significantly worse off in terms of disposable income; and that the public spending cuts will have also hit them hard' (Reed 2012, p. 9). Average earnings are also diminishing for the poorest and accelerating for the very richest. Save the Children's report on *Child Poverty in 2012: It Shouldn't Happen Here*, for example, argues 'Low-income families are also bearing the brunt of austerity, with spending cuts hitting the poorest tenth of the population 13 times harder than the richest tenth' (Reed 2012, p. 3). Many more people are now struggling to feed themselves. The UK's largest food bank network, the Trussell Trust, has seen the number of people receiving its food parcels double in the past year, and it predicts further increases, from 128,000 people last year to half a million by 2016 (Haddad 2012, p. 17). Poverty is set to increase and inequality is on course to reach unprecedented levels under the austerity programme.

Austerity measures are not only disproportionately affecting the poorest in society but also women and the disabled. Record numbers of women are currently out of work. Benefit cuts, notably childcare support, are affecting women's incomes far more than men's, particularly those on low incomes. Social care and support services for women are being scaled back. A report by the Fawcett Society on *The Impact of Austerity on Women* in March 2012 argued 'the cumulative effect of fiscal measures taken to reduce net public spending will have a disproportionate effect on women, making many women poorer and less financially autonomous' and that 'Austerity risks turning back time: fewer women working, more women living in poverty, the gap in women's and men's incomes and earnings widening, women's financial autonomy undermined and women's basic rights to safety and justice under threat' (Fawcett 2012, pp. 3, 39).

In fact, according to the House of Commons Library, 7 per cent of cuts announced in the 2010 Emergency Budget will be met from women's incomes, against 28 per cent from men's (Haddad 2012, p. 4). The *Guardian* also noted in March 2012 that

> An analysis of Treasury data by House of Commons Library researchers shows £11.1bn of the £14.9bn raised from the five spending reviews since 2010 comes from women even though they earn less than men on average. Planned changes to tax credits, child benefits and public sector pensions are largely to blame.
> (Martinson 2012)

Evidence also suggests austerity measures are having a substantial effect on the welfare of disabled people from radical reductions in social care programmes and cuts in disability and non-disability related benefits (Duffy 2013). A report from the Hardest Hit coalition, representing over 90 disabled people's organisations and charities, details the impact of austerity measures on disabled people and argues that they are having a profound impact of individual disabled people's lives (Hardest Hit 2012).

In 2010 Chancellor George Osborne observed 'Too often when countries undertake major consolidations...it is the poorest – those who had least to do with the cause of the economic misfortunes – who are hit hardest. Perhaps that has been a mistake that our country has made in the past. This Coalition Government will be different' (Osborne 2010). But the economic and social policies pursued under the banner of austerity-as-national-interest are having a disproportionate and deleterious effect on the country's most vulnerable people. It is very difficult to reconcile a conception of national interest proffered by the state with the pernicious social impact on those on the margins of affluent society: those in poverty, disabled, old and unemployed. National interest as protection of a 'way of life' and 'standards of living' ring hollow.

This forces us to ask questions about the concept of national interest in relation to the coalition austerity programme: whose interests are we talking about when we invoke the 'national' interest? Who is the national interest for and who is it framed by? Who represents and speaks for the 'national interest'? The breadth and pace of the current programme justified by invoking the national interest is evidently not in the 'national interest' of these sections of the national community that are often politically, socially and economically marginalised. This reflects profound political disagreement about the relationship between national interest and social and economic justice within the national community. It has been brought into sharp relief by the biggest squeeze in living standards for a generation. It highlights the deeply political act of framing the national community and its collective interests in particular ways, notably in terms of whether and how deficit reduction should be pursued.

It is useful here to apply the notion of human security to the national community, a concept usually applied by the governments of the developed North to the developing and underdeveloped South rather than their own populations.[5] As a developed, urban-industrial, affluent country, the institutions of the British state are able to meet the legitimate human security expectations of most of its citizens, most of the time. But there are clearly areas where the UK state does *not* provide such security for its citizens, or discriminates in doing so, notably through structural socio-economic vulnerability that can be a cause of acute and enduring insecurity as well as institutionalised modes of discrimination.

The government states that protecting, securing or defending our way of life underpins a basic conception of national interest. If we extend that general theme to the way of life of the most vulnerable in our society then it shifts our conception of national interest to one centred on social justice, equality, welfare and life chances of all members of the national community. When we see that austerity policies and effects are dramatically undermining the human security of those at the bottom of the social ladder by reproducing and aggravating seemingly endemic forms of structural violence (political, social and economic structures of built-in repression that leave people in 'a permanent unwanted state of misery' [Galtung 1990, p. 293]), then we must question the idea of an objective 'national interest' exercised for the benefit of all. Instead, we should examine how national interest as human security for the citizenry, or national security as social development might differ from the more orthodox conceptions of these terms. That, of course, would be a deeply political programme.

Permanent war on terror

Active participation in the US-led 'global war on terror' in response to the 9/11 attacks has defined conceptions of UK national security ever since. The Labour government responded in a number of ways in the name of the national interest, notably by attacking Afghanistan and Iraq and ramping up surveillance of the citizenry and the anti-terrorism powers of the state. To reiterate, national security is routinely framed as national interest by definition, both in terms of conceptions (what we understand national security to mean) and policies (actions undertaken in the name of national security). Military intervention under the war on terror was legitimised by Blair's conception of 'enlightened self-interest' and his doctrine of the international community unveiled in Chicago in 1999. This stipulates that in a globalised world we must be continuously prepared to use military force to address and prevent violent conflict in key regions of the world alongside the US not only for our own national self-interest but also as a global public good for all (Ministry of Defence 2003).

Central to this is the notion of national security risk. Since 9/11 the international security environment has been characterised as uncertain, complex and loaded with multidimensional, interdependent security *risks*. Risk can be defined as a product of the integration of states and societies into globalised economic, social, military and political processes and relationships and subsequent vulnerability to system changes and shocks. Vulnerability generates risk that fosters insecurity (Williams 2008). Risks cannot be eliminated or significantly reduced, only managed or displaced. Since the 1998 Strategic Defence Review 'national security' has morphed into a form of Western globalised national security risk management through military force and control. Security risks are dealt with by attacking distant sources of insecurity with military force if necessary. The invasion of Iraq in 2003 can be viewed in these terms (Shaw 2005, p. 94). The logic here is that a stable and secure international system is a vital national interest (little argument here perhaps) and that this can only be guaranteed by Western military predominance and military intervention to manage global security risks on behalf of the international community, with 'international community' frequently reduced to a Western/NATO 'risk community' (Coker 2002). This interpretation of national security threat and risk generates a national interest in a foreign policy of violent intervention supported by expeditionary military forces.

Defining national security threats, risks and appropriate responses is a discursive act, as noted above. There is an inescapable relationship between politics and security: security is essentially what political and military elites say it is (Wæver 1995). Defining national security as national interest in a particular way generates particular effects. These effects have consequences that are justified in the name of our collective national interest. Consequences of our embrace of Washington's war on terror include the deeply problematic and hubristic liberal, democratic, free-market state-building programmes in Afghanistan and Iraq that currently have very uncertain outcomes after more than a decade of massive investment and horrendous violence at enormous human cost. It also includes a re-militarisation of international politics and the emergence of endless war as military-led risk mitigation generates new and potentially more dangerous risks deemed susceptible to further military solutions (Rogers 2002, p. 14; Greenwald 2013); dispersal of al-Qaeda's core but a flourishing of franchise operations in the Middle East and North Africa (Rogers 2013); heightened risk of further terrorist attacks at home as noted by former MI5 Director General Eliza Manningham-Buller (2010); and curtailment of civil liberties and securitisation of daily life in the name of essential and effective counter-terrorism (Perrigo 2010).

It is not obvious that these outcomes have been in the collective interests of the citizenry let alone those upon whom our violent actions have been visited in the name of our interests. The malign consequences of the war on terror challenge the rhetoric of 'enlightened self interest' that implies the exercise of UK military force as a 'force for good' will lessen security risks to the British state and citizenry by resolving current security threats and pre-empting future risks. It forces us to ask whether sacrificing the lives of 179 soldiers' and Ministry of Defence (MoD) personnel in Iraq and 444 in Afghanistan to date; participating in the killing of several hundred thousand Iraqi and Afghan civilians with a disproportionate number of women and children losing their lives; decimating the immediate human security of several million others through injury, displacement, persecution and trauma; and sparking long-term trends of rising crime rates, property destruction, economic disruption, deterioration of healthcare resources, and food production and distribution capabilities, all while providing profits for largely Western corporations through arms deals and service contracts and private military contractors, constitutes being a 'force for good' when the outcomes of major military interventions have proven indeterminate at best.

This has all been done in the name of our collective national interest, but the relationship between actions and interest is murky. Given the impact of military interventions under the war on terror it is important to question how they relate to ideas of national interest and national security. At a basic level government is required to protect the population from external attack, particularly attacks threatening the existence of the state. We can be satisfied this is the case. As the 2010 National Security Strategy concluded: 'for the foreseeable future it is unlikely that any state or alliance will have both the intent and capability to threaten the independence, integrity and self-government of the UK militarily' (Cabinet Office 2009, p. 66). This is not to say a major state-based military threat cannot re-emerge to the point where the existence of the state is under acute threat, but that is not the case now and the prospect appears remote. It is therefore difficult to claim that actions conducted under the war on terror, notably military invasions, are *essential* to our collective national interest/national security. Gordon Brown's argument that the exercise of military force in Iraq and Afghanistan was crucial to keeping the streets of Britain safe from terrorist attack rang hollow with the public with little evidence to support the claim (Hennessy et al. 2009). This challenges the apparent necessity of 'hyper-interventionism'. Reviews of national security tend to highlight the dangerous uncertainties of a globalising/fragmenting world brimming with multiple threats and risks. The 2010 National Security Strategy and the MoD's Development, Concepts and Doctrine Centre's *Global Strategic Trends – Out to 2040* documents paint a frightening picture that justifies continuous use of military force in the national interest. A more balanced assessment reveals that:

- The UK is militarily more secure than it ever has been: it enjoys a prosperous, secure and stable regional neighbourhood and no longer faces the threat of harm from a major, sustained external attack as during the Cold War.
- High casualty terrorist attacks are rare and do not constitute an existential threat to the state or 'way of life'.
- Incidence of inter-state and intra-state war continues to decline and there has been a pronounced downward trend in the number of battle deaths.
- Non-state conflicts are concentrated in only a small number of countries and are increasingly short-lived.
- The number of democracies continues to rise and the number of autocracies continues to decline.

- The world's average Human Development Index increased 18 per cent between 1990 and 2010 (41 per cent since 1970), reflecting large improvements in life expectancy, school enrolment, literacy and income. Almost all countries have benefitted.
- Extreme income poverty has fallen substantially, with the number of people living on less than $1.25 a day having declined from a high of 1.9 billion in 1981 to a low of 1.4 billion in 2005. In relative terms, the proportion of people living in extreme poverty dropped from 52.0 to 25.7 per cent during this period.
- Measures of state fragility indicate a marked decrease in state fragility over 1995–2010.
- The growth of intergovernmental organisations (IGOs), NGOs, transnational advocacy networks and telecoms (mobile phone and internet access) continues to intensify global, regional and local social system formation, interconnectivity and subsequently social democracy and political accountability (Marshall and Cole 2011; UNDP 2011; Human Security Project 2010; UN DESA 2010).

This is not a plea for best-case thinking, hoping the worst never happens, teleological idealism or 'presentism'. The truism of future uncertainty cannot be escaped but it is vital to acknowledge that the militarised response to 9/11 and more general use of the military instrument for global risk management operations are operations of political *choice*. They are not *requirements* generated by some objective or inevitable distillation of national security and national interest. The suite of operations of choice as defined by the MoD in 2010 include 'Peace Enforcement', 'Military Assistance to Stabilisation and Development', 'Power Projection', 'Focused Intervention' and 'Deliberate Intervention' (Ministry of Defence 2010, pp. 48–49). These go far beyond the set of standard military tasks that are generally considered necessary, legitimate and uncontroversial in direct support of the UK state and citizenry, tasks like assistance in civil emergencies, evacuating UK citizens from overseas, residual protection from direct attack, protecting UK airspace and waters, and a maritime contribution to global protection of sea lanes of supply upon which the UK economy is highly dependent (Ministry of Defence 2010, pp. 44–50). Once again, if we place the national citizenry at the centre of questions about national interest then it becomes far from clear how the consequences of our optional militarised response to 9/11 and wholesale embrace of Washington's war on terror relate to a conception of national interest that is meaningful to the national community in whose name the consequences are justified.

Role obsession

Part of our hyper-interventionism is about reproducing a Blairite notion of the UK's contemporary international role as a 'pivotal power' with global responsibilities by virtue of our history, power, influence and values. (Blair 1998, 2000, 2001, 2003; Ministry of Defence 2003, p. 4; Wheeler and Dunne 2000). This notion claims that a combination of Britain's innate responsibility for international security plus the interdependence of global security challenges means we have an obligation to actively intervene in international conflicts to protect civilian populations, defend the values underpinning 'international community' and enhance national and global security (Blair 2001). Blair framed this narrative in such a way that the only alternative identity was an isolationist Britain and 'a doctrine of benign inactivity' that would only bring insecurity (Blair 2006). It is for these reasons that Britain must remain a country that is prepared to use military force to intervene in the world as a self-appointed force for good (Ministry of Defence 1998). It requires military expeditionary forces of global reach that are fully interoperable with the US across 'the full spectrum of capabilities' even as those capabilities are cut or scaled down (Cabinet Office 2010b, pp. 16–18). In fact, being a country that does hard as well as soft power is intrinsic to the political and defence establishments' conception of the UK's national role (Blair 2007). Blair defined this enlightened self-interest as 'hard headed pragmatism' (Blair 2002). This became a 'hard-headed internationalism' under Gordon Brown and continued under David Cameron as a liberal-conservative narrative of responsibility, interdependence, shared values, international community and military intervention (Brown 2007; Cabinet Office 2008; Cameron 2010; Hague 2009, 2010).

From this we can see how a particular framing of UK national identity by the state and its interpretation of UK history, culture and role generates a 'national interest' in military interventionism as a necessary and inescapable function of who we are and therefore how we act.[6] But it is not necessary or inescapable. This national role conception is a political construction. It naturalises a Blairite view of the UK as an unquestioned 'pivotal' power with a special responsibility to uphold international peace and security by virtue of what Hill labels 'inherited notions of indispensability and grandiosity' (Hill 2010, p. 12). It swallows the self-congratulatory force for good Kool-Aid without a moment of critical reflection. It constructs a world of endless and multiple threats generated by the networks of globalisation – a rampant globalism that serves up endless pathological political forms that induce unacceptable vulnerability necessitating a military response and perpetual violent conflict. It conflates military operations of choice with military operations of necessity. It clings to military power projection as an essential tool of sovereign power in the sovereign's interest.

It hides the fact that UK national security policy and practice is largely an extension of a US hegemonic, militarised, global guardian doctrine ostensibly based on liberal political ideology. It is a doctrine that sees direct and implacable threats emanating from the world's untamed illiberal spaces on the peripheries of globalisation. UK national security interests have subsequently become a de-territorialised, unbounded and open-ended extension of a US global constabulary doctrine (Porter 2010). By reproducing this narrative, we, collectively, risk naturalising a state of continual values-based military activism, destabilisation and intervention as normal practice somehow constitutive of who we are. This role and the actions that flow from it exaggerate the efficacy of military force when the role of military power in meeting the challenges of complex and interdependent security risk is on the wane (Jenkins 2010). It appears oblivious to the counter-productive outcomes of open-ended conflict against illiberal political forms and of the neo-liberal nation-building projects. It represents a self-defeating securitisation and militarisation of risk in the name of reproducing a favourable world order.

In fact it points to a need for *downgrading* the military instrument in our national security culture in favour of the exercise of arguably subtler and more effective forms of power (Niblett 2010, p. 2; Smith 2006). It challenges a culture of national interest and national security that conflates hyper-interventionism with influence in the institutions of global order. It asks us to acknowledge the contingency of the set of national interests constructed in response to 9/11 and the US-led war on terror and the actions and consequences that followed. It questions whether and, if so, how an interventionist, military-oriented, state-centric, global risk management doctrine and the risks it can generate will stabilise and transform the international rules-based system into a more equitable and sustainable form that is surely in the long-term interests of UK citizens and global human society.

The problem is that although we can say these things and there can be nods of agreement, in official national security discourse these things are almost taboo. Robinson, for example, highlights how military interventionism has now become 'a "hard policy path", with a momentum of its own that makes it almost impossible to challenge from within the defence community' (Robinson 2005, p. 12). Robinson and others challenge the benign, post-imperial force for good mantra; they uncomfortably foreground the deep extent to which we are culturally embedded in US security thinking (of which the UK–US Joint Strategy Board established after the 2010 Strategic Defence and Security Review is particularly symbolic, PASC 2012, Ev. 17); they expose the contingency of national role conceptions and ask difficult questions about security for whom and to what end; and they expose the jingoism that emerges from a party political fear of being branded weak on defence.

Parting shots

Where does this leave us? First, any discussion of 'a' or 'the' national interest must ask whose interests we are talking about when we invoke the term. Assumptions of a unified national community with an objectively knowable hierarchy of collective interests are problematic once discussion moves beyond basic requirements for the continued functioning of the state. Everything else is contested and often controversial. Defining interests in terms of practical and aspirational ends, appropriate and legitimate means, and associated allocation of resources is a political project. This is especially so when the reproduction of national role conceptions and elite systems of social and political control are added to the mix.

Second, it means acknowledging the ways in which actions justified in the national interest on the two major issues addressed here (the response to the financial crisis and 9/11) are perpetuating forms of structural violence at home and abroad through systematically diminishing the life chances of society's most vulnerable and embedding a culture of violence through a re-militarisation of international relations. Atkinson describes this in the context of austerity as 'the economic violence born of the neoliberal capitalist orthodoxy' and 'the economic crisis in everyday life' (Atkinson 2013, p. 29). From a more radical perspective it means identifying and resisting austerity-as-national-interest and hyper-interventionism-as-national-interest as forms of state control at home and abroad. This critical perspective suggests that reproducing our modern urban-industrial state requires political stability and popular acquiescence. This requires elite management of risks and threats to the functioning of the global economy in populations and spaces on the fringes of globalisation, some of which stem from the pathological effects of global capitalism itself. Controlling these risks and threats is essential both at home and abroad, and violently if necessary. Stability of the global capitalist system and elite control is the ultimate and enduring elite 'national' interest (Rogers 2007).

Third, competing conceptions of national interest rest on different understandings of ends, means and resources. I suggest in this exploratory chapter a more progressive foundation that places human security at the centre of 'national interest' conceptions. This suggests a shift in focus away from concern with relative position and national role and away from 'a narrative of exceptionalism...characteristic of British policy-makers' attempts to define the country's international significance', and towards privileging human security (Harvey 2011, p. 4). It entails movement towards a more egalitarian idea of national interest in which our 'role' isn't to 'be' anything but to 'do' things for the national community and the wider global human community. It means placing far greater emphasis on the human security impact of our excessive use of military violence both for those on the receiving end and in terms of the long-term human security impact for our national community of a permanent 'long war' and post-9/11 re-militarisation of global politics.

This is the basis of a quite different understanding of 'enlightened' self-interest, one in which long-term security for us on these islands (the purview of our elected representatives) rests upon human development and social cohesion that privileges the poor and immiserated at home and abroad, concerns itself more deliberately with political, economic and environmental justice and equality, seeks to reduce direct political violence, and prefers cooperation across state and cultural boundaries to develop an inclusive multilateral rules-based international order rooted in conflict management, transformation and resolution that progressively delegitimises the use of force. The challenge is to think through a viable political programme towards these ends in an era when the state and society are enmeshed in interdependent networks of global social relations that bring opportunity as well as risk.

Notes

1. These map loosely on to what Neuchterlein (1976, p. 248) described as defence interests, economic interests, world order interests and ideological interests.
2. Frankel (1970, p. 31) distinguished between objective and subjective interest with the latter based on a particular aspirational and cultural vision of the 'good life' to be pursued in general terms over the long term. Charles Beard (1977) developed a distinction between objective and subjective national interests.

3. Nye (1999, p. 23) defined national interests as 'simply the set of shared priorities regarding relations with the rest of the world'.
4. Compulsory austerity was the original subtitle. Selective is more accurate and was helpfully suggested by Eric Herring.
5. Human security was defined in the UN Development Program's 1994 *Human Development Report* as a universal, holistic people-centric rather than state-centric security framework based on a range of interdependent categories of security challenges, including economic, food, health, environment, personal, community and political security. It also encompasses a number of broad local and structural security threats including population growth, economic inequality, migration, drug trafficking, international terrorism and environmental degradation and climate change.
6. MccGwire (2006, p. 644) observes that 'the role a state chooses (or settles for) [based on dominant collective identities within the policy elite] ultimately defines both the national interests that need protecting or promoting (the basis of foreign policy) and the parameters of its security concerns (the basis of defence policy)'. On the relationship between identity, interest and appropriate actions see Wendt (1999, pp. 231–233).

6
Critical Perspectives on the Concept of the 'National Interest': American Imperialism, British Foreign Policy and the Middle East

David Wearing

The 'Occupy' protests that began in New York on 17 September 2011, and spread to London and many other cities around the world through the autumn of that year, introduced a new phrase to the political lexicon: 'we are the 99 per cent'. What the protesters aimed to convey to the wider public with that slogan was an explicitly class-based critique. The global economy was being run in the interests of wealthy elites and corporations, particularly banks – in other words, the 'one per cent' – and not in the interests of the general public, the '99 per cent'. Governments were failing or refusing to prioritise the 'national interest' and were instead acting as state managers for a capitalist ruling class (Mason 2012).

Though not emerging from a pre-existing, permanent organisational structure, these protests had a clear political heritage. One notable antecedent was the global justice movement (often wrongly described as the 'anti-globalisation movement') that arose in the late 90s in response to a particular form of globalisation, characterised by the 'Washington Consensus' around the pursuit of the neo-liberal economic model. Again, governments were seen as being preoccupied with the interests of big business, often at the expense of the public in countries subjected to IMF-led structural adjustment programmes and market reforms effected through the WTO (Klein 2008). The international anti-war movement that later confronted the Anglo-American 'war on terror' drew upon a closely related worldview, according to which the purpose of the invasions of Afghanistan and Iraq was not to defend the domestic populations from the threat of terrorism, nor to bring democracy to the countries in question. Rather, it was to pursue the geopolitical interests of the aggressor states, which in turn was seen as an objective strongly influenced by the class interests of what would later be called the 'one per cent'. What was being objected to was neither anti-terrorism or 'humanitarian intervention' but, as the protesters saw it, a modern form of imperialism (Milne 2012b, pp. 52–60).

The intellectual roots of these twenty-first century movements are perhaps less readily identifiable as belonging to a particular school of thought than was the case for their twentieth century predecessors. An Occupy protestor in September 2011, while probably familiar with the work of contemporary Marxists such as David Harvey, was just as likely to be found reading non-Marxists such as Naomi Klein or Noam Chomsky, who are less concerned with elaborating deeply theoretical accounts of the workings of capitalism than they are with applying a fundamentally class-conscious perspective to the task of empirical policy critique on the subjects of war and globalisation. The same can be said of the British historian Mark Curtis, whose critical account of British foreign policy under New Labour, 'Web of Deceit' (Curtis 2003), was published shortly after the invasion of Iraq in 2003. Having said this, despite the intellectual eclecticism of these social movements, the perspective best elaborated by their members in the academic field continues to be that rooted in Marxist theories of political economy and imperialism.

Theories of imperialism, globalisation and the state

Although Marx did not himself dwell specifically on the nature of imperialism, subsequent historical materialists have regarded global capitalism and imperialism as being closely intertwined, and logically so in the present historical circumstances. As Hobsbawm says, 'A world economy whose pace was set by its developed or developing capitalist core was extremely likely to turn into a world in which the "advanced" dominated the "backward"; in short into a world of empire' (Hobsbawm 1987, p. 56). The development of Marxist theories of imperialism has served 'to make Marx's research programme more concrete by building onto it an evolutionary theory of successive stages of capitalist development' (Callinicos 2009, p. 34). For Marxists, 'imperialism must be explained in terms of the development of capitalism', which is essentially a structural critique (Brewer 1990, p. 11).

There was general agreement between early theorists such as Hobson, Hilferding, Bukharin and Lenin on the connection between the rise of monopolies, the export of capital and the outbreak of inter-imperialist rivalry in the late nineteenth and early twentieth century, though the exact nature of the connection was the subject of some dispute. Hobson argues, as Brewer has said, that 'the emergence of widespread monopoly is said to lead to under-consumption (or over-saving), growing foreign investment, and imperialist expansion' (Brewer 1990, p. 73). For Hobson, the 'taproot of Imperialism' is that domestic 'growth of the powers of production...exceeds the growth in consumption...more goods can be produced than sold at a profit, and more capital exists than can find remunerative investment', thus driving states to secure foreign markets for goods and services by force (Hobson 1938, p. 81). Imperialism does not make overall economic sense for the country, but it does serve certain narrow interest groups (especially financiers, but also exporters, the shipping trade, arms manufacturers and the military) who stand to gain from it. (Brewer 1990, pp. 74–83). In Hobson's words (echoing Smith), 'The business interests of the nation as a whole are subordinated to those of certain sectional interests....This...is the commonest disease of all forms of government' (Hobson 1938, p. 46).

In the post-war period, Marxist and historical materialist perspectives integrated particular conceptualisations of globalisation and the state. In terms of globalisation, as Michael Cox notes, 'the apparently novel thesis that national economies have become mere regions of the global economy and that the productive forces have expanded far beyond the boundaries of the nation state, is not novel at all', its fundamentals having been set out by Karl Marx and Friedrich Engels in *The Communist Manifesto* (M. Cox 1998, p. 451; Marx and Engels 2004).

Historical materialists regard the state as being integrated into, and thus reflecting the balance of social power in, the broader capitalist political economy. The state is penetrated by ruling class interests and yet, while playing a role complementary to those interests, does so in a distinct and autonomous way. Specifically, the state manages class conflicts, absorbs challenges to the system, and performs a management function in the interests of the system as a whole (Callinicos 2009, pp. 86, 91; Linklater 2005, p. 136; Dunleavy and O'Leary 1987, pp. 203–270; Hay 2008, and for a UK-specific analysis, Miliband 1969, 1982). The state, ruling class and capitalist systems are all buttressed by the dominant ideology or 'common sense' of the day, which is itself a reflection of where the power to shape intellectual activity lies. The hegemonic ideology under capitalism obscures class antagonisms, and presents the state as the protector of the 'general interest' (Carnoy 1984, pp. 89–127). Thus the leading states and inter-state institutions of the global north perform the state's domestic management role at an international level.

Robert Cox describes globalised capitalism and the state as tied together in an international system comprising a three-level configuration of social forces, states and world orders, with each element acting and developing in such a way as to reproduce the others, and the system as a whole (R. Cox 1986). The relationship between productive and class relations, governing institutions, and the balance of power internationally is a mutually constitutive one. Central to this is the Gramscian notion of consent, whereby the system holds together because it has acquired a sufficient degree of legitimacy, not merely within the state and ruling class of the leading nation, but across a range of power-centres, decision-makers and social classes internationally. Arrighi takes up this theme, describing how the global political economy has passed, in the modern era, from one period of hegemony to another, with the *pax Britannica* of the nineteenth century being replaced by the middle of the twentieth century with the *pax Americana*, with each successive period of hegemony reflecting a particular stage of capitalist development (Arrighi 1994; see also Arrighi and Silver 2003).

Parenthetically, it may be noted that support for this critical perspective can be found in a perhaps surprising place: the writings of the Scottish Enlightenment philosopher, Adam Smith. Smith is of course best known for advocating the liberalisation of markets, but what is less well known is that he shared some of the key concerns of today's critics of neo-liberalism. His most famous work, *The Wealth of Nations*, offered a powerful political critique of the 'one per cent' of his day, repeatedly emphasising the role of power, influence and class in distorting government policy to serve the interests of a narrow elite.

Smith noted that the 'English legislature has been peculiarly attentive to the interests of commerce' because policymakers were continually 'imposed upon by the sophistry of merchants'. The vested interests 'like an overgrown standing army...have become formidable to the government, and upon many occasions intimidate the legislature' (Smith 1999a, p. 517, 1999b, p. 44). The class power of wealth and big business makes the elite the 'principal architects' of policy, 'an order of men, whose interest is never exactly the same with that of the public, who have generally an interest to deceive and even to oppress the public, and who accordingly have, upon many occasions, both deceived and oppressed it' (Smith, quoted by Rothschild and Sen 2006, pp. 328–329). Smith repeatedly stressed that while the status quo of his day did not serve the public interest, it did benefit the 'principal architects' of policy; an assessment with which the various activist movements mentioned above would readily agree (Smith 1999b, pp. 29, 72, 92–93, 197).

Smith's work is a reminder that there is no fundamental, philosophical impediment to liberal scholarship contributing to the sort of class-conscious critique of modern political economy, and the interrelation between concentrations of socio-economic power and the state, that is discussed in this chapter. Nevertheless, it is predominantly the Marxist and historical materialist schools that have engaged with this task. The following brief discussion outlines some recent contributions to the theoretical debate surrounding the making of foreign policy, and of British foreign policy in particular.

Theorising imperialism today

Callinicos identifies a theoretical division between contemporary Marxist and historical materialist scholars such as Hardt, Negri and Robinson, who hold that, since capitalism is now organised along transnational lines, geopolitical competition amongst states is no longer relevant and the interstate system itself may not be strictly necessary any longer; and those such as Panitch, Gindin, Harvey and Wood, who maintain that nation states still matter, (aside from any disagreements on whether geopolitical competition has been negated under US hegemony) (Callinicos 2009, pp. 16–17).

For Hardt and Negri, 'the United States does not, and indeed no nation-state can today, form the centre of an imperialist project' (Hardt and Negri 2000, pp. xiii–xiv). Empire under capitalism has transcended state rule and now operates as a transnational system of power, constituted across states, institutions and classes. Against this, Wood describes 'capitalism [as] a global system organized nationally'. States have not merely persisted in spite of capitalism; they have been, and continue to be, central to its development. For Wood, 'the universalization of capitalism has also meant... the universalization of the nation state. Global capitalism is more than ever a global system of national states, and the universalization of capitalism is presided over by nation-states, especially one hegemonic superpower' (Wood 1999). Panitch and Gindin agree, arguing that 'states, rather than being the passive victims of globalisation, have been its authors and enforcers'. They point to 'capital's dependence on *many* states' and 'the pre-eminent role of the American state in the making of global capitalism' (Panitch and Gindin 2005, p. 101).

For Harvey, there are two logics of power at work: territorial and capitalist. One seeks to maintain or expand the space in which state power can exert itself, while the other is driven towards capital accumulation. The two logics are distinct but their relationship is dialectical; sometimes complementary, sometimes antagonistic (Harvey 2005, pp. 29–30). Similarly, Callinicos says that 'capitalist imperialism is constituted by the intersection of two forms of competition, namely economic and geopolitical', state rivalry and competition between concentrations of capital (Callinicos 2009, p. 15). In other words, imperialism under capitalism is about both state and economic interests. Harvey describes how these two logics can combine in the concept of the 'spatial fix' whereby, when the rate of profit falls and capitalism faces a crisis of over-accumulation, the geographical expansion of the imperial system offers a solution, allowing capital to move into areas where the possibilities for profit making have not been exhausted. Another solution of course is to redistribute wealth domestically, but this is ruled out on grounds of potential disruption to class relations (Harvey 2005, pp. 89, 94). Again, the contradiction between the 'national interest' and the interests of the dominant class are evident in the behaviour of the state, according to the Marxist perspective.

US imperialism during and after the Cold War

Under the historical materialist perspective, UK foreign policy today (particularly in the Middle East) must be analysed within the context of an era of US-led capitalist-imperialism, and Britain's commitment to maintaining that international system. Stokes observes that, with Washington finding itself in a unique position of strength at the end of the Second World War, 'the post-war US national interest was articulated around a dual vision; the maintenance and defence of an economically open international system conducive to capital penetration and circulation, coupled with a concomitant global geo-strategy of containing social forces considered inimical to capitalism, including but extending far beyond alleged Soviet-aligned communists' (Stokes 2005, p. 221; see also Chomsky 1991, pp. 45–64; Mann 2005, p. 49). Stokes describes how 'US planners constructed a liberal international economic order integrated with (and largely beneficial to) other leading capitalist powers under the tutelage of the US state...US hegemony relied upon consent as well as force' (Stokes 2005, p. 222).

The balance between consent and coercion was radically different from the global north to the global south. In the latter, largely acting through 'pre-existing state structures and local ruling classes', the US was prepared to act forcefully to deal with the threat of 'indigenous nationalisms that looked likely to terminate the incorporation of markets on terms favourable to Western capital, or to present potentially alternative models of non-capitalist development' (Stokes 2005, pp. 222–223). Chomsky argues that democracy itself – given that it empowered popular, independent nationalism – was regarded by US planners as a grave threat to American power and global capitalism; Blakeley shows how state terrorism has been used systematically as a policy tool to deal with independent challenges to imperialism; and Grandin reviews the way in which Latin America became the testing ground for an 'informal imperialism' that employed techniques of coercion and state terror to neutralise independent forces without the need for direct colonialism, a model that would become US imperialism's preferred *modus operandi* elsewhere in the world after 1945 (Chomsky 1991; Blakeley 2009; Grandin 2006). Therefore, while broad consent is recognised by Marxists and historical materialists as a crucial element of US hegemony, relations between the capitalist core and the global south (of which the Middle East is understood to be a part) are seen as often exploitative, coercive and violent.

The end of the Cold War removed a key external justification for US leadership of the capitalist world, but conversely, enhanced its dominant position (Anderson 2002, p. 7). The demise of the USSR granted US imperial power a much freer hand to impose its economic vision – the Washington Consensus – of further deregulation, financialisation and the erosion of the social contract (Amin and Luckin 1996, pp. 252–253). 'The Third Way version of neoliberalism fitted well with the catechism of the "international community" and its shared devotion to universal human values'. Free markets, free elections and human rights (as a justification for military interventionism) were the legitimating trademarks of American power (Anderson 2002, pp. 9–10).

An important dimension of US imperialism, in the historical materialist view, has concerned the geopolitics of oil. Achcar quotes Chomsky summarising this view of the significance of the Middle East to US imperial strategy,

> the major interest lies in the energy reserves of the region, primarily in the Arabian peninsula. A State Department analysis of 1945 described Saudi Arabia as 'a stupendous source of strategic power,

and one of the greatest material prizes in world history.' The US was committed to win and keep this prize.

(Chomsky cited in Achcar 2004, p. 18)

It is a point of broad agreement across the literature that the exceptional material and strategic value of this region and its resources meant that maintaining US influence and power there was key to Washington's ability to wield power on the global stage (Achcar and Chomsky 2007, pp. 54–55; Stokes 2005, p. 230). As Gowan, writing shortly after the Gulf War of 1991, observed,

> the control of oil supplies to both Japan and the countries of Western Europe has always served the US as a crucial political lever in relations with these states. They are, after all, more reliant upon Middle East oil than is the United States, and would undoubtedly increase their independence if their sources were not under the latter's 'protection' but under that of a regime not itself dependent on the US.
>
> (Gowan 1991, p. 48)

Callinicos additionally argues that a major pillar of US hegemony has been the strategic control over oil, not least due to the dependence of the other main centres of capitalism in the global north. This was formalised in the Carter Doctrine, declared in 1980, which stated that any attempt to gain control over the Persian Gulf would be seen as an assault on the vital interests of the US and subject to a potential military response. Thus, according to Callinicos, 'securing the Middle East has proved to be the main axis of US military intervention in the past quarter-century' (Callinicos 2009, p. 182). The rapid growth of energy-hungry China, which is expected to exceed US rates of consumption by 2020, only further enhances the strategic value of the region (Harvey 2005, p. 228). Harvey puts the point simply: 'whoever controls the Middle East controls the global oil spigot and whoever controls the global oil spigot can control the global economy, at least for the near future' (Harvey 2005, p. 19).

The other key aspect of the Gulf region's centrality to global capitalism has to do with its role in the financial system. Gulf petrodollars played a major part in the financialisation of global capitalism and the move to neo-liberalism. Following the oil crisis of 1973–1974 and the renegotiation of regional oil contracts, the sharply increased revenues enjoyed by the oil producing states were invested in the Western banking system. An explicit deal was done in 1978 whereby the Saudis would sell their oil solely in US dollars and ensure that OPEC continued to do the same, and in return the US would offer the kingdom extensive military and political support (Hanieh 2011). Financial deregulation dovetailed deliberately with the rise in oil prices to ensure that petrodollars were drawn into Wall Street and the financial system of the global north (including the City of London), as part of the shift from the Bretton Woods settlement to the new neo-liberal order (Harvey 2005, pp. 128–132). Over the last ten years, Gulf investments have played a central role in the globalised world economy, not least in the development of East Asia. Hanieh notes that total foreign assets held by Gulf state companies, individuals and ruling families came, in 2011, to an estimated $2.2 trillion (Hanieh 2011).

In sum, therefore, the Marxist and historical materialist perspective regards the Middle East as a prime material and strategic prize under the system of capitalist imperialism currently dominated by the US. The implication of this for British foreign policy will be explored below.

Britain in the era of the American empire

How does British foreign policy fit into this picture? For the historical materialist, analysis 'must start from the structure of social relations, not from individual choices or motivations' (Brewer 1990, p. 11). In this view, Britain is a capitalist state with a corresponding, hierarchical class system that reinforces and reproduces itself in a variety of different ways. These include, for example, the privileged route taken by individuals from a wealthy upbringing through the elite centres of education to the higher reaches of the state and corporate worlds, the ability of the privately owned media to shape debate and set the agenda according to its class interests, and the power of big business and capital to influence government more generally (Miliband 1969, 1982). What results is a system of government that is dominated by class interests, and which pursues policies aimed both at serving those interests in a narrow sense, but also at maintaining the broader capitalist system (even at the expense, occasionally, of a particular business lobby). In terms of this latter function as it pertains to the international scene, the US has been regarded since 1945 as Britain's best hope of maintaining and expanding a global liberal capitalist system that works in the interests of the British state and British capital.

Thus, Britain and its foreign policies are understood by historical materialists in the context of the UK's position as a member state of the consenting core of major capitalist powers under US hegemony. Since

Britain's own capacity to maintain its imperial role essentially collapsed in the three decades between 1914 and 1945, London has perceived its own interests to be best served by supporting Washington's leadership in consolidating and extending the reach of global capitalism, while working to advance the interests of the British state and British concentrations of capital to the greatest feasible extent within those overarching parameters (Curtis 2003, pp. 101–119; and for a broader theoretical view of second-order powers under US leadership, Callinicos 2009, pp. 218–219).

London has sought to maximise its influence within the new US-led order in the post-war era in a number of ways. The City of London remains at the heart of global finance (Harvey 2005, p. 134), and Britain's membership of NATO, its role as a leading arms exporter and its status as one of the main second-order military powers, all afford it a seat at the table in respect of major global security issues (Callinicos 2009, p. 215; Curtis 2003, pp. 101–119, 180–206). Its simultaneous membership of the EU and closeness to Washington also give it a central role in discussions between the core capitalist states.

As the leading historical materialist focusing on British foreign policy today, Mark Curtis has documented the role Britain has played in the global south during the period following the Second World War, dealing coercively with threats to the US-led order as and when they arise, and acting as advocate in the international economic forums for the advancement of global capitalist interests and the integration of the south into that transnational system (Curtis 2003, 2004, 2010). British foreign policy in the Middle East falls under the heading of its relations to the global south, and, as ever, the role that it plays is complementary to US strategy (Curtis 2003, pp. 253–284). As Curtis notes,

> Oil is, of course, the fundamental Anglo-American interest in the Middle East, and was described by British planners in 1947 as 'a vital prize for any power interested in world influence or domination'.... Oil is designated to be controlled by Western allies in the Middle East to ensure that industry profits accrue to Western companies and are invested in Western economies. A traditional threat in the past has been that the nationalist regimes would use oil wealth primarily to benefit local populations and to build up independent sources of power to challenge US domination over the region. Traditionally, such regimes have been overthrown or prevented from arising by British and US power.
>
> (Curtis 2003, pp. 15–16)

Britain therefore helps to maintain a US-led, conservative regional order conducive to the interests both of itself and of the broader capitalist-imperial system.

As noted above, Gulf oil money has played a central role in today's highly financialised global capitalist system, since the oil crisis of 1973–1974. By attracting the surge in oil revenues from the Arab producer states into its economy, the British state was able ultimately to turn that series of events to its advantage. In the last days of the 1970–1974 Conservative government and the early days of the subsequent Labour administration, Britain and Saudi Arabia sealed what Curtis describes as 'a profound economic alliance, the consequences of which are still evident' (Curtis 2010, p. 115). As well as investment in the British economy, and investment opportunities for British industry in the Gulf, Whitehall also sought a wider influx of surplus oil revenues in the financial system, whereby recycled petrodollars would perform the same stabilising function as the recently expired Bretton Woods system. In 1975, Harold Wilson was briefed to tell Prince Fahd, 'Your country now has a major stake in Britain and you will naturally be closely interested in the progress of the British economy'. By that stage, the Saudis held the equivalent in today's prices of around £20 billion worth of investment in the British economy, as well as supporting the pound by holding large proportions of their surplus funds in sterling (Curtis 2010, p. 118).

These financial ties reinforced the key strategic interest perceived by the British state in supporting the rule of the autocratic regimes in the Arabian peninsula. Throughout the 1970s, the Saudi National Guard continued to be trained by the British army for their duties protecting the king, while the Saudi oil minister was guarded by a team of former SAS personnel. According to Curtis, 'In 1973, Britain signed a £250 million deal with the Saudis to train its air force pilots and service its aircraft' (2010, p. 120). Today, Britain's major arms sales contract with Saudi Arabia (al-Yamamah) is thought to be the 'single largest arms deal in history' (Hollis 2010, p. 159), while Britain also provides arms and training to the security forces of the various Gulf regimes (Curtis 2003, pp. 253–269).

Britain and Iraq

The case of the invasion and occupation of Iraq can be used to illustrate how the Marxist and historical materialist perspectives may be applied to contemporary issues in British foreign policy. Historical materialists take the view that the US and Britain sought a post-Saddam

Iraq integrated economically and militarily into the US-led regional order, even if this contradicted the wishes of the Iraqi people. The conduct of coalition forces in the years after April 2003 is seen as making more sense viewed from this perspective than if seen as being based on the liberal assumption (see for example, Fisher and Biggar 2011) that humanitarianism and democracy promotion were the key policy aims.

For Callinicos, the war was about 'tightening Washington's grasp on the oil supplies on which all its rivals depend more than it does' (Callinicos 2009, p. 15) while Harvey observed that the occupation would establish a 'powerful US military bridgehead on the Eurasian land mass' to help counter any possible emerging power bloc loosely comprising France, Germany, Russia and China (Harvey 2005, pp. 84–85). For Anderson, a successful act of regime change would 'give Washington a large oil-rich platform in the centre of the Arab world, on which to build an enlarged version of Afghan-style democracy, designed to change the whole political landscape of the Middle East' (Anderson 2002, p. 17).

Here, it is crucial from the Marxist or historical materialist perspective that what Anderson refers to as 'Afghan-style democracy' is correctly understood, in its imperial context. Robinson argues that, while the notion of ' "democracy promotion" ... plays a key legitimating function' in Western foreign policy, what was favoured by the occupiers of post-Saddam Iraq 'is more accurately termed polyarchy ... a system in which a small group actually rules on behalf of (transnational) capital and mass participation in decision-making is limited to choosing among competing elites in tightly controlled electoral processes' (Robinson 2006, pp. 441–442). The post-2003 Iraqi state and governing elite was formed under Western occupation and tutelage in such a way as to be penetrated by, and thus to represent, the will of the occupying states and the interests of the globalised economic order in Iraq (Harvey 2005, pp. 197, 214–215, 217; Herring and Rangwala 2005; Klein 2008, pp. 323–382; Muttitt 2012). A government representing the sovereign will of the Iraqi people would be undesirable since, as Achcar observes,

> There are no reliable US allies in Iraq with any real credibility ... Iraq, like other Middle Eastern countries, thus only confirms what Samuel Huntingdon called 'the democracy paradox: adoption by non-Western societies of Western democratic institutions encourages and gives access to power to nativist and anti-Western political movements'.
>
> (Achcar 2004, pp. 42–43)

Achcar continues: 'This is a "paradox"... only in the eyes of those who believe that democracy goes hand in hand with submission to the West'. Given the history of imperialism in the region, he says, 'it is entirely natural that if the majority of the people could express itself freely and truthfully at the ballot box in Muslim countries, it would elect governments hostile to Western domination' (Achcar 2004, pp. 42–43).

Although opinion polls taken in circumstances such as Iraq's post-2003 should be regarded with caution, the many surveys that were conducted consistently revealed significant popular opposition to the occupation (Chomsky 2006, pp. 163–165). Britain should have been aware of this. One poll carried out for Britain's Ministry of Defence (MoD) in August 2005 found that 82 per cent of Iraqis 'strongly opposed' the presence of coalition troops (Rayment 2005). The fact that the occupation continued against the wishes of most Iraqis, according to the best evidence available, seriously undermines the democratic credentials of US-British policy at the time. That the same MoD poll showed less than 1 per cent of Iraqis crediting coalition forces with improving security, 72 per cent having no confidence in them and 67 per cent saying they made them feel less safe does not sit well with the image of British and American troops providing humanitarian protection to liberated Iraqis.

Emerging evidence of detainee abuse by occupying troops helps to explain the Iraqi perception (Hersh 2004; Cobain 2012), as does the more general conduct of coalition forces. One striking example was the November 2004 siege of the rebel-held town of Fallujah (Steele and Jamail 2005). American troops instructed civilians to leave Fallujah before the assault began, but men aged 15–55 were denied exit, leaving one in six residents remaining with water and electricity cut off. The hospital was captured as an early priority to deny the media the most practicable site for documenting casualties. Around half the city's homes were damaged and a quarter destroyed. Five months after the assault, half of Fallujah still had no electricity. Estimates of civilian deaths ranged from 650 to 1,300 (Muttitt 2012, pp. 113–114). British officers on the ground are reported as having expressed their horror at the Americans' general treatment of Iraqis (in April 2004 one said the US troops viewed Iraqis as 'untermenschen' [Rayment 2004]), but British forces were nonetheless deployed to assist their coalition allies in blocking escape routes from Fallujah and preventing supplies entering once the siege had begun (Steele and Jamail 2005).

Commercial considerations also influenced coalition policy, and hence Iraqi perceptions of it. Muttitt notes that, before any elections had been held and in violation of the occupiers' obligations under international law, the coalition,

> through a series of executive orders... removed all restrictions on foreign investment, allowing 100 per cent outside ownership of Iraqi companies and the repatriation of all profits. 'National treatment' prohibited the government from favouring local companies over foreign ones, throwing the sanctions-battered economy open to competition that would likely destroy it. Tariffs, duties and import taxes were suspended. Income taxes were reduced from 40 per cent to a flat rate of 15 per cent on businesses and individuals. Iraqi state-owned enterprises were prepared for privatisation. Former World Bank economist Joseph Stiglitz described the programme as 'an even more radical form of shock therapy than was pursued in the former Soviet world'.
> (Muttitt 2012, p. 89; see also Klein 2008, pp. 323–382)

Moreover, the centrality of oil as a material and strategic prize under the historical materialist perspective has been noted above. Indeed, when Baghdad was comprehensively ransacked by looters after Saddam's fall, with even hospitals and museums stripped bare, the only building protected by coalition forces was the Oil Ministry (Muttitt 2012, pp. 44–51).

Britain was also closely involved in policy discussions on the oil industry, using its privileged position as occupier to advise Iraq's post-Saddam authorities on commercial relations with oil multinationals and the structure of its industry (Muttitt 2012, pp. 118, 125–127). It did not do so from a neutral perspective. Several meetings were held in Whitehall prior to the invasion where oil and gas multinationals were reassured that Britain was 'determined to get a fair slice of the action for UK companies in a post-Saddam Iraq' (Muttitt 2012, pp. 3–5). A Foreign Office paper noted that 'the future shape of the Iraqi industry will affect oil markets, and the functioning of OPEC, in both of which we have a vital interest' (cited by Muttitt 2012, p. 38 – obtained under the Freedom of Information Act).

A poll in 2007 showed a popular preference amongst Iraqis for state over foreign management of the oil industry by a majority of two-to-one. (Muttitt 2012, p. 156) This was not a view acceptable to the coalition, which was heavily involved in the drafting of the proposed new oil law. The IMF had the right to review drafting progress on a quarterly basis (Muttitt 2012, p. 173), and British and American officials are reported to have seen the draft law in July 2006, when oil multinationals were also able to provide their input at a meeting in Washington. However, the Iraqi parliament did not see the draft until March 2007 and the Iraqi public did not see it until July of that year (Muttitt 2012, p. 199). In the event, public concern over the direction of Iraq's key industry under the occupation led to the law's passage stalling in the Iraqi parliament.

This was the first of two significant political defeats for the occupiers and their Iraqi allies. The other was the failure to agree a long-term US military presence in the country, akin to that in South Korea (Muttitt 2012, p. 243). Despite enormous pressure placed on them, including by the Obama administration following Bush's exit, Iraqi politicians refused to sign a Status of Forces Agreement with the US (Muttitt 2012, pp. 273–274). This was probably because they were aware that the majority of the public would not accept the arrangement, a fact Washington was effectively urging them to ignore (Muttitt 2012, pp. 273–274).

More generally, historical materialism anticipates that democratic pressure from Arab publics will be regarded by Western powers as a threat to be contained. In Iraq, internal Coalition Provisional Authority (CPA) memos warned that 'elections could create a legitimate counter authority to the CPA, making its ability to govern more difficult' and would 'largely sacrifice Coalition control over the outcome' of the post-Saddam transition. American law professor Noah Feldman, who worked on the transition to democracy in Iraq, warned that 'if you moved too fast the wrong people could get elected' (Chomsky 2006, p. 131). Appointees were instead chosen to form an 'Iraqi governing council' though real power continued to rest with the occupiers (Muttitt 2012, pp. 76–77). Yet the CPA was not able to control the process entirely. In January 2005, elections were held at the insistence of the Shia Iraqi leadership, backed by large popular demonstrations, in spite of, in the words of the editors of the *Financial Times*, the CPA's preference to 'shelve or dilute' them, (cited, inter alia, by Chomsky 2006, p. 160).

In sum, according to the historical materialist assessment, Britain invaded and occupied Iraq as part of a coalition that: ignored an Iraqi majority wish for it to leave; pressured the Iraqi government to overrule that majority; attempted to shape a political and economic transition that suited coalition preferences, not the public's; worked to marginalise that public where necessary; and often deployed brutal force to suppress resistance. In terms of Britain's own role, according to the historical materialist view, there is a distinction to be made between her national interest and the actual interests pursued by the British state in Iraq. It is worth noting that the British government was warned by the security services in February 2003 that al-Qaeda represented by far the greatest threat to national security, and that this threat would be heightened by military action against Iraq (Press Association 2003).

Britain's response to the Arab uprisings

In respect of the various uprisings that have taken place across the Arab world since the end of 2010, Marxists and historical materialists would derive certain expectations, based on their shared theoretical principles, on how Britain would respond to these events. According to this view, the UK was likely to welcome the prospect of regional democratisation in rhetorical terms, in accordance with the dominant liberal discourse, but in practice to take a more interests-based approach. Challenges to allied regimes would be met either with renewed support for those allies or, where this was unlikely to be successful, with attempts to ensure that successor governments were composed of reliable elements, willing to maintain the economic, military and strategic orientation of the status quo ante. In the case of uprisings against regimes not allied to the Atlantic powers, support for the opposition would be more willingly provided, with the crucial proviso that such forces represented a better option going forward than the status quo. These theoretical expectations can be applied to subsequent events in a number of ways.

In the case of Libya, once the future direction of the state was thrown into question in February and March 2011, the Atlantic powers including the UK moved quickly to ensure that the eventual outcome would be a reliable state, friendly to Western interests. The defection to the opposition of a number of figures from the Gaddafi regime who had led on the rapprochement with the West and the advance of neo-liberal economic reforms in the preceding years, coupled with Gaddafi's ongoing resistance especially to economic change and his general unreliable nature, made the choice to back the Eastern-based opposition a fairly clear one for NATO (Prashad 2012). There has been some disagreement amongst historical materialists as to the effect of the NATO intervention on the humanitarian situation, at least at the start of the conflict (Achcar 2011). However, they broadly agree that NATO sought to commandeer the Libyan uprising to ensure that it served its own interests.

In Syria, the opportunity to topple or undermine a regional adversary and leading ally of Iran was offset by two factors. The first was the unreliability of the opposition, both in terms of the rise of jihadist elements within the domestic armed rebellion and in the persistent difficulties in shaping a coherent and purposeful external, political opposition (a task which had been easier to achieve in the Libyan case). The second consideration was the danger that direct or indirect military intervention could worsen the conflict, with wider, destabilising regional effects. There has been some disagreement amongst historical materialists as to whether the Syrian conflict should best be understood in terms of its domestic roots (Maunder 2012) or with regard to the role of outside forces (Milne 2012a). However, the point that the Atlantic powers (and therefore the UK) were motivated by geopolitical calculation rather than humanitarian principle is again the subject of broad agreement.

In the case of Bahrain, a large and broad-based pro-democracy uprising in the spring of 2011 was violently crushed by internal security forces (Slackman and Audi 2011), with the support of a Gulf Cooperation Council (GCC) intervention force led by Saudi troops reportedly trained by the UK (Kirkup 2011). Notwithstanding the cancellation of some British arms export licenses for Bahrain in response to these events, what followed over the next two and a half years was a discernible recommitment to Britain's alliances with the GCC states, including the energetic pursuit of deeper economic ties, increased arms sales, greater military cooperation and the signing of new defence agreements with Bahrain (and also with the UAE) (Clarke, Stansfield and Kelly 2013). The agreement with Bahrain reportedly contained provision for cooperation on 'internal stability' (Al Arabiya 2012), of particular concern given that the regime's priority in terms of internal stability appeared to be protecting itself and its privileges from the population. These developments further reinforce the historical materialist perspective on the nature and commitments of British foreign policy in the Middle East.

Conclusion

This chapter has set out to explain British foreign policy in the Middle East in terms of a theoretical reading of modern political economy and international relations shared and subscribed to by a number of prominent activist movements over the last 15 years. This view holds that states in general, and the British state in particular, are not committed to the pursuit of the national interest but to serving the interests of a ruling class within a global capitalist economic system. This leads those states to pursue certain foreign policies in order to maintain, extend and entrench that system internationally. In the economic and political climate that has prevailed since the great financial crash of 2008, this understanding of the state – that it is subject primarily to class interests different from those of the general public – is one that will continue to have relevance for many analysts and activists around the globe.

7
Why America?[1]
Robin Porter

Introduction

On 4 December 2010, the *Guardian* published a front-page piece, claiming to be based on confidential cables between the US's London embassy and the government in Washington. The cables had been published in *WikiLeaks* a short time earlier. Dating from before the 2010 British election, the cables revealed that William Hague, later to become foreign secretary, had offered the ambassador a 'pro-American government' if the Conservatives won, while Liam Fox made clear his desire to buy more armaments from the US to achieve interoperability, 'since the US and UK will continue to fight together in the future' (*Guardian* 4 December 2010). This statement of intent has been mirrored in the foreign policy of the 2010 coalition government. It also represents continuity with the policies of the Blair government towards the George W. Bush administration, only the three years of Gordon Brown's government posing a question mark for a time over the closeness of cooperation. It is remarkable that these ties survived the transition from Republican to Democrat in the US, and from Labour to Conservative here in the UK. In many ways, a pro-American stance seems to be the default setting of Britain's foreign and defence policy.

So what is it that is so special about the 'special relationship'? Has it always been a fundamental pillar of British diplomacy? How does it accord with the stated first principles of Britain's foreign policy? Is it truly in Britain's national interest to be so close to the US?

The special relationship in historical perspective

For much of the past 200 years, US and British foreign policies have not coincided, and it may be instructive to recall very briefly some of the issues which have divided the two countries, if only as a reminder of how recent the special relationship actually is. Following the American Revolution of 1776, US attitudes to Britain were hostile for much of the nineteenth century. The relationship was marked by the war of 1812–1814 between Britain and the US in Canada, by US support for the Fenians and other rebellious movements in Britain's Canadian colonies in the 1830s and 1840s, by the 'Manifest Destiny' campaign for the annexation by the US of British North America in the mid-1860s after the American Civil War, and by America's determination to extend its influence at Britain's expense through the rest of the nineteenth century. Although in the twentieth century the US and Britain were allies through a part of each of two world wars and in Korea, the partnership was at times an uneasy one. The US declined to take part in the League of Nations between the wars, in the formation and functioning of which Britain played a leading role. Even after the first articulation of the 'special relationship' by Winston Churchill just after the Second World War, as has been noted elsewhere, the relationship has had its ups and downs (cf. Baylis 1997; Wallace and Phillips 2009). At the time of the Suez crisis the US failed to support Britain, and in the Falklands conflict was ambivalent, while Britain determinedly refused to become involved in the Vietnam War.

While the Cold War may have united UK and US interests for a time following the defeat of the Axis powers, Britain's commitment to containing the Soviet Union was always less ideological than that of the US. Britain's nuclear capability was seen by the US as being of uncertain utility and her intelligence gathering operations as unreliable, prone to leaks and subject to betrayal. US Defence Secretary Robert McNamara in particular was hostile to the independent British nuclear deterrent throughout the arguments in 1962 over the replacement of Skybolt by Polaris. US Secretary of State Dean Acheson's famous remark in his 'West Point' speech of December 1962, that Britain had 'lost an Empire and not yet found a role' (cf. *Spectator* 5 January 2013) caused a sensation in London, and is mirrored by the reported embarrassment of the US embassy in 2010 at the 'paranoia' of senior British politicians over the state of the special relationship (*Guardian* 4 December 2010).

Indeed, it is arguable that the notion of the 'special relationship' has for at least 50 years had little currency on the western side of the Atlantic, though US policymakers have learned to reference it when it serves a purpose to do so. Only in the UK, it would appear, is the notion taken more seriously, and advanced as a reason for involvement in military adventures which may not be in Britain's interest.

Moreover, it sometimes seems that initiatives undertaken in the name of the special relationship can lead to events (military action which is illegal under international law, Guantanamo, 'special rendition', indifference to civilian 'collateral damage', etc.) which reveal how far apart the UK actually is in terms of circumstances, values, beliefs, diplomatic objectives and interests from its American allies. There have been brief periods, following the 2003 intervention in Iraq for example, when the term 'special relationship' seemed to figure less prominently in British discourse on diplomacy. In 2006, under Nigel Sheinwald as foreign policy and defence adviser to the prime minister, for example, and again the following year when Douglas Alexander, then at the Department for International Development, called for a more 'multilateralist' approach (*Guardian* 14 July 2007). Later the same year, however, David Miliband, by then foreign secretary, publicly reaffirmed that the US was 'the single most important bilateral relationship for Britain' (Miliband 2007). This renewed acknowledgement of US leadership, past experience suggested, might sit uneasily with any notion of pan-European cooperation, NATO notwithstanding.

While the inauguration of Barack Obama as America's first black president brought a wealth of promises on domestic policy, changes in US foreign policy have been more subtle.

From the UK's point of view, the administration's tendency to extend the term 'special relationship' to a number of other countries at different times (notably Israel, France and Germany, among others, during reciprocal visits by leading statesmen) has suggested a process of moving away from what the UK had felt was its privileged status in American eyes. US National Intelligence Council scenarios for 2025 'assume a coherent European partner, with scarcely a reference to bilateral relations with the UK' (Wallace and Phillips 2009, p. 283). Ironically, the recent 'no' vote in parliament to David Cameron's projected British military involvement in Syria may well have encouraged the Obama administration in its desire to have a special relationship with Europe as a whole, while at the same time reflecting for perhaps the first time ever the power of ordinary citizens in a democracy potentially to reverse a government's decision on a fundamental issue of foreign policy.

It should also be noted that on a personal level Obama himself has no real ties with the UK; indeed if anything his father's Kenyan background during the British colonial administration there, coupled with the Irish origins of one of his eighteenth century antecedents, which he chose to celebrate during his 2011 visit to Dublin, may be possible reasons for a degree of wariness in dealing with Britain and its aspirations.

First principles of British foreign policy

If we are to judge the appropriateness of the demands of the special relationship to Britain's present circumstances and objectives in foreign policy, we should first perhaps reflect on what we believe to constitute British 'national interests' in the twenty-first century. The concept of the national interest is, of course, a controversial one, and by and large it is not the purpose here to engage with the extensive theoretical debate on what a 'national' interest in the abstract might look like, or even whether such a thing can exist. It is indisputable, however, that successive British governments in the past *have* based their foreign policy on a conception of what is 'good' or 'bad' for Britain. Moreover, for the diplomat in the field, decisions about different courses of action are even today similarly informed by a desire to advance the interests of the country they represent, even though these national interests may not always be explicitly articulated.

A close study of British foreign policy initiatives from roughly the Congress of Vienna of 1815 down to the present day suggests that, historically, certain fundamental principles have guided British foreign policy as the country sought to protect and advance its interests in its relations with other states. For example, a belief in the rule of law has been paramount, specifically international law, manifest in treaties between nation-states, the treaty system that developed in the nineteenth century (notably from the Congress of Vienna onwards) and the League of Nations and UN systems of the twentieth century, along with the resolution of disputes through these mechanisms, and more recently the application of human rights law through international courts.

There is also evidence of a primary concern with the international politics of Europe, and the need to secure peace there, to minimise threats to Britain through encouraging a balance of power. Concern with the politics of Europe has its roots in the experience of centuries of warfare, both between England, or later Britain, and other European powers (Spain, Holland, France, Germany), and within Europe, and has expressed itself through attempts to prevent warfare. The Congress of Vienna settlement of 1815 and the less successful Versailles Peace Conference of 1919, in both of which Britain played a major part, were precursors to Britain's efforts in more recent times to find a modus vivendi with her neighbours in Europe through the EU. Geopolitics – the simple facts of Britain's geographical location – have determined that Europe should be a cornerstone of British policy. The promotion of Britain's economic interests overseas has long been a priority. In earlier times this meant the expansion and naval protection of trade, the acquisition of raw materials, the development of markets and in the nineteenth century especially the appropriation of territory overseas in the form of colonies which could satisfy these needs. The military defence of the realm, and in the nineteenth and twentieth centuries also of far-flung parts of the British Empire, has also been fundamental. So has the maintenance of freedom of movement internationally for British subjects, and the guarantee of this through the dominance of sea lanes by the Royal Navy.

There have been strong echoes of these concerns in the 'global objectives' of Britain's foreign policy in recent times. It is the contention of this chapter that the principles encompassed in these objectives are as close as it may be possible to come to an explicit statement of the UK's 'national interests' as they relate to our foreign policy today.

In 2007, the Foreign and Commonwealth Office defined its global objectives as follows:

1. A world safer from terrorism and weapons of mass destruction.
2. Protection of the UK from illegal immigration, drug trafficking and other international crime.
3. An international system based on the rule of law, which is better able to resolve disputes and prevent conflicts.
4. An effective EU in a secure neighbourhood.
5. Promotion of UK economic interests in an open and expanding global economy.
6. Sustainable development, underpinned by democracy, good governance and human rights.
7. Security of UK and global energy supplies.
8. Security and good governance of the UK's Overseas Territories.
9. High quality consular services to British nationals abroad. Effective regulation of entry to, and settlement in, the UK in the interests of sustainable growth and social inclusion.

(Foreign and Commonwealth Office 2007)

These global objectives, while not the most recent, have been chosen deliberately, because they come prior to what many have perceived to be a growing sense of confusion as to what UK foreign policy objectives should be. During the latter part of the Blair premiership, and indeed under both the Brown and Cameron governments, there appears to have been an increasing loss of clarity over what should constitute Britain's foreign policy objectives. This is reflected in evidence to and conclusions of the Foreign Affairs Select Committee in 2011 (FAC 2010, 2011). One element of this was the attempt to make the objectives conform to the requirements of public service agreements, imposed on all government departments, which for a time also contributed to the confusion (2 FCO Priorities, FAC 2010, 2011).

Of the objectives cited above, 3, 4, 5 and parts of 6 have particular resonance with the earlier conceptions of the British national interest previously noted. The belief in the international rule of law remains fundamental to the thinking behind much British diplomacy. The politics of Europe and Britain's relations with the EU, though recently bedevilled by the eurozone crisis and by a rather impoverished public debate over the risks and benefits of EU membership, are still of critical importance to the UK. Britain remains committed to an open global economy and the promotion of its economic interests in the international arena, primarily through trade, and outward and inward investment. Concern for democracy and individual rights, while not always in the mainstream of British policymaking historically, has been put forward by some with influence on Britain's foreign policy process in support of what were perceived to be liberal movements for national self-determination, notably by Lord Byron in Greece in the 1820s, and by Gladstone with respect to Italian unification in the 1850s and 1860s. This was also the case during the Versailles peace process of the early twentieth century, and of course more recently in the Balkans. Of the other objectives, 8 and 9 are related to the UK's responsibilities towards its overseas and domestic populations. Objective 2 in part represents an extension of a longstanding concern over international criminal activity (the trafficking of drugs and people and the laundering of money now, piracy and the slave trade in the past, for example), though the emphasis placed on illegal immigration is more recent.

Objectives 1 and 7 in the list above are more problematic, however. Terrorism and weapons of mass destruction on one hand, and energy supplies on the other, have not been *dominant* concerns in British foreign policy until quite recently, but have become so for the most part since the presidency of George W. Bush and the 9/11 attacks on New York and Washington in 2001. The impact of the Iraq War is also significant here. Indeed, it is arguable that the UK's willingness under the Blair administration to countenance the fabrication of evidence relating to weapons of mass destruction, and then to commit British troops to the invasion of a sovereign state without proper sanction from the UN, far from promoting Britain's interests, has been immeasurably damaging to Britain's reputation. Moreover, the decision to commit

Britain to support the US in the Iraq adventure clearly acted as a provocation, radicalising many younger British Muslims. It was disingenuous of the Blair government to argue that this was not the case, and indeed, whether British Muslims *should* have been radicalised in this way is also beside the point. The Iraq invasion is now commonly perceived to have heightened the threat of terrorism to the UK – a threat most evidently realised with tragic consequences in the 7/7 London bombings of 2005, and most recently in the events at Woolwich.

While Iraq may *now* harbour people with ill intent towards the UK, at the time of the invasion it was largely irrelevant to the campaign against global terrorism. As the British army began to say, ever more vociferously, Iraq was also a distraction in the battle for hearts and minds in Afghanistan. The UK could have, and as was suggested by some at the Foreign Office at the time,[2] should have, made it abundantly clear to the US administration in private that it would *not* support unprovoked military action against Iraq. Such a stand would have been consistent with repeated affirmation of the UK's stated belief in international law. What is apparent here is that the strong desire of Prime Minister Tony Blair to demonstrate loyalty to President Bush following 9/11 has led to a distortion of longstanding principles of British foreign policy, with, some would argue, catastrophic results for Britain in terms of the loss of British lives over the years, the expenditure of treasure and damage to Britain's international reputation.

Many recent UK military interventions have been undertaken under what has come to be called the Responsibility to Protect (R2P). Essentially, this doctrine, which has evolved over the last 20 years, requires states to protect their populations from genocide and other 'crimes against humanity', and holds that other states have a duty to intervene if they do not. This is not the place to discuss this concept in any detail, but while R2P might perhaps be given some legitimacy if acted upon through the UN or some other multilateral body, the deployment of military force bilaterally or even unilaterally must surely carry much less moral or legal weight. Moreover, the doctrine fundamentally challenges the concept of sovereignty, and the whole basis of international relations as we know it, grounded in the Westphalian system.

Finally, it is possible that concern about energy supplies may also have been a factor in the decision to go to war in Iraq, at least for the Bush White House. For the UK, objective 7, security of UK and global energy supplies, would normally be understood to mean a guarantee of the security of energy supplies for which sale has been agreed and contracts signed rather than seizure. Indeed, any attempt to seize territory in order to try to control supplies would have been inconsistent with the basic principles of Britain's international diplomacy.

Community and conflict within the special relationship

In the second decade of the twenty-first century, the established powers of previous decades, the US, Russia and the nations of Europe, including Britain, find themselves confronting a wholly different world, a wholly new context for the conduct of their international relations. The rise of China as a global power, and its engagement with the international community for the first time ever, fundamentally alters the locus of power in the world. The dramatic economic ascendancy of Brazil in Latin America, the shift of India towards involvement in the international economy and the prospects for economic and technological progress in other parts of the world traditionally seen only as providers of raw materials and markets for the 'developed' world all make the pursuit of national interests through foreign policy much more challenging. Moreover, all political and economic activity must now be conducted against a backdrop of climate change, of diminishing supplies of energy and other resources (despite discoveries of shale oil and gas), and of course of international terrorism.

In these circumstances there is all the more reason why every country should examine the pattern of its international relationships with much greater care and, in a globalising world, should look in particular to multilateral solutions to problems which can only be solved through common effort. In this new situation, it may well be that the special relationship which Britain believes it enjoys with the US should be brought under scrutiny. Today, it can be argued, there are dimensions of US policy which are incontrovertibly opposed to the national interests of the UK. If we look again to the UK's list of global objectives for 2007 as a benchmark by which to judge the degree of coherence between UK and US priorities, there are a number of points of divergence. Among these, it has been suggested that the ways in which the US and UK have seen the struggle against terrorism (objective 1) have been different. Robin Niblett, for example, has observed that the UK's tendency to see the threat as 'not exclusively external' means that it potentially has more in common with its European partners on this issue than it does with the US (Niblett 2006). This may still be the case, recent events in

Boston notwithstanding. Moreover, successive US administrations have been vociferously critical of the UN and of its efforts to resolve disputes and uphold international law (in contrast to the UK position, objective 3). From its beginnings as an alliance of powers opposed to the Axis in 1942, the UN has laboured under the contradiction between its mandate to uphold international law and the tendency of the great powers, notably the US, to see it as an instrument through which to achieve their desired policy outcomes. The Iraq War brought this problem sharply into focus.[3]

It is arguable that the George W. Bush White House, at least, saw Europe more as a potential competitor both politically and economically than as a positive force in world affairs (in contradiction to UK objective 4). It should also be remembered that the US is a determined competitor for Britain in the commercial sphere (in opposition to UK objective 5), and that there is a strong lobby in the US in support of protectionist policies which stand in contradiction to the UK's belief in free trade. In its refusal to contemplate until almost the end of the Bush presidency the possibility that carbon emissions consequent on human activity could be a key factor in causing climate change, the US administration often sought to discredit the work of those in the UK and elsewhere in Europe who were determined to tackle this problem, while consistently pursuing the largest possible share of the world's remaining oil supplies (reference UK objectives 6 and 7) (see R. Porter 2008).

In addition, successive US administrations have at different times over the years taken a contrary view and at times spread contrary messages about a range of projects of international scientific collaboration in which the UK has been engaged, notably the International Thermonuclear Experimental Reactor (ITER) project, the European Galileo satellite project which the UK has supported, projects on stem-cell research, genetically modified crops (many of the patents for which reside with US corporations), space research and a variety of other issues. Finally, it may be noted that the 'interoperability' which conditions Britain's defence relationship with the US seems very frequently to mean the purchase of military equipment by the UK from the US; there seems to be very little quid pro quo for this. Despite some earlier purchases by the US – the Harrier jump jet being a case in point – and some ongoing joint weapons development work, in 2005 the UK Defence Manufacturers Association is said to have complained that Tony Blair had not pressed hard enough to win defence equipment orders from Washington for UK manufacturers.

Isolation or independence in a context of global uncertainty?

Isolation – the celebration of it, and later the fear of it – has been a consistent factor haunting decision-making on British foreign policy throughout the nineteenth and twentieth centuries, and into our own era. It may be appropriate here, then, to address the possibility that the fear of isolation is behind the belief that a special relationship with the US is essential. In the nineteenth century, a policy of isolation assiduously and deliberately cultivated for decades proved not so 'splendid' as the century drew to a close. Britain narrowly avoided having no friends in Europe in the early years of the twentieth century, and faced the prospect of the Franco-Russian entente combining with the triple alliance of Germany, Austria and Italy, leaving Britain not just isolated but under serious threat. This was resolved by various means during the first decade of the twentieth century. In the emergency of the First World War, we also called on Canada, Australia, New Zealand and ultimately the US to help us. Yet again to all intents and purposes alone in the 1920s and 1930s, the US having returned to its own isolationist stance, the UK was unable to prevent another conflagration which would see it emerge much weaker than before. The past 60 years have also been hard for the UK. No longer (partly by choice) a power broker in Europe, Britain has also suffered the psychological impact of the loss of empire, appears as well to have lost interest in the Commonwealth, and remains destructively ambivalent towards the EU – a project in which it might once have played a leading role. Against this background, a special relationship with the US has, in many senses, been an attractive option.

It is not the case, however, that the only alternative to being a great power is being in a supplicatory relationship with America. So why do British foreign policy elites now seem to feel that this is the only option? What is it that motivates Britain's apparently default position of support for the US?

There are first what might be considered to be intangible factors. The UK and US share a common language, and to some degree a common culture. Through the medium of film and television especially, the American way of life feels familiar to many Britons. US brands are ubiquitous, and corporate and financial ties reinforce the relationship. Yet it is predicted that the US may be the world's largest Spanish-speaking nation in just a few decades from now (*El Pais* 3 February 2011), with a Latin constituency with no particular empathy for Britain. Indeed, much of what we think we know about the US in this age of globally distributed television programmes and social media may be more illusory than real. If there is a residual affection for the UK in the US, it may be largely confined to pockets of the Eastern Seaboard and parts of California. This is not to say that Americans dislike the British; rather that we just don't really register with them. For our part, it may not be unreasonable to combine affection for individual Americans with a healthy scepticism towards the intentions of the American state. Moreover, it may be worth recalling that in literature the outstanding example of a projected total merger between the US and Britain is in the work of George Orwell; in his novel 1984, Orwell groups the US and Britain together in a political entity which he calls 'Oceania'.

Another factor which may have pushed successive governments towards America in recent years has been the popular perception in the UK that Europe is 'foreign', a perception of which parliamentary Eurosceptics have not hesitated to take advantage. Europeans speak foreign languages, which we seem reluctant to learn. Europe has been a major historical source of conflicts into which the UK has been drawn. A significant part of Britain's political spectrum has been influenced by this 'little England' strand of thinking, which has long maintained that the UK should hold itself apart from continental entanglements. Rather than making a robust case for a foreign policy rooted in the geopolitical circumstances of Europe, where we are geographically located, successive recent British governments have preferred the politically safer (or more popular) option of alignment with the US. Little wonder, then, that some of the UK's other allies feel that the UK is often an advocate for the American agenda – a kind of 'fifth column' within Europe for the interests of the USA.[4]

A third consideration that drives British foreign policy is that we can no longer conceive of major decisions related to UK intelligence and defence policy and operations which are not closely linked to those of the US. Earlier work has identified in detail the extent and nature of UK military and intelligence assistance to the US in the form of US military bases and intelligence gathering installations on British soil, both in these islands and overseas, and the depth of collaboration with GCHQ – what Wallace and Phillips refer to as 'an embedded military and intelligence substructure' – all of which involve significant derogations of UK sovereignty (Cf. Wallace and Phillips 2009, pp. 263–284). Yet intelligence is not without an agenda, and again it may be naïve to assume that the US agenda is going to be automatically appropriate for the UK, or even that intelligence supplied will not be shaped in some way to produce a desired policy response on the part of the UK.

There is an argument that the UK owes the US a debt of gratitude for the intelligence the latter provides, with the implication that we must accept the imperatives that the US intelligence community feel arise out of this information. This may have been true during the Cold War, when there was a clear need perceived in both countries to monitor the activities of the Soviet bloc. But in the present day the habit of close cooperation on intelligence matters may in fact be impeding the development of an independent British foreign policy on a range of issues in which the US has no interest, or on which it takes a diametrically opposite view. Recent revelations by Edward Snowden about the extension of US intelligence gathering to the ordinary citizens, and even the leaders, of supposedly friendly European countries render British involvement in US intelligence gathering toxic in the eyes of many of Britain's European neighbours. Moreover, there is a degree of circularity about these intelligence arguments. UK involvement in US-led military expeditions overseas in recent years may have exacerbated for Britain precisely the problems for which US intelligence is said to provide a partial solution, in that these foreign wars have actually contributed to inciting minority populations within the UK.

A fourth factor, and the reason often given in recent times for supporting America's foreign policy and defence initiatives, is that the UK can thereby exercise influence over US policy. Prime Minister Tony Blair, concerned about the Bush administration itself becoming more isolationist, put forward the view that the UK could be a 'go-between', or a 'bridge' between the US and Europe. This formulation was used throughout the last years of the Blair premiership, but most notably in Blair's 'Mansion House' speech in November 2004 (see Blair 2004). Journalist John Kampfner, however, believes that Blair overestimated the influence he could have on Bush, observing that neo-cons in the administration were interested in 'US primacy above all' (Kampfner 2004). Patrick Porter argues persuasively that a loss of influence, rather than an increase in influence, is what resulted from Britain's military involvement in Iraq, in a campaign which he describes as 'mission impossible' (Porter 2010, pp. 355–375).

As is now commonly known, the Iraq War threw up a number of issues which placed the 'special relationship' under strain – Basra, Diego Garcia and 'extraordinary rendition' to Guantanamo and other places being just a few. In the case of Basra differences of view as to the approach to be taken on the ground and in the other two cases the compromise of British sovereignty caused tension between Britain and the US. Nor was there any obvious 'payback' in policy terms with respect to climate change, the Middle East or other matters. The parliamentary report *British Foreign Policy since 1997* summed up the views of one group of critics by saying they saw the prime minister's approach as 'sincerely intended but fundamentally misguided'. Further, that,

> [Tony] Blair had strayed too far during his premiership from the central objective of British foreign policy, which was a clear-sighted pursuit of the country's national interest.
>
> (House of Commons Library 2008)

The consequence of all of this is that, in extremis, the UK may or may not be isolated, but it has certainly lost much of its sovereign independence, as well as having put at risk its ability to exercise 'soft power' – the basis for respect for Britain by others, and its influence over other states. Military actions are not divorced in their implications from actions to promote a positive relationship with other sovereign states, and may serve to sour the atmosphere in which negotiations for a range of soft power initiatives must be carried on.

Conclusion: In search of a mature bilateral relationship with the US

It is sometimes suggested that the UK has no credible alternative but to continue to follow America's lead in determining its foreign and defence policy, that Britain is hostile to Europe and has nowhere else to go. Yet it is clear that the present US administration at least does not welcome the Eurosceptic tendency in British politics, as the US assistant secretary for European affairs indicated in a speech in 2013 in Dublin (*Guardian* 10 January 2013). It is in Britain's own interests to mend fences with Europe, which has always in the past been its primary focus of military and diplomatic concern. Accepting this, Britain still has a choice. Recognising that the UK is now a pre-eminent mid-sized power with very many positive attributes, but no longer a great power, it may seek to adopt a more limited set of diplomatic and defence objectives which can be pursued independently. Or, alternatively, it may seek to continue to play a significant global role, but in company with its immediate neighbours in Europe. Chapter 3 in this volume explores this question further.

In the light of this, how should the UK arrive at a mature bilateral relationship with the US? Defence policy, and the evolving debate around the future of UK strategy, may offer some indications here. Strategy should ideally begin with a definition of what the UK is trying to defend, or to achieve internationally in terms of its essential national interests and aspirational international interests. These surely should proceed out of Britain's geopolitical situation, located as it is in Europe, its economic circumstances and its need to preserve its sovereignty, in all senses of the word, and see the values in which we genuinely believe preserved at home and promoted to the extent possible internationally.

Despite the uncertain world of global hyperconnectivity in which we live, Britain's essential interests will continue to be influenced by the basic facts of its situation: that Britain is an island nation firmly located in the European region of the globe; that it has reduced capability militarily, economically, diplomatically relative to that of other powers, but now also reduced responsibilities. It is also important to recognise that while the UK has less influence politically and commercially, it may in recent years have increased its capacity for influence in terms of what is often referred to as 'soft power': respect internationally for its political institutions and legal system, its science and technology, its engineering and architectural achievements, its business acumen, its educational practices, its culture – theatre, dance, literature, cinema – its sporting achievements, and so on; activities through which the particular skills and values of the British people are expressed.

Policies which display these skills and promote these values abroad should be the foundation of British diplomacy, as they encourage respect for the UK internationally. Conversely, policies which are led by military intervention abroad, especially when it is not sanctioned by the very international institutions and legal framework in which Britain professes to believe, would appear to do the exact opposite. This is in contradiction to the Blair position, which was that one cannot exercise soft power without exercising hard (or military) power (Blair 2007).

In sum therefore, it is essential that we define what we in the UK see as our fundamental national interests, and the values we wish to project, in order that we are not led unthinkingly to support and reinforce foreign and military policies which express values that are not our own. Support for this approach has come in the past from leading figures in the world of British diplomacy. Sir Rodric Braithwaite, former prime ministerial adviser and former chairman of the UK Joint Intelligence Committee, in 'End of the Affair' (*Prospect* May 2003) urged upon the UK, in dealing with the US, 'the need to be prepared to walk away', something which, he says, British prime ministers have been 'loath to contemplate'. Michael Ancram, former shadow foreign secretary, shadow defence secretary, and member of the Intelligence and Security Committee, expressed his opposition to 'romantic dreams of curing the world', or an 'unquestioning acceptance' of US policy. Rather, he urged a respect for what is 'in the British national interest' (Hansard HC Deb. 20 July 2006, c541).

If the UK can do this, its relationship with the US, instead of being problematic, could end up as one in which each side genuinely valued the other, and, where there *was* a genuine convergence of interests, each side treated the other with the respect due to sovereign equals.

The US is of course entitled to its own foreign policy, and has its own interests to protect; it follows that US methods and intelligence are not without an agenda to them, and that agenda is to promote American interests – it could not be otherwise. But they are not necessarily Britain's interests, and it should not necessarily be Britain's agenda.

Notes

1. It is recognised that there is a significant existing body of work on the 'special relationship' between Britain and the US. See, for example: Baylis (1997), Danchev (1998), Dunn (2008), Wallace and Phillips (2009), Porter, P. (2010), Freedman (2006), among many others. The present piece acknowledges this literature, but departs somewhat from the approach conventionally taken in an academic article in that it is an analytical essay by a former practitioner intended to promote debate of the issues involved, primarily among practitioners. The opinions expressed are entirely the author's own, and do not in any way reflect the views of the Foreign and Commonwealth Office.
2. Author's private correspondence, January 2003.
3. An examination of voting patterns at the UN suggests that in the 1950s and early 1960s the US was able to achieve its objectives there by pressuring other states (especially in Latin America) to vote as a bloc in support of US positions. In subsequent decades, as many former European colonies achieved independence and it was no longer possible to control the voting in the General Assembly in this way (nor even in the Security Council), the US increasingly tended to downplay the UN, or just ignore it. On Iraq, for a radical critique, see Gowan (2003).
4. The author's private conversations with European diplomats in Beijing and in Brussels.

Part III
Strategy and Planning

8
Organising for British National Strategy[1]

Alexander Evans

Foreign policy strategy requires an understanding of long-term national interests (Strachan 2011, pp. 1281–1296). However, 'the national interest' is a catch-all term that can be both meaningful and meaningless. Political leaders do try to define the national interest. Some will veer towards a minimalist reading, favouring limited national goals. Others may push for a maximalist reading, moved by principle or universalism. The balance between values and interests – and the definition of interests – is determined at the level of strategic foreign policymaking in the British system, as in other democratic societies. The prime minister, foreign secretary and cabinet, supported by civil servants and no doubt influenced by the small band of writers and thinkers who are actually read, now regularly set out a formal foreign policy strategy. Thinking about Britain's interests, values and role in the world was once largely articulated through speeches and articles or in debate on the floor of the House of Commons. Today it has moved into the terrain of official strategy documents, although speeches remain important markers.

Strategy is 'a plan of action designed to achieve a long-term or overall aim' (OED 2013). Yet most plans fail. Plans often fail to define challenges accurately. Plans that predict the future rarely get it right. And plans are rarely useful at key decision points for political principals. So much strategy has to be about dealing with the unexpected and promoting coherent international policymaking in a changing world. But who services this strategising? Which advisers can help political leaders navigate a complex and competing array of interests and arguments? And where does thinking creatively about the past and the future – thinking in time – fit into foreign policy formation?

This chapter explores the formulation of the 'national interest' by looking at the machinery of government, with a deliberate focus on how policy planning evolved within the Foreign and Commonwealth Office (FCO). Before turning to the policy planning staff, this chapter briefly looks at three specific problems of foreign policymaking. These are the challenges of 'thinking in time' (Neustadt and May 1988), taking a strategic perspective on foreign policy and thinking creatively.

Hunting for the long-headed

In December 1968 the Harvard Professor Ernest May asked how the US government could access 'long-headed' staffers to provide greater strategic depth to foreign policy.[2] Across the Atlantic the British had also been grappling with the problem of long-term foreign policy. Harold Macmillan appointed a committee chaired by Lord Plowden to review overseas representation in 1962–1963 (CRSO 1964). The resulting report was critical of the Foreign Office:

> In the past some policy problems have not been anticipated or prepared for sufficiently. This is easy to say but difficult to legislate for. Some situations are unpredictable and surprises cannot be eliminated. Nevertheless, many issues can be foreseen at least in outline and it is better to prepare for these in advance than to improvise when they have arisen.
> (CRSO 1964, p. 55)

Thinking in time is hard to do because it requires a fuller appreciation of the past and harder thinking about the future than officials have time or patience for.

Short-termism in foreign policy is a persistent problem, not least because foreign policy is often reactive. The operational and immediate dominate. Long-term perspective is difficult when short-term priorities crowd the inbox. Governments are measured by what they do, not how they think. Strategy can be neglected. Even when there is a holistic foreign policy vision, ministers and senior officials will spend much of their time making decisions.

Many problems flow from this focus on the present. It reduces space for reflective thinking about Britain's interests and role in the world, and about the means to advance them. It fosters an insider culture among officials who work on foreign and security policy; this culture can be impatient of outside views that appear inconsiderate of the demands of policymaking or unconscious of the ability (or otherwise) of government to execute particular policy choices.[3] It diminishes the little appetite that exists to consider recent or historic policy failure, and incorporate lessons learned into current and future policymaking (May 1992, pp. 331–354). It reduces the chance of meaningful conversations between scholars and practitioners.[4] It can reinforce many of the behavioural biases in policymaking: optimism bias (Camerer and Kunreuther 1989, pp. 565–569), overconfidence (Tetlock 2005) and groupthink (Janis 1972).

One further challenge is 'recentism', a focus on the immediate past at the expense of a longer view. Recentism can make officials and politicians cautious when they should be bold, and bold when they should be cautious. Meanwhile diplomats and national security officials, like all professionals, face difficulties in dealing with information that contradicts existing beliefs (Sherman and Cohen 2002, pp. 119–123). We are all prone to not recognising our own areas of incompetence.

Who can take the broader view?

The second challenge relates to taking a strategic perspective on foreign policy. A classic tension in bureaucracies is the competition between generalists and specialists. The stereotype is that generalists lack depth, but bring breadth and judgement, while specialists lack broader perspective but bring expertise to bear (Laski 1931). The debate about specialisation in diplomatic services is unhelpful, as many generalists are de facto specialists by virtue of repeated spells working on a region or issue. Many specialists, meanwhile, may be better 'thinkers in time' about a particular thematic or regional problem than generalists.

Both generalists and specialists rarely work on the full sweep of British policy interests in the course of a single posting. In foreign and security policy few roles cover the waterfront. Among them are private office staff of the foreign and defence secretaries, officials at the heart of the cross-Whitehall national security machinery, senior press office officials, the director-general political and the policy planning staff in the Foreign Office. To this list one could add a select band of ambassadors and senior diplomats in a few key chanceries overseas, including Washington and Brussels. 'Big picture' positions are among the most heavily loaded jobs with the least time to read or reflect. Hours are long and the work intense (Rhodes 2005, pp. 3–25). However, for thousands of British officials working away on national interest-related topics, their viewpoint is likely to be limited by the field of their department, team or diplomatic post.

Imagination and dissent

The third problem is how to cultivate imagination and dissent when policy, by its nature, is driven by recent events, consensus and committees. This can cultivate a culture of pragmatism. As Anthony Forster and Alasdair Blair point out, this reflects 'the pressures under which senior civil servants operate, especially in respect of the need to focus on policy implementation, the increasing reliance of politicians on external advice as a means of challenging civil servants, and the consensual style of interdepartmental cooperation' (Forster and Blair 2002). A bureaucratic culture that encourages imagination and dissent can help diplomats and politicians better handle surprise and policy failure.

Many crises emerge with little notice. Some are self-inflicted, some 'flow from the unintended consequence of policy' (Crocker 2008, pp. 99, 177–185). Many crises are driven by a complex interplay between multiple factors that can generate a war, humanitarian crisis or multilateral division over an issue of consequence. Imagination alone cannot predict future crises, but it can improve the capacity of policymakers to think their way through potential second and third-order consequences of current policy choices. It can inform scenario planning. If used well, it can incorporate a better understanding of surprise into medium and long-range policymaking.

Dissent, meanwhile, can properly challenge existing and proposed policies. A strong policy submission to ministers contains robust arguments about the advantages and risks of different policy options. Ministerial submissions may need to reconcile different views within a single department like the FCO or a range of cross-Whitehall views. Those charged with responsibility for a policy area are not always ideally placed to cultivate dissent. They may be too attached to a particular path of action. They may not be able to bring a broader perspective of current or future UK national interests to bear.

The policy planning staff

The policy planning staff of the FCO was established in order to have a longer-term, broader perspective on British interests that could nonetheless still contribute to current policymaking. Established in its modern form in 1964, it has been known by various names. Today it is the 'policy unit', but it has most frequently been called the policy planning staff or just 'planners'. This small group of diplomats – later leavened by external appointees from *Financial Times* journalists to Oxfam managers – was meant to generate longer-term thinking on

British interests and policy. Sir Crispin Tickell was the first member of the independent foreign policy planning staff, initially split off as a group of three officers from the Western European department in 1963.[5] He later described his role as,

> Writing long-term policy papers. For example, we wrote papers on future relations with the Soviet Union. I was also joint secretary of a Cabinet Office working group on the shape of the world 10 years ahead.... The Planning Staff also wrote a paper about relations with Cuba. We did several papers of a kind that spanned the interests of several departments. There was then a body called the Permanent Under-Secretary's Steering Committee which considered broad policy issues, and I was secretary of that.
> (Tickell 1999)

Tickell later returned to broader themes in foreign policy while on sabbatical at Harvard (1975) and All Souls, Oxford (1981). Sir Michael Palliser, who took over as head of policy planners in 1964, was determined 'to make a success of it'. His strategy was based on influencing the foreign secretary,

> I said I wanted an office, I wanted to be involved in all the Secretary of State's policy meetings, I wanted our offices to be in the same area of the Foreign Office as the Foreign Secretary and I was determined that we should not be too large. It gave us an access which I consider to be indispensable for planning. The other reason why, and here again I am saying all this because I don't know how planning is run now but I don't think the principles that were being developed then were wrong. The other reason I wanted to be small was because I was quite convinced that the only way you could get planning ideas, or, if you like, new ideas, slightly radical ideas, effectively injected into the system was if you could persuade the department responsible for the work that you were on their side and trying to make life easier for them.
> (Palliser 1999)

The pursuit of fresh thinking through external networking, another policy planning task, was a shock to Foreign Office traditionalists. Sir Robert Wade-Gery recalled,

> [what] the Planning Staff was there to do was to develop links between the Foreign Office and the foreign affairs community who

weren't the Foreign Office. That is to say, academics, businessmen, Chatham House, journalists and the military, all of whom had ideas to contribute, and most of whom had been kept at arms-length by the old fashioned Foreign Office who thought that Chatham House was a nest of communists, and journalists were people you should never speak to, soldiers were too stupid to bother with and academics were wholly irrelevant.

(Wade-Gery 2000)

Sir Brian Crowe, head of policy planning from 1976–1979, took external engagement one step further, beginning the process of externally recruiting a member of the staff from outside. Helen Wallace, an academic at the Civil Service College, was brought in for a year. Crowe recalls how difficult this was:

Towards the end of my time in the Planning Staff I made her appointment possible in a difficult negotiation with the Trade Unions. They said if we wanted an academic in Planning Staff we didn't need to go outside. In Research Department there were lots of academics. I said that's not quite the same, the whole idea is cross fertilization, bring people in from outside. But that is exactly the job of all these academics in Research Department, they said, they could do all that for us, we could have as many as we liked from Research Department.

(Crowe 2003)

The *Economist* journalist John Plender was another early external recruit, joining in 1980 (Plender 2002). This was during a period when cross-Whitehall exchanges between the Foreign Office and other departments were still rare. Alyson Bailes, later deputy head of planners, spent 1979–1981 on secondment to the Ministry of Defence and was struck by the 'still small' number of FCO people who did likewise (Bailes 2005, p. 193). Bailes later emphasised that this 'boundary blurring and jumping has nothing but positive connotations', making the case that each time she was 'returning with useful ideas from outside as well as a clearer view of the FCO's own strengths' (Bailes 2005, p. 193). The practice of engaging outsiders gathered pace during the 1980s, often in the form of small seminars run for or on behalf of the foreign secretary or senior officials. Sir Sherard Cowper-Coles (member of policy planners 1983–1985) gives a classic example,

The thing I'm proudest of in the Planning Staff was that I wrote a paper for a seminar Mrs Thatcher had at Chequers on intervention. She was very upset about the way the Americans invaded Grenada and she was worried that they would do the same with Nicaragua. She believed in the rule of law, and she convened a seminar on this at Chequers in the format of outsiders being present in the morning, including Dame Rosalind Higgins, Professor of international law at the LSE. Then there was a lunch and then, in the afternoon, conclusions were drawn for policy.

(Cowper-Coles 2011)

Members of the planning staff enjoyed their tours. Sir Jeremy Greenstock (in planners in 1978) thought that 'being a Planner was extremely interesting. You saw a different side of Diplomatic Service life and work. You were given time to think and write' (Greenstock 2004). Some of this thinking contributed to speeches. According to Sir Rodric Braithwaite, who was head of planners in 1979–1982, Lord Carrington's 'main interest in the Planning Staff was that we should write speeches that had at least three quotations in them so that people who were listening to them, this is what he said, would think that he occasionally read a book' (Braithwaite 1998).

However, two challenges to planners became apparent in the 1980s. The first was the lure of the operational. By 1981 planners were responsible both for long-range papers and for crisis management, and the latter dragged officials away from strategy. One example was the Soviet invasion of Afghanistan, when policy planners stepped in and dealt with the crisis. As Sir Rodric Braithwaite head of policy planning 1979–82 recalled,

For five or six weeks we were the sort of executive arm of the Deputy Secretaries, and so on, who were dealing with it. That was very interesting. The same thing happened during the Falkland crisis after I left when Christopher Mallaby was in charge of it. In fact to an even greater extent. So that the Planning Staff was acting as a sort of airportable brigade, or perhaps, because it is so small, something like an SAS Squadron. And that is a useful function. I mean, I don't want to underestimate the other function of producing alternative ideas but one must not exaggerate. You have to be very good; you have to have a very powerful intelligence and ability to advocate before people will listen to you when you are starting from such a weak base.

(Braithwaite 1998)

As Lord Jay (member of planners in 1981–1982) set out, the crisis management role also included responsibility for the G7 as then was (Jay 2007). Working on crises or drafting speeches guaranteed greater likelihood of working directly to ministers – important for ambitious diplomats – whereas long-term papers ran the risk either of being ignored or of upsetting policy leads in the relevant geographic or functional departments. Sir Sherard Cowper-Coles wrote speeches for Margaret Thatcher and Geoffrey Howe (Cowper-Coles 2011). Speech-writing mattered in a system that valued (and values) good writing. A deftly written paper could make a diplomat's reputation. Zara Steiner is right when she points out that the 'more prolific or more intelligent writers' were not always the most influential diplomats – but they were often best *known* within the system (Steiner 1969).

Members of planners drafted papers on subjects where they lacked expertise. Papers were often designed to be provocative (or prophetic). When they forecast the future, they were invariably proved wrong. Policy influence rested with the line departments as they generated most of the ministerial policy submissions. They also controlled the resources in Whitehall and out in the network of overseas posts. As Sir David Gore-Booth, head of planners 1987–1989, put it,

> one of the troubles of being a planner is that you aren't a Sovietologist otherwise you would be in the Sovietologist bit and it is quite difficult to challenge the expertise and that is actually what one is doing all the time. You were challenging people who knew better than you and you didn't always win. The success was probably rather limited but worth trying.[6]

Papers written by non-experts could be seriously wrong. Sir Brian Crowe recalls that,

> Planning Staff had the function of challenging or questioning the policy advice other people were producing, which was interesting. I remember one policy paper I produced with my staff because it was so wrong, one on South Africa. We got South Africa completely wrong, deciding in our wisdom that majority rule could never be achieved and looking at territorial partition options instead. It illustrates one of the problems of Policy Planning Staffs, that of trying to write policy on issues about which none of us had any experience or real knowledge. They wanted us to write a paper on South Africa.

None of us in the Department knew anything about South Africa. We had to look it all up from scratch. You develop ideas and in the end we got it all wrong.

(Crowe 2003)

The relative autonomy of policy planning may also have limited its influence. As Michael Palliser observed, proximity to the foreign secretary was crucial. Yet unlike other policy planning staffs, FCO policy planners did not operate either as a personal staff of the minister or as an alternative 'cabinet' of advisors. It remained on the whole a 'small and rather junior body within the Foreign Office', in the words of Sir Rodric Braithwaite, who was told when he first joined it that,

> the Planning Staff was rather like an irregular force operating ahead of the main army, out of uniform and doing pretty much what it liked. And that is fine and it can be useful. But if it starts being irritating to the main force the first thing they will do is put regular officers in charge of it. And if that does not work they will take it out into the forest and shoot it. So you have to be a bit careful. You work out how to sell your wares to people who think they know at least as much as you do about the subject. Very often they do, actually. Just being original for its own sake is, of course, a waste of time.
>
> (Braithwaite 1998)

The Foreign Office was not – and is not – devoid of original thinking. If anything, such thinking flourishes in a culture that values high-quality political reporting and strong policy advice. However, this brief reprise of a selection of oral histories from UK policy planning suggests that the reality often fell short of the ideal when it came to a dedicated unit focused on planning inside the FCO. The contemporary policy unit continues the tradition of writing broader papers on strategic foreign policy – along with providing a challenge function to existing policy. Over the past decade it has also been closely involved in the drafting of successive published UK foreign policy strategies. Moreover, it is now a crucial part of the contribution the FCO makes to the National Security Council (NSC), acting as a channel for FCO papers flowing into the Cabinet Office. The policy unit has also led on 'diplomatic excellence', the initiative to revive core diplomatic skills and improve expertise within the service.

The role of White Papers and speeches

Readers in search of definitions of the UK national interest or a foreign policy strategy can draw on two types of documents. The first are speeches, a regular source of 'bigger picture' thinking by prime ministers and foreign secretaries past and present. The second are White Papers, of which there have been fewer, and not all focused on the broadest sweep of UK interests. Recent examples include *UK International Priorities: A Strategy for the FCO* (2003) and *Active Diplomacy for a Changing World* (2006). These were both FCO documents, although the second was agreed by the entire cabinet. The national security strategy, *A Strong Britain in an Age of Uncertainty* (2010), marks the third iteration of a cross-government document. These papers are the products of months of cross-Whitehall negotiation, expert consultation and political decisions by ministers on tone, judgements and forward commitments.

The advantage of White Papers is they can set out the broad sweep of UK strategy. They can provide organising goals around which UK government activity can be shaped, and a story that can help diplomats and officials. The choices made as a result of, or informed by, these processes are important. Alliance preferences have the potential to shape Britain's role and influence in the world. Priorities will shape the nature and goals of the diplomatic network. Defence budget choices can have a cascading effect over decades because of the defence procurement cycle. Approaches to trade, climate, intervention, the use of force, multilateral institutions and development have ramifications for UK security and prosperity. And finally, these documents can help the UK tell a story about what contemporary Britain seeks internationally – and how it plans to pursue these goals. The disadvantages of White Papers and speeches are that unclassified documents drafted by committees can lack personality, precision and frankness. They have a short shelf life. They can favour consensus views of the national interest and duck hard choices about trade-offs. They can accentuate the positive.

Meanwhile parliament has also been engaged on the question of foreign policy strategy. Select committees have been active on and around the subject, with a series of inquiries and reports by the House of Commons, defence, foreign affairs and public administration select committees (PASC 2010). Such reports can be influential, not least given the strong criticism by the Public Administration Committee (PASC) that 'no-one' does UK grand strategy. The PASC wrote: 'As things stand there is little idea of what the UK's national interest is, and therefore what our strategic purpose should be.'[7] Hew Strachan has criticised what he regards as an overly operational focus of the UK NSC: 'The NSC has not conducted a dialogue with itself, with other parts of government, or with outside opinion as it has sought to think about security over the longer term' (Strachan 2013). In the FCO the policy planning staff have tended to lead on work on White Papers and, more fitfully, contribute to speeches and internal department priorities. One lesson from strategic planning is that while the plans themselves rarely prove enormously useful, the *process* of planning can help develop a shared understanding of the British national interest.

Lessons from the US

'The problem is not having the big ideas. It's making policy on a day to day basis to carry out these ideas.' Ambassador Richard Boucher, former US Assistant Secretary of State, George W. Bush administration (Boucher 2012).

The most comprehensive set of essays on US policy planning identifies many of the same themes identified in the UK: the lure of speech-writing and operational work, the challenge of influence when the decision is not immediate, the problem of planners being viewed as gadflies, generalists, interlopers or wrong (Drezner 2009). Senior decision-makers in the US have packed schedules; what gets 'seventh floor' attention at the State Department is the product of ruthless filtering. Strategy papers defer to decision memos.

However, policy planning at the State Department enjoys great internal and external prestige, despite its mixed record of policy influence.[8] The reputation began with George Kennan. Yet Kennan made his name with the Long Telegram, which was written while he was in an operational role – deputy head of mission to Moscow – not when he headed policy planning. As Richard Fontaine and Brian Burton write in a thoughtful analysis of State Department policy planning, 'Kennan left his post [as head of policy planning] deeply frustrated. The fact that his office's work was not formally linked to "line of command" authority in the regional and functional bureaus, he believed, separated policy planning from policy implementation' (Fontaine and Burton 2010). Fontaine and Burton argue that one way to make strategy more directly relevant to policymaking is to 'bring the future into the present; that is, to outline mid- to long-term strategies for seizing future opportunities or avoiding future problems, and then connecting those strategies to decisions policymakers must make today' (Fontaine and Burton 2010).

One former Clinton administration assistant secretary argues that for countries like the US and Britain, strategic foreign policy is even more difficult because 'there are a few countries in the world where no matter what happens, there has to be a response'.[9] This obligation to comment on or respond to everything reduces time (and attention) for longer range thinking. Others argue that the problem is a lack of interest, not time. One former NSC staffer from the (first) Obama administration suggested: 'You can't plan for what you don't appreciate. The problem is there is no appetite in the Administration or Congress for long-term planning on issues abroad.'[10] People and personalities may matter more, in the bruising daily inter-agency debates about policy, than ideas. As one former ambassador ruefully observes, 'the force of personality of an individual is more important than the title or position he or she held' (Chamberlin 2012). Meanwhile another problem lies in the nature of different institutional cultures across the interagency field. As one former US Department of Defense official said:

There was a joke that State couldn't plan whereas the Joint Staff would produce a 1,000 page plan that nobody could use. The Office of the Secretary of Defense dealt with longer-range issues because of the DNA of long-term planning around procurement. The State Department would come up with esoteric, conceptual reporting.[11]

One alternative is to place policy planning at the centre of government in the NSC. A series of senior officials were tasked to do this under the George W. Bush and Obama administrations, among them Bob Blackwill, Zal Khalilzad and Derek Chollet, all formally given a strategic planning role in the White House (Khalizad 2012; Blackwill 2012). But each found urgent operational work trumped long-range thinking. Operational work was visible, and guaranteed time with the president and senior cabinet officials. Strategic work was less visible unless tied to a specific operational challenge.

Current and former officials the author has interviewed, including a former deputy secretary of state and a number of assistant secretaries and members of the White House national security staff from the Kennedy administration through to the (first) Obama administration hold varying views on the value of strategy. Most agree that it is useful to have strategic thinkers involved in the policy process, with a robust sense of history (Andrew 2004, pp. 1900–1960) and good access to expertise. But some argue that strategy work in government is inevitably ephemeral: favouring tone over content, speeches over execution. Policy choices are, they point out, largely operational. Crucial choices escalate to the principals committee of the NSC, and the president with (or without) the cabinet then makes a decision. At this level, several interviewees emphasised, strategic policy documents are less important than the nature of the individual decision-makers, their style and the people and advice that they value.

Thomas Hughes wrote on decision-making in government while assistant secretary of intelligence and research in 1965. He argued that most discussions in government are between four types of people:

- competent men with viewpoints;
- incompetent men with viewpoints;
- competent men without viewpoints;
- incompetent men without viewpoints (Hughes 1969).

These characteristics are not mutually exclusive. Today's competent woman or man with a view can be tomorrow's incompetent woman or man without a view. Depending on the discussion and other dynamics, individual policymakers can exhibit any of these four types. Hughes captures well a dilemma of policymaking. Foreign policy strategy is often about the people who make decisions and those who advise them as much as framing documents, strategies or systems. The latter can help. They can provide message and policy discipline. But a strategic approach to foreign policy may well depend on individuals as much as systems – which suggests that a reformed approach to strategy in foreign policy should take a harder look at organisational culture.

Conclusion

Organising government for strategy and policy planning then may not be the problem of the day. Fiddling with the bureaucratic hard-wiring will not resolve the tensions that this brief review of British and US policy planning exposes. Policy will always be driven by the urgent and immediate. Critics will cast aspersions on whether policymakers and their advisers are sufficiently mindful of history, the future and a broader view when they come to decisions. Practitioners will push back: even where they accept a 'strategy gap' exists, they may argue that time pressure is a persistent reality for decision-makers. There will however always be a need for broader strategic thinking on foreign policy. Ministers will want to set out their goals and launch new initiatives. In a complex, austerity-influenced cross-Whitehall environment, defining Britain's interests and organising policy accordingly is essential.

What are the lessons for contemporary British diplomacy? This chapter suggests that the organisational may be less important than the cultural. Insights from the history of policy planning in the UK (and US) suggest there is no easy institutional fix to the challenge of strategic thinking. In concluding, this chapter tentatively offers eight suggestions for the future.

Invest in people as much as systems. A former White House official suggests that 'at the end of a day, it's all about the people'.[12] Diplomats and national security officials need opportunities to take a broad look at UK interests, particularly at the early stages of their careers. One option could be a more systematic approach to learning and development with an internal course on the evolution of British foreign and security policy, including dissident and critical perspectives on how future strategy should be constituted. The value of time to think means that, episodically, some officers should be given the opportunity to step aside from operational roles to reflect and consider broader questions of policy, practice and strategy. From a budgetary perspective this is difficult to justify. While the FCO funds elements of this, it is limited in comparison with State Department opportunities where diplomats regularly spend spells at a military college, university or think tank on their government salary. One study in 2011 concluded that this US effort remains insufficient. (Stimson Center 2011, p. 11). Even if the FCO cannot pay for similar opportunities, there could be a more systematic effort to encourage alternatively funded sabbaticals or training.[13]

Mainstream strategy in operational parts of policymaking. Ambassadors have the advantage of representing *all* UK interests, but there are only a few major countries in which every UK national interest is present. There is only one way to foster a broader understanding of (and debate around) British strategic interests, and that is to involve a wider set of practitioners in it. Geographical and functional directors in the FCO can also make room for strategic thinking, including through assembling informal ginger groups on longer-range subjects. This approach gains support from Democrat and Republican national security officials in the US[14] and is already in evidence in the current FCO.

Keep a wonk space, but make it punchy. A policy planning staff has value. Perhaps the greatest value is not in the potential for grand strategy, but for the functional duties it can perform: policy challenge, a contribution to speech-writing and cross-Whitehall documents, generating new ideas, encouraging learning, connecting with non-officials and engaging in bilateral and multilateral policy-planning talks with counterparts. Despite the risk of ritualised exchanges, these latter talks can provide insight into how other governments are thinking about international affairs at large. Moreover, policy planners can act as an incubator for tomorrow's senior diplomats, who need breadth of experience and an understanding of all policy issues. As Michael Palliser, one of the first planners, reputedly said, it is a 'gather ye rosebuds' job, and one should squeeze everything one could out of it (Braithwaite 1998). The challenge is how to recycle this learning back into the foreign policy machine. Robert Gallucci, a member of the State Department policy planners during the Carter administration, argued 'the best you can do is try to compress long-range thinking into a form and modality that can be consumed by assistant secretaries in a way that is useful' (Gallucci 2012). This is a strong case for niche interventions and provocative short memos.

Use history. Access to history, including internal diplomatic history, can help decision-makers take a long view of a problem. Lessons from past policy failures can be bluntly reviewed and used to inform current policy. Policy planning cannot fulfil this task: but creative use of historians within and beyond Whitehall can. This can work in practice by working through past cases with current officials and diplomatic historians as part of diplomatic training, or exploiting Foreign Office archives to better understand the evolution of other foreign policy elites that the UK will need to deal with in future.

Encourage heterodoxy. Peter Hennessy suggests that 'a certain promiscuity of approach is valuable, too, because of the necessary humility this brings' (Hennessy 2011). The advantages of plural approaches to strategy are well documented (Dixit and Nalebuff 1998). Greater intellectual and methodological pluralism in policymaking advances most when the conversation itself is broadened. This recommends involving more people from outside government, if necessary through a security-clearance process as 'adjunct' advisers. A more diverse diplomatic service and national security establishment – in every meaning of the word – can strengthen Britain's capacity for strategy.

Strengthen central capacity, but don't rely on the centre alone. In the UK the central cross-Whitehall function has grown, a tendency towards the centre that is also occurring in the US. The Cabinet Office is at the heart of a collective view of the national interest, but it is also at the core of national security operations. 'Strategy cannot be with the operators because part of the problem is to get strategy back from the operators' advises George Percovitch, a senior US think-tanker (Percovitch 2012). But he argues the place to put it is high up in the heart of a US NSC, in order to make sure it has traction. Making space for strategic policy at the heart of the Cabinet Office and NSC process in the UK is crucial.

Foster 'in and outers'. Whitehall has been a relatively closed machine for decades, with little boundary-crossing out to academia, the private sector or charities. Policy recruitment into government has generally been through the civil service fast stream; later movement has tended to be one-way, with officials exiting government rather than moving in and out. The impartiality of the civil service is important and needs to be maintained, but the fixed boundaries of officials versus outsiders can and should be less formidable. The best way to understand a different perspective is to live it: one rationale for diplomats in the first place. A more porous diplomatic service can benefit the quality of strategic thinking on British interests.

Prove the value of strategy and policy planning through better advice and impact. As Lord Kerr, a former head of the diplomatic service said:

> What Whitehall respects is not the linguistic skills of the Foreign Office, not the beautiful drafting of the Foreign Office, though it is still miles above the standard of the rest of Whitehall, what Whitehall really respects is the Foreign Office that can produce on tap a stream of really good advice on what makes people tick in country X on issue Y, and which people there we should be trying to influence, who you should speak to today, and we happen to know that he is in his office now.
>
> (Kerr 2004)

Advice and impact will be the true measure of improved strategic capacity in the FCO and across Whitehall. Aligning policies with strategic goals is also just as important as setting goals[15] and this is one area in which government tends to be better on specific country or issue strategies than with strategic foreign policy as a whole.

The FCO has already done much to advance this agenda. A sustained campaign on 'diplomatic excellence' has seen a series of initiatives including better in-house training, action to establish a diplomatic academy, improved use of specialists and a revival of investment in language and regional expertise. In 2011 the Foreign Secretary set up the Locarno Group of former senior diplomats to advise him[16] and the FCO has also set up a series of alumni groups to draw on the cumulative advice of officials. There is a reinvigorated role for policy planners, research analysts and historians. Meanwhile, in parallel, Cabinet Office structures have been strengthened through the creation of a formal NSC and national security adviser.

However, a brief survey of the archives, secondary literature on policy planning and interviews with former UK and US officials suggests that people matter more than systems when it comes to nurturing longer-headed officials. From the perspective of past members of policy planners, the reality often fell short of the goal. As Sir James Cable wrote, 'foreign policy planning seems likely to remain the art of a small minority: its exponents a little outside the mainstream of decisionmaking; its preoccupations a trifle esoteric; its impact limited and intermittent' (Cable 1994, p. 115). Yet policy planning played a crucial role in shaping British foreign policy. It prepared successive generations of diplomats to think about the broader UK national interest. It allowed diplomats time to think and to network externally. It gave a group of mid-level officials access to the heart of Foreign Office policymaking, particularly if the relationship with the permanent under-secretary was strong.

The contemporary challenge is how to foster strategic, anticipatory and innovative thinking among all those who work on British foreign policy. This is about people, above all, for diplomats need to think in time, take a broader view and cultivate imagination and dissent.

Notes

1. The author would like to thank John Gaddis, Paul Kennedy, Ryan Irwin, Charlie Laderman and Chris Miller for their encouragement at Yale, and the Asia Society, as selected interviews cited here were conducted during a Bernard Schwartz fellowship in New York in 2012. This chapter was written in a personal capacity and does not reflect the views of the UN or the Foreign and Commonwealth Office. This is a revised and updated version of an article that first appeared in *International Affairs*, London, vol. 90, no. 3 May 2014, pp. 509–524, and is reproduced with permission.
2. Letter from Ernest May to Henry Kissinger, 6 December 1968. Nixon Library archive, NLN 03/211. www.nixonlibrary.gov/virtuallibrary/documents/dec10/66.pdf
3. Part of the challenge here is stylistic. There is a sharp contrast between staccato, action-oriented policy briefs and longer academic or journalistic articles.
4. This is already difficult enough, amplified – according to Robert Gallucci, the president of the John D. and Catherine T. MacArthur Foundation – by the theoretical turn in international relations which has made dialogue between academics and practitioners more difficult (Gallucci 2012).
5. 'There was no independent Planning Staff.... It was a section of a department called Western Organisations Department, of which I later became

head, many years later. It was called Western Organisations and Planning Department, and the little planning section within it consisted of three people.' Sir Crispin Tickell, interview by Malcolm McBain, Churchill Archives Centre, British Diplomatic Oral History Programme, 28 January 1999.
6. Sir David Alwyn Gore-Booth, head of policy planning from 1987 to 1989, Churchill Archives Centre, British Diplomatic Oral History Programme.
7. Public Administration Committee (2010), p. 26.
8. The author has discussed this with four former heads of US policy planning, along with a number of former members of the staff.
9. Interview with the author, October 2012.
10. Interview with the author, October 2012.
11. Interview with author, October 2012.
12. Interview with author, October 2012.
13. A positive trend is the small number of British diplomats taking funded mid-career fellowships like those provided by Harvard, Princeton and Yale. Similar opportunities are rare in the UK because of funding restraints, although two senior diplomats have taken the LSE IDEAS Executive Masters.
14. Former Clinton administration NSC official, interview with author, New York, September 2012 and former George W. Bush administration NSC official, telephone interview with author, September 2012.
15. Former George W. Bush administration NSC official, telephone interview with author, September 2012.
16. https://www.gov.uk/government/news/foreign-secretary-announces-first-meeting-of-locarno-group

9
UK Nuclear Interests: Security, Resilience and Trident

Benoît Pelopidas and Jutta Weldes

Over the last eight years, discussions about the UK's national interest have set the goal of building a 'resilient nation' (Omand 2005). The idea of 'resilience' has, or seems to have, superseded 'security' as a primary way of defining the UK's national interest. Resilience was thus at the heart of the Conservative Party platform in 2010 ('A Resilient Nation') and remained at the core of the two key strategic documents published in 2010: the National Security Strategy (Cabinet Office 2010a) and the Strategic Defence and Security Review (Cabinet Office 2010b). In each, resilience appears as one of the two overarching goals that the UK has set as its national interest. In their foreword to the National Security Strategy, David Cameron and Nick Clegg thus state: 'at home, we must become more resilient both to external threats and to natural disasters' (Cabinet Office 2010a, p. 4).

The requirements of resilience arguably differ fundamentally from those of security in terms of both the scope and the timing of action when confronted with the prospect of disaster. While security is understood as protection and implies preventive action aiming at avoiding disaster, resilience assumes and accepts that its referent object is vulnerable and will face disaster sooner or later. The goal is not to prevent disaster from happening, or even necessarily to delay it, but rather to limit the damage and facilitate recovery. So a re-framing of the UK's national interest from the logic of security-seeking to that of resilience-seeking suggests a major change that will be assessed in this chapter.

Is there actually a shift from security to resilience in the understanding of the UK national interest? This question matters for a variety of reasons, including that the ability to produce national resilience is not, its supporters notwithstanding, unproblematically a 'public good'

(Omand 2005, p. 14). The acceptance of resilience as a public good depends on two factors:

- the consistency between the discourse of resilience and the actual policy put in place in the name of the national interest;
- the acceptance by the public of exposure to danger and its justifications.[1]

As we will show, some recent academic analysis assumes that the turn from security to resilience is actually occurring, but that analysis tends to neglect the fact that the two concepts can actually be articulated in multiple ways rather than being strictly opposed. They can be pursued simultaneously, resilience appearing as the goal of plan B when the efforts to keep the nation secure have failed; resilience can appear as a condition for security, in which case security follows from the recognition of the resilient character of a given community; and finally, resilience can be one among many ways to mitigate risk. Clarifying which one of these relationships is used in the framing of the UK's national interest in terms of resilience is key to assessing the scope of the shift from security to resilience.

The debate over the renewal of Trident offers a good case study to assess this shift for three reasons. First, Trident, as the only pillar of the UK nuclear deterrence strategy, has so far been portrayed by the government as a core instrument serving the UK's national interest. The 2013 *Trident Alternatives Review* states explicitly that 'nuclear deterrence has a unique role in deterring extreme threats to the UK's vital interests which cannot be countered by other means' and 'any change to the UK's nuclear deterrent system and/or its posture may have the potential to impact...our...national interests' (UK Cabinet Office 2013b, pp. 3, 9, 13). Second, the debate concerns one of the most important areas of possible change in the UK's strategy to promote its national interests. Third, the discourse of resilience, which was absent from the 2006 Defence White Paper (UK MoD 2006) and not associated with Trident in the 2010 Strategic Defence and Security Review and National Security Strategy, has arrived in discussions about Trident in the *Trident Alternatives Review* published in July 2013 (UK Cabinet Office 2013b).

Nonetheless, we argue that the debate and policy decisions related to UK nuclear weapons demonstrate that the shift from security to resilience is more rhetorical than real both because the framing of Trident is not in fact fully compatible with the requirements of resilience and because other possible systems which could meet resiliency requirements are neither contemplated nor prioritised. These findings matter for both theory and policy. If we are right, the scholarly worry about a shift from security to resilience does not apply to nuclear weapons policy in the UK. As a consequence, given the destructiveness attached to those weapons and their expected role in the national security architecture, talking about a radical shift from security to resilience in the framing of UK security and nuclear interests is not convincing. In the UK's current strategic planning and understanding of its national interest, the notion of resilience only suggests that there is a plan B in case of a failure of standard security policy, and both are pursued in parallel. In policy terms, we show that the disconnect between the principles of resilience and the practices of nuclear weapons policy suggests that UK policy elites have still not publicly recognised all the risks of major accidents and other mishaps involving nuclear weapons.

To show this, we start by documenting the rise of resilience in the discourse about UK national interests and reflect upon its possible articulations with the concept and goal of security. Our aim is to make sense of what a shift from security to resilience would entail. We then assess the practices of UK nuclear weapons policy, and Trident in particular, in relation to the requirements with which a resilient nuclear weapons policy would need to comply. We conclude by arguing that the current understanding of the requirements of deterrence as a communicative practice both limits the opportunities for conceptual innovation in nuclear thinking and in large part explains the missed opportunity regarding the acknowledgement of the risk of a nuclear accident and the possibility of a consistent shift towards resilience as a national priority.

Redefining UK national interests: From security to resilience?

National interests, whether the UK's or others', are socially constructed. That is,

> national interests are social constructions created as meaningful objects out of the intersubjective and culturally established meanings with which the world, particularly the international system and the place of the state in it, is understood. More specifically, national interests emerge out of the representations – or, to use more customary terminology, out of situation descriptions and problem definitions – through which state officials and others make sense of the world around them.
>
> (Weldes 1996, p. 280)

In recent years, various academic and policy literatures have argued that we live in a 'risk society' (for example Beck 1992, 1990) and that we therefore have moved, or should move, from constructing UK (and other) national interests in terms of a 'security' discourse – which focuses on (putatively) objective threats, protection, defence, prevention and/or deterrence – to constructing those interests in terms of a discourse of 'risk' and 'resilience'.

Indeed, prominent academics and public intellectuals talk/write as if they assume that a turn to resilience is in fact occurring. As a result, many debates have focused on the *effects* of such a shift from security to resilience. Responses have been twofold. On the one hand, some scholars have made this shift something to be opposed because moving from security to resilience exposes lives to vulnerability instead of trying to protect them. In other words, resilience would do, or already does, away with security.[2] On the other hand, security experts and some public intellectuals have embraced resilience and have advocated the shift from security to resilience (for example, Taleb 2012). In either case, the debate takes the shift from security – and threats, protection, defence, prevention and/or deterrence – to resilience for granted, focusing on whether it should be embraced or resisted, based on a discussion of its effects.

This focus on resilience emerges out of the prominence of concerns over risk and uncertainty. It is the 'obsession with risk' (Krahmann 2011, p. 354) and uncertainty in the discourse of 'risk society' that demands we be, or become, resilient. In contrast to what Cameron and Clegg called 'the brutal certainties of the Cold War – with an existential danger that was clear and present' we are now represented as being 'in an age of uncertainty, we are continually facing new and unforeseen threats to our security' (2010, pp. 3–4). In this discourse of 'risk society', the UK must shift its focus from manifest threats to possible risks and, more concretely, to risk assessment, which opens space for framing the UK national interest in terms of resilience (Edmunds 2012; Hammerstad and Boas 2012; Ritchie 2011).

Identifying and prioritising risks requires technologies of risk assessment. Risk can, in this sense, be understood as 'a measure of the level of insecurity calculated by the probability of a hazard multiplied by its impact' (Krahmann 2011, pp. 354–355). The UK National Security Strategy concurs (Figure 9.1): assessing risk, it asserts,

> involves making judgements about the relative impact and likelihood of each risk in comparison with others... This methodology involves

consideration of the impact of an event (based on economic consequences, casualties and social/structural factors); and the likelihood of this event occurring over a determined timeframe.
(UK Cabinet Office 2010a, p. 37)

Based on this logic, the UK National Security Strategy announced that 'we have conducted the first ever National Security Risk Assessment (NSRA) to assess and prioritise all major areas of national security risk – domestic and overseas' (UK Cabinet Office 2010a, p. 25).[3] The NSRA 'compare[d], assess[ed], and prioritise[d] all major disruptive risks' to UK national security over the 20 years to come. Specific risks were allocated to three 'tiers', with 'hostile attacks on UK cyber space', an 'international military crisis between states, drawing in the UK', 'international terrorism' and 'a major accident or natural hazard which requires a national response' comprising the highest-priority Tier 1 risks (UK Government 2010e). A possible nuclear attack – the risk whose realisation Trident is designed to deter – is the first risk mentioned in Tier 2.

The demand for resilience follows directly from this discourse of uncertainties and risk, and especially from technologies of risk

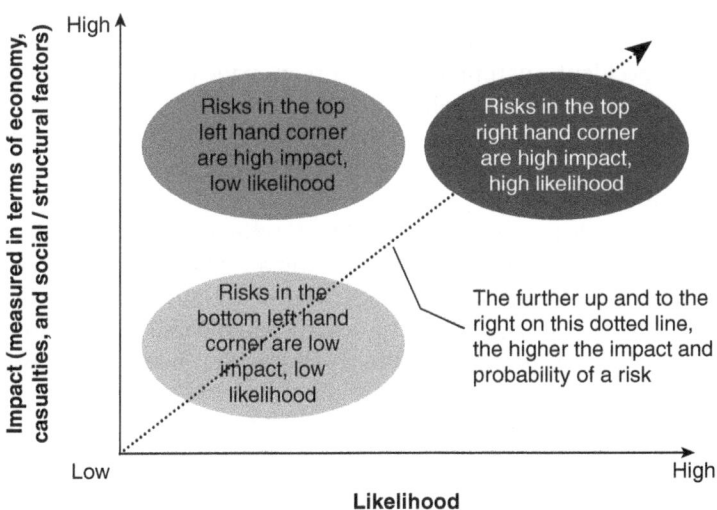

Figure 9.1 From 'Fact sheet 2: National security risk assessment' (UK Cabinet Office 2010e) (see https://www.gov.uk/government/uploads/system/Factsheet2-National-Security-Risk-Assessments.pdf)

assessment. Because there is no such thing as zero risk (as opposed to the absence of a specific threat) and because the 'potential range of imaginable risks is infinite' (Krahmann 2011, p. 356), risk can only ever be managed and/or mitigated. As one former senior UK civil servant put it, 'we must continue to be honest about risk management – not risk elimination... [We must] not be under the illusion that the risks can be eliminated at any acceptable cost' (Omand 2005, p. 17). The UK National Security Strategy therefore insists that 'To ensure that we are able to recover quickly when risks turn into actual damage to our interests, *we have to promote resilience, both locally and nationally*' (UK Cabinet Office 2010a, emphasis added).

Resilience offers a 'science of complex adaptive systems and an operational strategy of risk management' (Walker and Cooper 2011, p. 143). Resilience requires that states prepare for when security policies – that is, protection, defence, prevention and deterrence – or major infrastructural systems – for example, critical infrastructure like electricity grids and cyberspace – fail, perhaps catastrophically (an example might be the spectacular failure of the nuclear power plant at Fukushima Daiichi in 2011). 'National resilience' is therefore 'the ability to resist, absorb, recover from, or successfully adapt to adversity or a change in conditions' (US Department of Homeland Security 2009, p. 111). It entails building the capacity 'to deal with the consequences that are common to most types of emergency, regardless of whether those emergencies are caused by accidents, natural hazards or man-made threats' (UK Cabinet Office 2013a). The requirement of resilience thus assumes vulnerability and emphasises, correspondingly, the survivability of people and infrastructure, and the mitigation of and recovery from the consequences of the realisation of risk.

At the very least, achieving national resilience requires creating resilient institutions and infrastructure, and a resilient population (Ellis 2010, p. 380). As Cameron and Clegg argued, 'in an age of uncertainty the unexpected will happen, and we must be prepared to react to that by making our institutions and infrastructure as resilient as we possibly can' (2010, p. 5). As a result, one of the major national security tasks identified by the Strategic Defence and Security Review was to '[p]rovide resilience for the UK' by providing the 'security and resilience of the infrastructure most critical to keeping the country running (including nuclear facilities) against attack, damage or destruction' (UK Cabinet Office 2010b, p. 12).

Resilient populations are also extremely important. According to Omand, resilient populations are those that understand:

- the full range of risks facing the nation;
- the 'type of protection and preparation that is considered necessary and proportionate';
- that there are 'limitations' in public security; and
- that individuals and communities all have a role to play (2005, p. 17).

As the National Security Strategy put it: 'Ensuring that the public is fully informed of the risks we face is a critical part of this approach' (Cabinet Office 2010a, p. 25). In short, the UK national interest requires a resilient UK population that:

- would accept their vulnerability to the full scope of risks, including nuclear risks, and the inability of the state to provide security; and
- would contribute to the mitigation and survivability in the case of realised risks.

Security and/or resilience?

Interestingly, despite quite vociferous arguments defending the claim of a shift in UK (and other) national interests from security to resilience, it is not clear in this discourse – and particularly in the policy documents we examined – what the relationship between 'security' and 'resilience' actually is. This relationship remains ambiguous and ill-defined, leaving open various potential renderings of the exact relations between these concepts. Are they contradictory, complementary or something else?

As indicated in our discussion of resilience discourse, the academic argument that a shift has occurred from security to resilience suggests that the UK national interest is or should be seeking resilience rather than seeking security. On this interpretation, resilience straightforwardly replaces security as the objective of national strategy and the core national interest. In the UK strategic documents we have examined, however, the UK seeks to be both 'secure and resilient'. This orientation is confirmed in the core of the National Security Strategy, which says that 'We must be a nation that is able to bring together all the instruments of national power to build a secure and resilient UK' (UK Cabinet Office 2010a, p. 10). The Strategic Defence and Security Review similarly sets resilience as the first of two key goals: '(i) to ensure a secure and resilient UK by protecting our people, economy, infrastructure, territory and ways of life from all major risks that can affect us directly' (Cabinet Office 2010b, p. 9).

In this second case, resilience is added to security as a second core national interest. The addition of resilience is necessary, as argued above, because of uncertainty and the unavoidability of risk. In this discourse, the UK national interest in security takes precedence, but resilience kicks in as plan B when security has failed, which it is sure to do at some point given that risks can never be reduced to zero. As the UK National Security Strategy made clear, 'whilst we will focus on early identification and mitigation of risks, we recognise that we cannot expect to eliminate risks altogether' (UK Cabinet Office 2010a, p. 22).

Third, resilience can be interpreted as part of being secure, as when it is claimed that 'we cannot prevent every risk as they are inherently unpredictable. To ensure we are able to recover quickly when risks turn into actual damage to our interests, we have to promote resilience, both locally and nationally' (UK Cabinet Office 2010a, p. 25). Here, the relationship involves the claim that we are more secure if we are also resilient. In this sense, the one objective, security, presupposes achieving the other, resilience. As Sir David Omand has argued in defence of resilience, 'We must work smarter: think strategically, prepare for the worst, ruthlessly target resources at risks [sic] and work with allies and partners to anticipate and prevent threats before they become real. This preparation is *in itself* a form of dissuasion as well as of defense' (2010, p. 13, emphasis added). That is, it is a prerequisite for security.

Finally, a fourth relationship is also possible: resilience can be viewed as one of a variety of means to mitigate risk, which, in turn, is as close to security as we can get in a 'risk society'. According to Omand, 'having a resilience capability framework' is a methodology for 'risk reduction' (2004). Elke Krahmann argues similarly that risk can be mitigated through a variety of strategies: prevention, pre-emption, avoidance, deterrence, protection and, finally, resilience (2011, pp. 369–370). On this interpretation, resilience is a much smaller part of a wider discourse of uncertainty and risk, which, as noted above, has (supposedly) replaced security as the national interest. This view resembles the UK National Security Strategy claim that 'providing resilience' is one of its eight 'national security tasks': 'Providing resilience for the UK by being prepared for all kinds of emergencies, able to recover from shocks and to maintain essential services' (UK Cabinet Office 2010a, p. 33).

Despite a widespread academic and policy discourse of 'resilience', then, its conceptual relationship to security remains unclear. So, in order to assess the assumed shift from security to resilience in the definition of the UK's national interest, we turn to a focused analysis of nuclear weapons policy and Trident, which has so far been portrayed by the government as a core instrument serving the UK's 'vital interest'.

UK nuclear policy versus the goal of resilience

What would a resilient nuclear weapons policy look like? Is it consistent with the way UK elites frame both resilience and the role of Trident? The prime minister and deputy prime minister have repeatedly invoked the metaphor of the 'ultimate insurance policy' (Cameron and Clegg 2010, p. 5)[4] to describe their understanding of the role that UK nuclear weapons are and should be playing in the national security architecture and the promotion of the national interest. The notion of an insurance policy fits with the framework of resilience in several fundamental ways: the two notions are opposed to prevention, they recognise vulnerability, and they focus on *ex post facto* damage limitation. And, as we noted in the introduction, at least since 2013, Trident itself has been framed in terms of resilience.

Beyond those rhetorical tropes, the above analysis suggests that a resilient nuclear weapons policy should be based on two principles:

- it should start by recognising the full scope of nuclear risks; and
- it should aim for maximum survivability.

The first principle requires further elaboration. The full scope of nuclear risks includes the risk of accidents, possibly resulting in the launch of a nuclear-tipped ballistic missile. In this context we can distinguish between technological accidents and accidents resulting from misperception. The first would be in line with the widely shared intuition that there is no such thing as a fail-safe (that is, risk-free) technology and that technological failure does not always result in a desirable outcome like the prevention of unintended nuclear use (Pelopidas 2013b). In the case of nuclear weapons, once the complex and tightly coupled nature of these systems is recognised, as well as the limit of the imagination of the engineers performing the reliability tests,[5] the causal chain leading to accidents becomes clear. As Charles Perrow writes,

> Since nothing is perfect... there will be failures. If the complex interactions defeat designed-in safety devices or go around them, there will be failures that are unexpected and incomprehensible. If the system is also tightly coupled, leaving little time for recovery from failure, little slack in resources or fortuitous safety devices, then the

failure cannot be limited to parts or units, but will bring down subsystems or systems. These accidents then are caused initially by components' failure, but become accidents rather than incidents because of the nature of the system itself; they ... are inevitable ... for those systems.

(1999, p. 330; See also Sagan 1993)

One might think that adding redundancy to the system would solve the problem of tight coupling. There are two issues with this line of reasoning, however. While redundancy would definitely address the problem of tight coupling, it would not entirely solve it, and it would address that problem by worsening the other feature of the system which makes it prone to accidents, that is, its complexity (Sagan 2004). It is true that the scenario in which a missile does not go off when it should because of a similar cascade of failures would also qualify as a normal or systemic accident. And in that case, one might argue that no casualties will follow. Several accidents involving British nuclear weapons between 1960 and 1991 described in the July 1992 report by Sir Ronald Oxburgh, the chief scientific adviser at the Ministry of Defence, fall in the category of failures without risk of nuclear explosion (Oxburgh 1992; Schlosser 2013a, 2013b). Even so, the possibility of such an accident should be taken seriously, if the focus on resilience is to be consistent, since an adversary might detect early signs of preparation for a launch and might react to them even if the launch ultimately failed.

Nuclear weapons could also be used as a result of misperceptions. If an enemy launch is detected and the object flies towards one's country, there is a non-zero chance that the response will be nuclear retaliation. As examples indicate – most famously during the NATO Able Archer 83 exercise in 1983 and in 1995 when Russian air defence mistook a meteorological satellite launched from Norway for a submarine-launched ballistic missile from the US (Pry 1999) – mischaracterisation of flying objects can and does happen, and the speed of ballistic missiles limits leaders' ability to realise that a mistake has been made (Podvig 2013). From a UK perspective, such a systemic accident or misperception would lead to a nuclear explosion on its soil if it happened in any nuclear-weapon states whose missiles target the UK. Given that, so far, no protection against a nuclear attack exists (see Pelopidas 2013a), the issue of unauthorised launch is not only a problem of the reliability of the national arsenal. If the accidental launch originated in the UK, it would become a problem only if the enemy identified it correctly as coming from there and decided to retaliate.[6] In a nutshell, the prospect for normal or epistemic accidents, in the UK or in any nuclear-armed state targeting it, as well as the prospect for misperceptions, keeps the likelihood of a nuclear explosion in the UK above zero even if one believes that nuclear deterrence works perfectly.

Recognising this vulnerability should be a pillar of a resilient nuclear weapons policy. The second principle, if understood in relation to the goal of building a resilient nation, leads to attaching survivability and the efforts to maximise it to the population itself – or parts of it – rather than only to the warheads as does classical deterrence theory (Cohn 1987). As a consequence, a nuclear weapons policy aiming at resilience should design an infrastructure aiming for maximum survivability and justify its construction in those terms.

Let us now confront those criteria – the recognition of the full scope of nuclear risks and the goal of maximum survivability – with the actual framing of UK nuclear weapons policy. First, the probability of accidental or erroneous launch based on a misperception in the UK or towards it is not acknowledged either in the 2010 strategic documents or in the 2013 *Trident Alternatives Review*.[7] Only two scenarios possibly involving nuclear use are considered: nuclear terrorism, and an unspecified 'uncertainty' against which the existence of British nuclear weapons work as the 'ultimate insurance policy' (UK Cabinet Office 2010b, p. 5). In both cases, malicious intent is clearly assumed. In the first case, it is the intentional use of a nuclear device by a terrorist group. Thus, the Strategic Defence and Security Review claims that 'there is a risk that some countries might in future seek to sponsor nuclear terrorism' (UK Cabinet Office 2010b, p. 37). Similarly, it is asserted that some actors might seize 'fissile material' to build a nuclear device or, possibly, a radiological dispersal device with a view to *'malicious use'* (UK Cabinet Office 2010b, p. 55, emphasis added). In the second case, the notion of threat, with its underlying intentionality, reappears in spite of the general shift from threat to risks discussed above. In the Strategic Defence and Security Review, one reads that 'We must not allow states [seeking to support nuclear terrorism] to threaten our national security or to deter us and the international community from taking the action required to maintain regional and global security' (UK Cabinet Office 2010b, p. 37). So, contrary to the requisites of resilience, the UK nuclear policy as stated in the two 2010 documents as well as the more recent *Trident Alternatives Review* fails to recognise all the risks related to nuclear weapons in practice.

Second, a resilient nuclear weapons policy ought to aim at survivability. If this aim goes beyond the mere survivability of the warheads and relates to the survivability of the 'resilient nation', one would expect to see expenditures and public policies justified in the name of survivability. Historically, two types of programmes have been developed to achieve this goal: civil defence programmes, that is, underground shelters, and anti-missile defences. One could also imagine other types of shelters, either under water or in space. However, the inefficacy of the civil defence programmes has been well-established (Garrison 2006; Clarke 1999, pp. 30–40) and none of those programmes is currently being considered. To the best of our knowledge, there are also no plans for under water or space shelters.

However, regarding missile defence, the Strategic Defence and Security Review states that the UK 'will...maintain [its] existing policy of close cooperation with the US and our other NATO allies on ballistic missile defences, and [it intends] to support proposals to expand NATO's role' (UK Cabinet Office 2010b, p. 28) because '[the UK's] strong defence, security and intelligence relationship with the US is exceptionally close and central to our national interest' (UK Cabinet Office 2010a, p. 22). Indeed, the UK participates in the deployment of the US nuclear security architecture in Europe: it hosts one ballistic missile early warning station and the European ground station for the Space-based Infrared System (Stocker 2004, p. v). In early 2012, the Ministry of Defence signed a contract with European missile manufacturer MBDA and charged it with developing a new missile defence system for the Royal Navy (*Guardian* 2012; Richardson 2013); and in March 2013 it was announced that Royal Navy Type 45 destroyers could join future missile interceptor testing conducted by the US missile defence agency (*Defense Update* 2013).

For the UK's participation in that effort to become consistent with the notion of survivability as a feature of resilience, one has to assume that the US will actually engage its anti-missile capabilities to intercept a missile targeted at the UK, and with a high enough success rate that increased UK survivability becomes possible. This consistency has become conceivable because of the evolution of the stated goals of the US missile defence system over the years.

From the peak of Reagan's ambition to make nuclear weapons and the ballistic missiles carrying them 'impotent and obsolete' (1983), by building a shield that the president even considered sharing with the whole world,[8] the ambitions of the project were diminished and its proponents came to recognise a whole set of vulnerabilities. In other words, the project, based on the logic of defence, became a way to enhance deterrence instead of replacing it (Rosenfeld 2009).[9] Thus, the justification for the now-cancelled US deployment of the European phased adaptive approach for its missile defence programme consisted in enhancing deterrence and 'strengthen[ing] regional deterrence architectures' rather than replacing deterrence with defence (US Department of Defense 2010, pp. v, 12).[10]

All in all, there are two ways to make UK nuclear policy even partially compatible with the criterion of maximum survivability, in spite of the lack of a project to build protected space for the population. The first would put its faith in the US mobilisation of its anti-missile capabilities to protect the UK if it appears to be targeted by a large-scale nuclear attack and to bet on a high enough rate of success to avoid the total destruction of the British Isles. The second scenario is the generally unspoken case of a small-scale nuclear attack on the UK consistent with the scale of the North Korean nuclear arsenal. In that case, the assumption would be that the strike did not destroy all of the UK's nuclear means of retaliation and these could then be used in the hope of restoring deterrence after its failure.

In a nutshell, the current UK nuclear weapons policy fails to meet the two criteria of resilience – the recognition of the full scope of nuclear risks and the goal of maximum survivability – and shows a lack of consistency between the rhetoric of resilience and the practice of nuclear weapons policy.

Conclusion: Deterrence against resilience?

As we have shown, the existing UK national interest discourse relating to nuclear weapons does not meet the requirements of a resilient nuclear weapons policy. There is no recognition of the full spectrum of nuclear vulnerability (that is, of the risk of accidental launch in the UK or towards it) and nuclear weapons themselves do not guarantee the survivability of the nation in case of a nuclear attack, except in a case in which the enemy only launched a few warheads and is deterred from launching the rest by the prospect of a retaliatory strike. The systems which could have been invoked to limit damage have either been abandoned, as in civil defence, or continue to be supported but as instruments of deterrence rather than defence, for example, US ballistic missile defence and the now-cancelled European phased adaptive approach. Finally, a lot of very optimistic assumptions about the efficacy of the missile defence system and the commitment of the US as an ally are needed in order for these systems to be a meaningful part of a nuclear security infrastructure closer to the imperatives of resilience.

Perhaps, then, some academics and public intellectuals have been too quick to radicalise the opposition between security and resilience and to talk/write as if a turn from the first to the second is actually occurring in defining the UK national interest. More than that, if such a shift is not taking place regarding the weapon system presented as the 'ultimate' security guarantee of the country, one might question what the whole idea of such a turn from security to resilience actually means.

Given that the lack of consistency between the rhetoric of resilience and policy practice comes from an incomplete recognition of the exposure to danger which is created or accepted by this policy, the idea that resilience is a public good appears problematic on both of the grounds we defined in the introduction:

- the consistency between the discourse of resilience and the actual policy put in place in the name of the national interest; and
- the public's acceptance of exposures to dangers and their justification.

This argument also holds if policymakers did discuss nuclear weapons accidents, but did so in secret, because the unjustified exposure to danger remains. Furthermore, this lack of consistency and the failure to recognise the risk of nuclear weapons accidents distorts the construction of the UK national interest regarding nuclear weapons. It privileges a pro-nuclear weapons position by removing the possibility of nuclear accident from public discussion (see, for example, Pelopidas 2011).

Ultimately, the current public discourse on deterrence remains an obstacle to the shift to resilience as a recognition of vulnerability because, as a communicative practice, it has two audiences with apparently contradictory expectations (Pelopidas 2013c). On the one hand, the adversary has to be convinced of the credibility of the retaliatory strike for a deterrent threat to make sense. If he doubts the resolve of the domestic leader, convincing him requires communicating that the situation might spiral out of control so that the retaliatory strike will take place even if the leader is not resolute enough to order it (Schelling 1960, chap. 6; 1966, chap. 3). This is exactly what current policymakers think domestic audiences do not want to hear. Therefore, even in contemporary democracies, populations are not consulted about which cause(s) would justify their exposure to nuclear disaster, so one cannot know what their answer would be. As a result, the imperatives of public acceptability of the discourse of deterrence as understood by political elites prevent the conditions of a shift towards resilience, which would at least publicly recognise the condition of global nuclear vulnerability.

Notes

1. After all, there are many systems that one might not wish to make resilient, including antibiotic-resistant bacteria, dictatorships, the global banking and bonus system, slavery and neo-liberalism, see Limnios et al. (2012).
2. The peer-reviewed journal *Resilience: International Policies, Practices and Discourses* takes this approach as its manifesto, see also Evans and Reid (2013, 2014) and Neocleous (2013).
3. In the UK National Security Strategy the term 'risk' appears much more frequently than does 'threat': risk and risks appear 478 times, while threat and threats appear only 69 times. The UK also established a National Risk Register (UK Cabinet Office 2012).
4. Following a visit to one of the Royal Navy's Vanguard-class submarines in Scotland, David Cameron reasserted that: 'having that nuclear deterrent is, quite simply, the best *insurance policy* you can have that you will never be subject to nuclear blackmail' (Cameron 2013).
5. For an elaboration of this idea and the notion of 'epistemic accident', see Downer (2011). He defines epistemic accidents as 'an emergent property, a fundamental consequence, of the structure of engineering knowledge. They can be defined as those accidents that occur because a scientific or technological assumption proves to be erroneous, even though there were reasonable and logical reasons to hold that assumption before (although not after) the event.' Most importantly for our argument, he adds that 'Epistemic accidents...are unavoidable because engineers necessarily build technologies around fallible theories, judgments, and assumptions' (p. 752).
6. In agreement with the Russian federation, the US has reprogrammed its missiles so that in case of unauthorised launch, they would head towards the ocean. We could not find evidence of such an attempt from other nuclear-weapon states (Schlosser 2013b, p. 478; Feaver and Thompson Sharp 2010, p. 45).
7. Lord Des Browne of Ladyton confirmed to one of the authors that this was not discussed when he was UK secretary of state for defence (interview with Des Browne, London, 16 October 2013). This is all the more surprising as the risks of accidents at nuclear power plants are recognised in the National Risk Assessment and in the 2013 *National Risk Register of Civil Emergencies* (UK Cabinet Office 2013c, p. 34).
8. Reagan voiced this idea in a meeting in the situation room on 3 February 1986 (Hoffmann 2009, pp. 240–241).
9. The shift from defending to strengthening deterrence as the key rationale for the US ballistic missile defence programme has been all the clearer since the US Congress passed the National Missile Defence project in 1999 with its focus becoming regional threats with a very specific emphasis on Iran and North Korea instead of any possible ballistic missile threat (Rosenfeld 2009, p. 205; US Department of Defense 2010, pp. iii, iv, 13). The focus on strengthening deterrence and not strictly protecting a territory is common to

all current missile defence programmes including the most ambitious ones in the US and Israel, in spite of money invested in the US ballistic missile defence programme and the Israeli Iron Dome, and the claims of supporters of the missile defence programmes. The French president, Jacques Chirac, expressed this very clearly on 19 July 2006 when he contemplated the participation of France in reflections about missile defence (see Kelleher et al. 2013).
10. For an overview of the phased adaptive approach as outlined by Barack Obama in September 2009 and updates on its implementation, see Arms Control Association (2013).

10
Complexity, Strategy and the National Interest[1]

Timothy Edmunds

In 2010, and in anticipation of a controversial and contested Strategic Defence and Security Review (SDSR), the UK House of Commons Public Administration Select Committee (PASC) issued a stinging critique of strategy making in the UK, accusing the government of having 'all but lost the capacity to think strategically' (PASC 2010, p. 3). Two years later, in 2012, it was still lamenting 'the government's inability to express coherent and relevant strategic aims' (PASC 2012, p. 38). These criticisms have been echoed in the strategic studies and foreign policy analysis literature, including calls for a revival of grand narratives of national interest to drive strategic practice (Layton 2012, pp. 59–60), for a new relationship between political decision-making and professional expertise in strategy making (Strachan 2006, pp. 77–80) and the reinvigoration of institutional capacities for strategic thinking and action in the Ministry of Defence (MoD) and elsewhere (Cornish and Dorman 2010, pp. 408–409). Related themes are apparent too in the burgeoning literature on risk, which identifies distinct challenges of strategic practice associated with contemporary patterns of complexity, uncertainty and interdependence and calls for better strategy making in response (Rasmussen 2006, pp. 203–206).

This chapter examines the politics and practice of strategy making in the UK in the face of these challenges. While recognising that strategic uncertainty and domestic austerity pose new problems for the strategic policy community, it argues that the criticisms of British strategic practice are often misplaced, for two main reasons. First, many of them posit their critique on a reductionist notion of unitary 'national interest' that fails to capture systemic patterns of complexity and contestation in the wider security environment and at home. Second, they underestimate or ignore the extent to which the UK strategic community is itself innovating in response to these themes, particularly since the last SDSR. This is not to argue that considerable challenges do not remain for British strategic practice. Chief among these include how to translate strategic innovation in departments and elsewhere into a coherent national strategic agenda; how to do this while maintaining institutional coordination and a shared sense of strategic purpose across government (and beyond); how to sustain and consolidate institutional expertise and experience in a rapidly changing civil service and at a time of continuing public austerity; and how to articulate and legitimate security policy decisions amongst a general public that is both disengaged from elite strategic discourse and sceptical of the efficacy of military force. Even so, the chapter concludes by arguing that it is possible to see the outline of an emergent and distinctive theory of action in contemporary British strategic practice, characterised by principles of adaptivity, anticipation, self-organisation and nascent cross-governmentalism.

An anatomy of the attack

The attack on British strategy making has been building for some time. Its immediate spur was the stuttering progress of the conflicts in Iraq and Afghanistan, though arguably it reflects structural tensions that have been present in British defence for decades (Edmunds 2010, pp. 393–394). In 2005, in the first of a series of seminal articles on the issue, Hew Strachan argued that Western strategy faced 'existential crisis' in the wake of Iraq, due to an inherent confusion in strategic thinking and a consequent failure to effectively link military action to clear political goals (Strachan 2005, p. 34). A series of public interventions by military officers and others over the following years accused UK policy specifically of having lost its sense of strategic purpose in Iraq and Afghanistan, to the point where the army risked being 'broken' by its experiences.[2] More recently, criticism of UK strategy has crystallised around the conduct and outcomes of the National Security Strategy (NSS) processes of 2008 (updated in 2009) and 2010 (HM Government 2008, 2009, 2010), and perhaps most particularly around the controversial and contested SDSR of 2010 (MoD 2010). The NSS documents were disparaged for their breadth, vagueness and perceived lack of focus (JCNSS 2012a, p. 3). For its part, the 2010 SDSR was widely derided for a lack of strategic coherence and a perception that it was led primarily by a hastily implemented and cuts-driven government spending review rather than by a measured consideration of the UK's strategic circumstances and requirements in the new context of austerity (Cornish and Dorman 2011, p. 3).

In one way or another, all these critiques call for a reconsideration of the manner in which the UK makes strategy. Strategy is variously defined in these and other literatures, but generally consists of the linking of ways and means to achieve specific ends. It is thus best considered as a theory of action; a rationale for employing the resources and assets at one's disposal effectively in order to deliver particular policy outcomes. Yet, as Strachan points out, the very breadth of potential offered by these definitions means that it has 'acquired a universality which has robbed it of meaning, and left it only with banalities' (Strachan 2005, p. 34). Strategy in this respect is most clearly understood as applying specifically to the circumstances of war; it is an iterative, realistic and purposive process, 'a compromise between the ends of policy and the military means available to implement it' (Strachan 2005, p. 52). In this context, the primary strategic failures of the UK since 2001 have related to the application of military force. They are concerned first and foremost with a failure to properly think through the desired political outcomes of the interventions in Iraq and Afghanistan, and then to deliver an effective and achievable commitment of military and other resources to achieve that effect.

However, the critique of British strategy making goes deeper and wider than this focus on recent military adventures. After all, the NSS and SDSR apply a much broader lens to the security and foreign policy of the UK, and address a different, albeit related, order of question to those concerning the use of military force. Indeed, many of the most pointed commentaries on these issues relate to what is often called 'grand' or 'national' strategy, that is the strategy of the state itself in delivering its national interests and creating security for itself on the global stage. As the PASC report has it, '[i]n modern politics, [national strategy] is about ensuring that the whole of government identifies and acts upon the national interest' (PASC 2010, p. 8). Similarly, for Colin Gray, '[G]rand strategy is the direction and use made of any or all of the assets of a security community, including its military instrument, for the purposes of policy as decided by politics' (Gray 2011, p. 292). Against these definitions, the perceived failure of UK strategy making has occurred as much at a systemic, institutional level as it has in the field in Iraq and Afghanistan. For the PASC and others, the UK has 'all but lost the capacity to think strategically' on these terms, and 'the ability to articulate [its] enduring interests, values and identity has atrophied' (PASC

2010, p. 3). To their critics, the 2008 and 2010 NSS are embodiments of this malaise, 'thick with description, and thin on the main question: the dialectic between the country's aims and its ability to meet them' (Porter 2010b, p. 6). They exemplify an overly passive and ultimately a-strategic understanding of the UK's place in the world by focusing too heavily on risks over opportunities; on reaction and preparedness over taking the initiative (Strachan 2011, p. 1284).

Against this background, it is tempting to suggest that 'good strategy' has emerged as a catch-all solution to the UK's strategic ills. Given its precipitous fall from fashion during the post-Cold War years in favour of the wider discipline of security studies, this return to the efficacy of strategy and strategic studies is perhaps ironic, and no doubt heartening for its few champions during the lean years. Yet this renaissance in strategic studies faces challenges of its own. While the literatures and commentaries cited above have been powerful in their critique of UK strategy and policy, they have been less articulate in explaining how the UK should actually go about making good strategy in the contemporary era. It is common for such contributions to return to the classic texts of strategic thought (Strachan 2005, pp. 34–40), or to historical example (Guldi 2006), or to exhortations to 'the national interest' (PASC 2010, p. 13) to make their points, with varying degrees of insight and success. Yet, and with some exceptions (Jermy 2011), there have been few attempts to translate the critique of UK strategic practice into an alternative theory or framework for strategic action. They have also spent less time considering the ways in which the UK strategic policy community has itself been innovating in response to strategic challenge, public austerity and a perception of institutional failure since the last SDSR in 2010.

National interest in an age of uncertainty

If there are two words that have become synonymous with the contemporary Western security environment, they are 'complexity' and 'uncertainty'. It is a rare national security review document or defence White Paper that can even get through the preamble without mentioning them. Of course, security policy has always been characterised by a degree of uncertainty to one degree or another, not least because it involves interaction with other states and actors, who themselves have autonomous agency in the international arena. Likewise, strategy, and perhaps particularly strategy in war, must inevitably grapple with complexity due to the constant interplay of different factors, actions and reactions which comprise evolving strategic circumstance (Beyerchen 1992–1993, pp. 66–72).

Even so, there is good reason to attach more than simple rhetorical significance to the role of complexity and uncertainty in modern strategy making. Complexity as a concept is employed by systems engineering, climate science, mathematics and other disciplines to describe environments which are systemically dynamic, adaptive and not subject to straightforward relationships of cause and effect (Ryan 2009, pp. 70–74). Certainly, the international security environment against which national strategy is premised shares many of these characteristics. It comprises a diverse network of risks, threats, opportunities and actors, many of which transcend clear boundaries of departmental and national responsibility, disciplinary expertise or even state competence. Examples include international terrorism, climate change, cyber-attack, the proliferation and use of weapons of mass destruction, and the spread of new, potentially transformative, military and non-military technologies, amongst many others. Such challenges are inherently complex, in the sense that they have multiple, frequently interrelated, causes and are likely to be multifaceted and unpredictable in consequence, with cascading effects (Yarger 2006, p. 23). They are also uncertain, in that they are often predicated against future eventualities rather than clear and present dangers, and, in conception and response, subject to interpretation, contestation and controversy. These dynamics are intensified by the densely interconnected nature of contemporary global affairs. Information technology, mobile communication and social media mean that the relationships between cause and effect, action and reaction, can be exceptionally rapid and wide-ranging, as can be seen by the spiralling consequences of political protest in Tunisia in 2010 and the subsequent events of the so-called Arab Spring and its aftermath.

The complexity of this environment means the strategic truism of linking ways and means to achieve specific policy ends is often easier said than done. This is perhaps particularly the case when it comes to the knotty issue of national interest, a concept which lies at the heart of many of the recent commentaries on UK national strategy. The PASC report, for example, places national interest at the centre of its critique. Steven Jermy, while recognising the role of complexity in contemporary strategy making, places national interest at the heart of his understanding of strategic action (Jermy 2011, pp. 138–139, 176). For Harry Yarger, an 'underlying assumption' of interest underpins any notion of strategy (Yarger 2006, p. 5), while Patrick Porter calls for the use of 'smaller and more bounded concepts of the national interest to rebalance ends and means' (P. Porter 2010b, p. 10). None of these contributions is necessarily incorrect in the broad direction of their analysis. As Yarger himself notes, all strategy is, to some extent, 'a process that seeks to apply a degree of rationality and linearity to circumstances that may or may not be either', and in some respects 'national interest' provides as good a measure against which to judge the rationality of particular actions as any (Yarger 2006, p. 1). Accordingly, the UK's strategic malaise is implied to stem from the inability of successive governments to recognise these enduring national interests for what they are, and on this basis to articulate a strong enough sense of national purpose against which clear lines of strategy can be drawn.

But there are also dangers in privileging national interest in this way. For national interest to have meaning as a framework for strategy making, it needs substantive articulation. Yet it is striking that many of the recent critiques of UK national strategy leave this question undefined, or at the very least requiring further definition, while still placing it at the centre of their critique. In so doing, they imply a concept of national interest that is at once objective and self-evident, yet also curiously disembodied from specific expressions of interest and purpose. While this critique may be tempting in its rhetorical clarity, it is inadequate as a guide to action and underplays the deeply political and contested nature of national interest itself.

In contrast to some earlier periods, the UK currently lacks a hegemonic national narrative such as empire or the Cold War to concentrate minds on the national interest and to unite British grand strategy around a powerful organising idea (P. Porter 2010b, p. 7). Instead UK foreign policy incorporates a range of sometimes complementary, sometimes competing strategic narratives of various strengths, whether these be Atlanticist, Europeanist, liberal interventionist, multilateralist, or whatever, in character (Gaskarth 2014). All of these narratives exist within the context of contemporary strategic complexity, in which direct threats are diffuse and uncertain, and in which the international environment itself is neither static nor especially predictable. Against this background, even when national interests are defined with any degree of clarity, they tend to present either non-hegemonic, and so inherently contestable, goals – such as free trade for example – or are cast at such a level of generality that their utility as a guide to strategy making is limited. Even on the specific issue of defence, and the more limited question of national interest within this, the complex nature of the contemporary security environment means that multiple interpretations of strategic priority are possible and perhaps likely. In the institutionally constrained context of the 2010 SDSR process, it is striking that different services and interests within the British defence establishment were able to promote quite distinct conceptualisations of strategic risk and interest to further particular priorities in the defence policy process (Edmunds 2012, pp. 272–275).

An even wider divergence is shown between elite narratives of UK security and those of the general public. One of the characteristics of UK military–society relations since 2001, and perhaps even since the end of the Cold War, is that popular engagement with the strategic narratives of the UK political and security elite, from both within and outside the immediate policy environment, has been tenuous at best, and actively hostile at worst. This dissonance was dramatically illustrated in the public and political debate surrounding the efficacy of military intervention in Syria in August 2013.[3] More widely, opinion polling consistently shows no clear consensus on the British national interest, beyond a broad and rather generic attachment to maintaining the UK's historical great power status (PASC 2013, p. 37). The public exhibits currents of Atlanticism, Europeanism and isolationism. However, all of these preferences are nuanced and conditional, and none appears to dominate – or come close to dominating – the popular consciousness. More specifically, the public remain ambivalent towards international activism on the part of the UK (whether military or otherwise) and have struggled to engage with strategic imperatives that are premised on uncertain, indirect, geographically distant or long-term risks to national security (Edmunds 2012, pp. 278–280). Of course, to its advocates, the concept of national interest has distinct and enduring qualities that rise above the mood of the public on any given day. However, it is equally the case that if strategy is to have meaningful purchase in wider society; if it is to convince the public and politicians to devote resources – financial, human and otherwise – to its achievement, then it needs to be grounded in some kind of collective sense of what is nationally important and why. In the absence of such broad consensus, the extent to which any given concept of the national interest can act as a suzerain driver for the making of strategy is likely to be constrained.

In the final analysis, and as Colin Gray notes, 'strategy can be oversold.... It refers to a function that no one can oppose: is it possible to argue against the importance of the three-way marriage among political ends, ways and means?' (Gray 2010, p. 168) The deceptive simplicity of this strategic trilogy of ends, ways and means risks imposing overly linear solutions to the complex, contingent and evolving security challenges and opportunities against which contemporary strategy is premised. The implication is that once suitably clear and robust national interests have been identified and translated into specific strategic ends, strategy making becomes a technocratic endeavour under which available ways and means are brought together to achieve these goals through a rationalist process of planning. But as Strachan observes, the danger of such an approach is that it introduces an overt determinism into the strategy making process, which then may struggle to comprehend or respond to strategic contingencies as they occur (Strachan 2011, p. 1296). Instead, such circumstances require flexible, adaptive responses; able to coordinate across complex policy networks and ideational domains and act accordingly (Verweij 2011). In this context, the idea that a kind of Palmerstonian *deus ex machina* of national interest is the solution to the UK's perceived strategic ills should, at the very least, be taken with a pinch of salt.

Strategic innovation

If a clear and hegemonic notion of the national interest does not provide a solid enough purchase for strategy making in the UK today, then what does? Part of the answer lies in the fact that interest does not go entirely undefined in either the NSS or the SDSR. The NSS, for example, talks explicitly about Britain's role in the world, albeit in terms – 'ensuring a secure and resilient UK' and 'shaping a stable world' – that are exceptionally broad and non-specific (HM Government 2010, pp. 10–11). However, it is also striking the extent to which the strategic policy community has, particularly since 2010, embraced strategic complexity as an organising framework to fill in some of these gaps. In so doing, they have faced an enduring challenge of complexity thinking: of how to translate a contextual recognition of complexity and uncertainty into a clear guide to action. The challenge is particularly pronounced given that the institutions which comprise the UK strategic policy community are large, often somewhat bureaucratic organisations, organised for the most part around traditional models of hierarchy and administrative decision-making. Such institutions incorporate an inherent bias towards linear, sequential approaches to problem solving and action, not least in order that their responses to what are often recognised to be complex problems can be effectively and reliably implemented across the organisation as a whole (Allison and Zelikow 1999, pp. 143–147). Moreover, the inherently long-term nature of much strategic planning – in which, for example, expensive and complex defence equipment purchases such as aircraft carriers and fast jets are conceived, developed, purchased, maintained in service and updated over timescales that are measured in decades – embeds a tendency towards inertia, inflexibility and path dependency into many aspects of their decision-making (Edmunds 2010, pp. 387–388). Under such circumstances, it is perhaps not surprising that long-established models of strategic organisation and planning have struggled to adapt to the complexities and contingencies of the contemporary era.

Even so, it would be wrong to assume that the UK strategic policy community has simply stagnated in response to the challenges of recent years. Indeed, since 2010, and even within the SDSR itself, there is considerable evidence that it not only recognises the strategic implications of complexity, but also that it is increasingly innovating in response. Most of these innovations remain relatively novel in application, immature in their impact on the policy process and subject to series of continuing challenges. However, they are indicative of the manner in which the UK strategy making system is transforming itself in response to change, and point the direction in which it is likely to consolidate in future. They fall into three broad categories: methodological innovations that aim to capture the dynamics of complexity in the security environment and attempt to impose strategic order and priority on decision-making on this basis; strategic policy developments that aim to further focus the analysis of the NSS and function as guides to action in specific areas of concern; and institutional innovations that aim to marshal organisational complexity and establish coherent modes of strategic practice that can cross departmental boundaries and exploit the range of expertise and capacity that resides in government and beyond.

One of the novel features of both the 2010 NSS and SDSR was their prominent use of formal risk assessment methodologies to comprehend the security environment, and to discipline strategic planning decisions on this basis (Edmunds 2012, pp. 270–272). Thus, for example, the narrative and conclusions of the NSS were premised against the findings of a newly implemented National Security Risk Assessment (NSRA). The NSRA compares and prioritises a wide range of national security risks against the twin criteria of likelihood and severity of impact. It then groups these risks into three tiers indicating their significance and priority for action. The NSRA takes place against the background of a wider National Risk Assessment (NRA) process, and, along with the NSS and SDSRs themselves, is reviewed at regular intervals.[4] This new approach has not been without its difficulties. The emphasis on risk arguably came at the expense of identifying strategic opportunity, leading to a charge from some critics that the two documents were ill-focused and overly reactive (JCNSS 2012a, p. 16). At the same time, and in the absence of a clear sense of strategic priority from above, the contestable and contingent nature of the NSRA findings provided a new framework within which old organisational disputes over resource allocation between the services and other interests could take place, to the detriment of national strategy as a coherent whole (Shaw 2013). Finally, and in contrast to the risk-based policy approach employed by the US in its 2010 Quadrennial Defense Review (QDR), the NSRA was essentially one dimensional in its methodology, focusing only on external security issues rather than considering these against other dimensions of risk such as those relating to, for example, organisational effectiveness or political legitimacy.[5]

Nevertheless, there was much about the risk-based approach of the NSS and SDSR that was genuinely innovative. The framework introduced a clearly articulated strategic rationale against which to discipline and prioritise difficult defence spending choices at a time of unprecedented public austerity, in defence as elsewhere. Thus, for example, the decision to withdraw the UK's fixed wing carrier strike capabilities until the introduction of new aircraft carriers in 2020 was made on the explicit basis of a risk assessment of likely security challenges and military requirements over this period (MoD 2010, p. 23). Similarly, new investment was targeted towards cyber security against a judgement of its continuing significance to national security in the coming decade. These judgements and decisions remain controversial. Even so, it is striking the extent to which they reflect an imperative to both recognise and impose a form of strategic order on a complex and uncertain security environment, and to make policy decisions and resource allocations on this basis (Cornish and Dorman 2013, p. 1192).

The SDSR has also become a regular, five-yearly process, rather than an intermittent exercise conducted according to the priority of the government of the day. The period between the 2010 SDSR and its predecessor, the 1998 *Strategic Defence Review* was over a decade; a decade which included the Kosovo and Sierra Leone interventions, the attacks of 9/11 and the 7/7 bombings, and the wars in Iraq and Afghanistan, and over the course of which the global strategic landscape changed beyond recognition. The introduction of a regular cycle for the SDSR process follows the US example with its QDR, and is an explicit recognition of the fast moving and changeable nature of the contemporary security environment. In the UK case, the run-up to the 2015 SDSR and possibly NSS[6] has been characterised by the continued development and application of the NRA/NSRA framework, alongside a series of other innovations that were designed explicitly to grapple with the problem of complexity. These increasingly draw on so-called 'foresight' methodologies, the aim of which is to provide anticipatory, often probabilistic assessments of future strategic trends against which decision-making can take place, using techniques such as horizon scanning, driver and trend analysis, and scenario planning.[7]

For example, the Development, Concepts and Doctrine Centre (DCDC) of the MoD produces a five-yearly Global Strategic Trends (GST) report, which is timed to coincide with the preparations for the SDSR. The 2014 iteration of this document aims to provide strategic context for decision-makers by considering the evolution of current and potential trends in the defence and security environment out to the middle of the century. DCDC's work in this area is wide-ranging and methodologically eclectic, drawing on a range of different approaches including: gap analysis of relevant existing literatures, the NSRA and previous GST reports; the commissioning of essays from and consultations with experts from the policy community, academia and industry; and a comprehensive mapping and analysis of global security trends and their relationship to each other (DCDC 2013). DCDC's work on strategic futures parallels similar exercises across government, albeit with specific departmental emphases and generally narrower foci, including those of the Defence Science and Technology Laboratory's Futures and Innovation group, the Cabinet Office's Horizon Scanning Programme, the Foresight Programme at the Department for Business, Innovation and Skills and the Department for Environment, Food and Rural Affairs' Horizon Scanning and Futures team. All of these groups and organisations aim to provide a detailed sense of context through which strategic risk and opportunity can be judged and against which decision-making can take place.

On their own, of course, this proliferation of new methodologies does not represent a new dawn of effective strategy making in the UK. However, they are indicative of a sustained, cross-governmental attempt to grapple with the contemporary strategic problematic. They underpin an emergent approach to British strategy making that avoids grand hegemonic narratives in favour of a strategic adaptivity bounded by futures-orientated analysis. They also illustrate a shift away from unitary, linear notions of national interest, reflecting instead a model of action that understands strategy as comprising a series of intractable, ongoing and even contradictory policy challenges, which in consequence lend themselves to an iterative process of positive adaptation rather than to definitive solution (Ryan 2009, pp. 74–86). This 'adaptable posture' in UK strategy making has not been without its critics, with the Joint Committee on the National Security Strategy (JCNSS) for example, arguing that it risks short-termism in government policy and is insufficiently convincing as a guide to action (JCNSS 2012a, p. 16). Such concerns seem less about the efficacy of the new strategic approaches pioneered by DCDC and others, which are by their very nature longer-term in outlook, and more about the manner in which they are translated into strategic practice. Indeed, it is clear that if these new analytical innovations are to have strategic purchase, and avoid repeating the most egregious pathologies of the 2010 SDSR, then they need to be able to be effectively coordinated, applied and prioritised in ways that both inform decision-making in the real world and mobilise action across government.

In fact, the period since 2010 has also seen a series of further developments intended to address these and similar issues. They include the development of sub-strategies to the NSS in priority thematic areas, such as the International Defence Engagement Strategy, the Building Stability Overseas Strategy and the Serious and Organised Crime Strategy, amongst others, the aim of which is to provide a more focused and purposive framework for action – and, where considered appropriate, cross-departmental working – than is the case in the NSS itself (JCNSS 2012b, pp. 4–5, 7–8). These documents go much further towards outlining the 'ways' of UK strategy; that is, the manner in which the defence and security establishment is to set about achieving the strategic goals outlined in the NSS. Other initiatives include the establishment of new cross-departmental structures for strategic decision-making, in particular the creation of a national security council (NSC) alongside new national security adviser (NSA) and two deputy NSA (for foreign policy and intelligence, security and resilience) posts. The civil service as a whole is introducing organisational and professional changes to facilitate working across departmental boundaries,[8] while defence specifically has also undergone a significant reorganisation under the auspices of the Levene Report on Defence Reform (Levene et al. 2011). This has seen the establishment of a stronger, more strategically orientated defence board, the aim of which is to take major cross-service decisions relating to the armed forces under the overall direction of the NSC; the creation of Joint Forces Command to oversee and implement joint military capabilities such as military intelligence and cyber warfare; and the devolution of greater autonomy to single service chiefs as part of a revised framework of accountability and governance in the armed forces as a whole.

Taken together, these initiatives represent the biggest revision of the architecture of British strategy making for decades, and signify a whole of government attempt to take seriously the challenges of contemporary strategy practice. Against this background, the claim that the UK continues to operate in a strategic vacuum is neither wholly true, nor entirely fair. Even so, it would be equally disingenuous to pretend that the problems of British strategy have been resolved. While the UK's new methodologies of strategic complexity offer a nuanced framework against which decision-making can take place, they remain only one component of the strategy making process, and their role is limited to informing strategic judgement rather than proscribing it. For their part, foresight and risk-based approaches certainly offer a compelling dimension to contemporary strategic analysis. However, they themselves have been criticised for the epistemological reliability of applying quasi-scientific and often probabilistic modelling techniques to complex social phenomena (Ryan 2009, p. 84); their capacity to deal with high-impact, low-probability, so-called 'Black Swan' events; and the extent to which they have been able to recognise and incorporate critical or non-orthodox perspectives. Such oversights were apparent in the previous NSS, where the JCNSS expressed its concern that 'central and uncomfortable' questions had been neglected, including the strategic and security impact of the eurozone crisis and the uncertainties posed by the planned referenda on Scottish independence and UK membership of the EU (JCNSS 2012c, pp. 4–5). More widely, and as noted above, there is a continuing danger that by placing risk at the heart of the strategy making process, the potential for recognising and creating strategic opportunity, whether security-related or otherwise, is missed.

These new approaches thus complement rather than replace the need for other forms of capacity in the British strategic policy community. These include regional and country-specific expertise, as well as ready access to specialist knowledge in areas like cyber security and climate change, and the corporate memory and experience to translate these analyses into effective policy. As others have remarked (Cornish and Dorman 2009, pp. 253–254), the decline in civil service numbers since the late 2000s, the shrinkage of indigenous departmental research capacities in the mainstream Foreign and Commonwealth Office and MoD, together with the increasing prevalence of new cross-departmental career paths for civil servants themselves, means that some of these functions have been eroded in recent years. Recent efforts have certainly been made to engage external expertise to meet these gaps, from academia, the think tank community and the industrial sector, whether through direct consultation or by jointly hosting specific research funding calls with the UK research councils. Even so, the manner in which such relationships are and will be able to influence British strategic practice remains to be seen, particularly with regard to their capacity to constructively challenge rather than simply validate policy orthodoxies, and their ultimate impact on policy itself (JCNSS 2012a, pp. 34–35; 2012c., p. 5).

Indeed, the second, and deeper, question underpinning many of these issues concerns the extent to which innovations in British strategic analysis, however well executed, are actually able to influence policy outcomes through the structures of decision-making. Here, the impact of institutional change in the strategic policy community has been more measured. Nowhere is this more apparent – or arguably more significant – than in the function of the NSC. In conception, the NSC was created in order to lead and articulate UK strategic thinking at a truly national level; able to both incorporate and surmount interests and perspectives from across government and beyond. Under the chairmanship of the prime minister, its permanent membership comprises eight cabinet ministers from key departments, with others, including the chief of the defence staff and the chair of the Joint Intelligence Committee, regularly invited to attend. The NSC structure also comprises a number of sub-committees that are formed to address specific issues such as nuclear issues or the Libyan intervention of 2011 (NSC[L]). Since its formation, the NSC and its sub-committees have certainly been active in areas ranging from the development of the NSS and SDSR to the conflicts in Afghanistan and Libya. In so doing, in the JCNSS's assessment, it has undoubtedly been able to function as 'a valued and important forum for collective discussion' across departments (JCNSS 2012c, p. 5).[9]

Nevertheless, the NSC has struggled to act as the engine for strategic thinking and direction for the UK policy community, at least to date. While it played an important role as a forum for brokering discussions and disagreements between individual departments during the SDSR process, it was not able to lead the review as a whole. Indeed, it only published the 2010 NSS, over which it had primary oversight, subsequent to the SDSR and so was essentially beholden to it rather than setting its agenda from the outset. The predominance of a brokering rather than a leadership role might be excused by the rapidity of the SDSR process and the new-born status of the NSC itself at that time. However, it is not clear that the committee has been able to fully assert itself on UK strategy making in subsequent years. Major strategic policy initiatives – such as the transformative Future Reserves 2020 and Army 2020 documents – have been driven by individual departments (in these cases the MoD), while the committee itself appears also to have devoted considerable effort to operational matters in Afghanistan, Libya and elsewhere.[10] At the same time, the NSC is largely dependent on the departments themselves for research and analysis and has only a limited capacity to undertake such work itself, or to commission it from outside.[11] While this avoids the problem of duplication across government, it also limits the extent to which the NSC is able to move beyond existing departmental agendas and mindsets and reinforces its strategic brokering rather than leadership role.

Finally, the NSC too is bounded in its remit and so limited in how far it can grasp a truly national strategic agenda. National security is itself only a component of national strategy in its broadest sense and, as Sir Peter Ricketts, NSA between 2010–2012, has observed, in this context, ultimately 'the only place where [national strategy] comes together finally is the Cabinet [itself].'[12] For the PASC, this represents a lost opportunity for the NSC to function as a 'deliberative forum with access to proper analysis and assessment' at a truly national strategic level against which the Cabinet discuss options and make decisions (PASC 2010, p. 18). Moreover, it also begs the question of how far the recent innovations in UK strategic analysis and assessment are actually able to feed into and influence decision-making at the highest levels of government.

Conclusion

The period since 2010 has seen considerable innovation in the UK strategic policy community, in ways that have built on and consolidated the approaches first introduced in the NSS and SDSR. There are other signs of a reinvigoration of strategic thinking in the UK too. It is striking, for example, that so much of the popular and parliamentary debate that led to the August 2013 defeat of the British government on the issue of potential military intervention in Syria, took place within the language of ways, ends and means, and made specific reference to the extent to which it could be understood to serve the national interest – albeit a national interest that was context-driven and evolving rather than hegemonic in nature, and in which the question of public legitimacy was prominent.[13] These innovations do not represent a 'magic bullet' solution to all the challenges that have been posed to UK strategy makers, and there remain a number of areas where British strategic practice could be significantly strengthened. However, they do reflect a concerted and serious attempt to accommodate the contemporary challenges of the global security environment and to articulate an appropriate organising framework for strategic decision-making in this context.

Against this background, it is increasingly possible to divine the contours of an emergent theory of action in the British strategic policy community. It addresses a world in which strategic context is rapidly changing, and which is, in important ways, inherently unpredictable. It also takes place in an environment in which resources are constrained and choices must inevitably be made between what strategic capacities can be funded and sustained and what cannot. In so doing, it is characterised by four key principles. The first of these is a focus on adaptivity, alongside a concomitant wariness of grand strategic narratives or hegemonic notions of the national interest. Second, it is anticipatory, in that it employs a methodologically eclectic range of analytical approaches to comprehend, order and prioritise contingencies within the strategic environment, in ways that are intended to better inform decision-makers in the face of uncertainty, and to bound the principles of adaptivity noted above. Third, it is self-organising and emergent, in the sense that it emphasises departmental, and even non-governmental, diversity and bottom-up strategic analysis to gain analytical purchase on the complex and multi-dimensional security challenges that confront British strategy makers. Finally, it is, at least nascently, cross-governmental, in that it establishes institutional structures such as the NSC, whose role is to cohere these principles into a process of national decision-making and make choices about strategic risk and priority on this basis.

Undoubtedly, significant challenges remain in consolidating this approach, particularly in terms of institutional coordination and engagement at the highest levels of strategic decision-making. Yet it is perhaps ironic, given the strength of the recent critiques that have been levelled at British strategic practice in recent years, that this dissipated and iterative approach to national strategy making in the face of a very modern kind of strategic complexity accords not only with historically grounded traditions of incrementalism in British policymaking but also with the nuanced and conditional position of the British general public in relation to core questions of national interest. It also suggests that the prospect of fashioning some kind of panoptic national strategy against which to drive policy is not only politically unlikely but, given contemporary dynamics of global complexity, may be strategically undesirable too.

Notes

1. This is a revised and updated version of an article that first appeared in *International Affairs*, London, volume 90, number 3 May 2014, pp. 525–539, and is reproduced with permission.
2. 'Sir Richard Dannatt: a very honest general', *Daily Mail*, 12 October 2006.
3. 'Syria crisis: the British public has its say as two thirds oppose strikes', *Independent*, 3 September 2013.
4. UK Cabinet Office, *Fact sheet 2: National Security Risk Assessment*, https://www.gov.uk/government/uploads/system/uploads/attachment_data/file/62484/Factsheet2 National-Security-Risk-Assessment.pdf, accessed 9 September 2013.
5. The 2010 US QDR for example employs a four-dimensional risk-based policy methodology, comprising operational risk, force management risk, institutional risk and future challenges risk. The British NSRA focuses only on what the US calls 'future challenges risk' (Department of Defense 2010, pp. 89–95).
6. Unlike the SDSR, the NSS is not subject to a formal five-year cycle, though at the time of writing there was an expectation that a new NSS would precede the 2015 SDSR.
7. Cabinet Office, *Review of Cross-Government Horizon Scanning*, 13 January 2013, https://www.gov.uk/government/uploads/system/uploads/attachment_data/file/79252/Horizon_Scanning_Review_20121003.pdf, accessed 11 September 2013.
8. Policy Profession Board, *Twelve Actions to Professionalise Policy Making* (October 2013), https://www.google.co.uk/url?sa=t&rct=j&q=&esrc=s&source=web&cd=1&cad=rja&ved=0CC4QFjAA&url=http%3A%2F%2Fwww.civilservice.gov.uk%2Fwp-content%2Fuploads%2F2011%2F09%2FTwelve-Actions-Report-Web-Accessible.pdf&ei=SEllUqqmDKOS0AWq1IHYCQ&usg=AFQjCNES7BAR6lNUV8HZd-aA0DaMYndKxg&bvm=bv.54934254,d.d2k, accessed 21 October 2013.
9. JCNSS, *The Work of the Joint Committee*, p. 5.
10. The NSC(L), for example, met 62 times over the course of the Libya crisis, a frequency that led the JCNSS to comment that 'any committee meeting over 60 times in a relatively short period of time is doing far more than looking at the strategic direction of the campaign' (JCNSS 2012a, p. 27).
11. Cabinet Office, in evidence to JCNSS, *First Review* (JCNSS 2012a, p. 32).
12. Sir Peter Ricketts, NSA 2010–2012, in evidence to the PASC, *Who Does UK National Strategy?* (PASC 2010, p. 18).
13. See, for example, Hansard, 29 August 2013, c. 1452.

11
National Interest and Strategy: An Ecologically Grounded Analysis
Max Taylor

Three influences can be identified that have shaped this chapter. The first is an unscripted speech given by Mary Robinson as part of the 150 years famine commemorations in 1995 at University College, Cork, Ireland, whilst she was president of the Irish Republic. No record of this speech exists, but in a powerful account of the influence of the famine on Irish thinking, Robinson made a number of important points about the practice of Irish foreign policy, and the way a small country like Ireland has to manoeuvre and compromise to achieve its foreign policy goals, in contrast to the way large powers can, through the exercise of power, shape more benign environments for themselves. These themes have been developed and extended since that speech, particularly linking the emergence of a distinctive Irish role to changes in the sense of Irish national identity. In essence Robinson drew attention to the significance of context and what in modern parlance we might refer to as the 'ecology'[1] of foreign relations. To put the point in other terms, as Schelling (1971) noted 'People need to do the right things at the right times in relation to what others are doing' (p. 62) to achieve desired ends, and they don't achieve those ends if they fail to do that.

The second influence relates to the growing recognition of the power of new technologies in both social and political realms particularly in relation to social media.[2] In many ways we are still coming to terms with the influence of these technologies. They have been characterised by unanticipated effects, and, once adopted, by unintended consequences, particularly in social and societal areas. As far as social media are concerned, what initially seemed to be an ephemeral means of communication primarily between young people using mobile phones has become a force that influences major political decisions. As a means of collecting together and expressing public opinion the use of Twitter, to take but one example, has become a factor in the decision-making process for the US government around military engagement, for example with Syria in 2013. Twitter is also increasingly used by both government and non-government agencies to disseminate information and opinion. During the September 2013 siege of a shopping mall in Nairobi, al-Shabab, which claimed responsibility for the siege, said on its Twitter feed that the 'Kenyan government shall be held responsible for any loss of life as a result of such an imprudent move. The call is yours!'. Al-Shabab, and other terrorist groups, recognise the significance of direct communication with their audience, rather than relying on news channel mediation. At a more mundane level, sites such as Facebook have become central elements in many people's lives, serving to maintain contact between friends and relatives, and to pass on information in a direct way.

What is significant about this, at least in the West, is that this activity occurs largely outside of traditional structures and hierarchies. In China, in contrast, active efforts are made to control the use of social media that are outside traditional structures, but even with such controls the Chinese government recognises the value of using social media to monitor the public mood. The Chinese government is thought to employ more than 2 million people to monitor web activity and control the internet. Chinese state media say that these monitors are to gather and analyse public opinions and to compile reports for policymakers, and are not necessarily engaged in censorship; however, it is clear that postings dealing with politically sensitive issues are deleted and websites outside China are also monitored. Notwithstanding these particular efforts at censorship, might we see this broad development as a modern expression of what Arendt (1958) identified as 'public space', in the contemporary sense of a virtual space where citizens come together to deliberate on matters of public concern? Actions and speech are the essence of Arendt's sense of public space, a metaphor that readily extends to contemporary social media.

There is however a further quality to social media of relevance to this discussion, which relates to time and temporality. The speed of growth, change and dissemination of new innovation has grown enormously over the past ten years. The growth in access to the internet[3] for example has been phenomenal: in 1995 there were an estimated 16 million users, in 2005 there were an estimated 1,018 million users and in 2013 there were an estimated 2,749 million users, which is around 38 per cent of the world population. In Europe internet penetration is around 63 per cent of the population; in the US it is around 79 per cent, with a clear skew in general towards younger people. The significance of these figures is difficult to comprehend, but of relevance to this chapter, and associated with such rapid growth, are the enormous changes in the speed of dissemination and uptake of innovation. And as a consequence, the process of change has also speeded up.

The third influence may be seen through Carl Jung's observation that – Nature *must not* win the game, but she *cannot* lose. (Jung 1967, p. 184). This quotation emphasises the significance of essentially dynamic ecological relationships and of adaptation as an instrument of change, but also the overriding significance of environment and context which drives the process of adaptation by natural selection. Clausewitz recognised the significance of adaptation in warfare when he said, 'Never engage the same enemy for too long, or he will adapt to your tactics', a point no doubt of relevance to international relations as much as to warfare. To extend the point further, Taylor (2012) notes how we might describe Clausewitz's sense of the environment of war as 'meaningful', in the sense that the environment is perceived and acted upon – it constitutes an ecology, a relationship rather than a state of being; a relationship between behaviour and the context in which that behaviour occurs. But what Jung's comment also does is emphasise the ephemeral nature of much of what we strive for. We as individuals and collectively are engaged in a process which exists outside of us, be it in terms of navigating our own way through our personal environment, or navigating a state's path through a complex international environment. And that process relates to choice and change, which in the context of the consequences of the new technologies and social media noted above suggests a potential acceleration of effect.

The nature of national interest

If we now turn to the issue of 'national interest', it seems reasonable to assert that, from a common sense perspective, there is an expectation at least within the liberal democracies that a nation should strive towards goals and have ambitions in order to protect and support its population, and furthermore a nation's leadership might be judged in terms of how it achieves those goals. In an environment where consent is required citizens, it might be argued, should reasonably expect no less. Collective action towards these ends is what we refer to as the pursuit of national interest; the source and nature of such goals, however, are complex as we will note later.

However, even the most cursory reading of the literature suggests that what is pursued as national interest seems to be full of confusion, lacks obvious evidential referents, and seems to have an intimate relationship with local political concerns. To identify just a few uncertainties: Is national interest an objective state of some kind that describes a personal and societal context (of perhaps, say, wellbeing, military dominance, ethnic or religious pre-eminence or economic benefit) to which we collectively do or should aspire and strive to achieve? If so, where does that aspiration come from – a political ideology, a religion, a moral or social imperative? Or is the critical element a form of the particularism identified by Huntington (1997) mediated by the new technologies in general, and social media in particular? Alternatively, is national interest some kind of higher-level point of aspiration that, whilst perhaps unachievable, transcends individual and sectional interests and makes reference to a notional, almost platonic, 'essence' of what a 'nation' should be competitively striving for, in contrast to what it currently is. But again, where might this aspirational state come from? Or, is national interest not a state of affairs in itself at all, but simply a reflection of a kind of inevitable meta-biological process, the working out of a nation-based homeostatic principle, where forces impacting on states ultimately result in the emergence of a condition of dynamic equilibrium – the inevitable result perhaps of a process of meta-balance of power. From a different but related perspective, perhaps all that can be identified is a set of rules that seem to apply in some general way that enables us to identify how we get to a sense of national interest, rather than identifying what that state actually is – in other words, do we see it as a process rather than an end state? In that case, is national interest simply the expression, at a collective level, of self-interest through economic and social power driven by temporary (and changing) expedience? However, perhaps all of the above just unnecessarily complicates things. Is the concept of national interest simply a rhetorical device with no objective meaning at all, other than something that is invoked as local need requires, to justify and define in political terms partisan (and presumably ultimately ephemeral) public policy, as Reicher and Hopkins (2001) imply?

One element of the conundrum we can be sure of, even if it adds to rather than limits our difficulties, is that the concept of 'nation' appears to be necessarily embedded in the concept of national interest. Indeed, Huntington (1997) asserts that national interest derives from national identity – 'we have to know who we are before we can know what our interests are' (p. 28). If Huntington is correct, there is certainly supportive evidence to suggest that a sense of national identity is a meaningful concept that influences us in terms of the behavioural choices we make. Recent work by Joyce et al. (2013) illustrates this by describing different forms of national identity expression and behaviour choices amongst Irish travellers and Irish students; and Lai et al. (2013) suggest that pro-social behaviour, such as volunteering, is strongly related to an empirically measured high sense of national interest, at least amongst a Chinese population.

But the idea of nation, of course, is a relatively recent invention (as opposed to other ways of identifying higher order collective focuses, such as family or religion), and this suggests both a degree of social construction to the concept, and a temporary quality given shifting ideas of what constitutes nationhood. If the idea of nation is a social construction, then a more fine-grain analysis has to consider within this form of aggregation which part of the 'nation', from which we might draw identity and allegiance, we might or should have regard to: the rich and wealthy? the most numerous social group? Which, if any, interest group can be or should be privileged in this way?

We might see the nature of social construction at work here, at least in the short term, in two ways. One sense might relate to how political rhetoric is used to construct meaning (Reicher et al. 1997). The other might relate to a popular sense of nation that draws on symbols, flags, the trappings of popular culture and emotion that might be used to engage with and illustrate in some sense what national interest is about. However, perhaps from our loftier perspective we would seek to distinguish between what Billig (1995) describes as 'Banal Nationalism' as the facilitator of an essentially ephemeral partisan process, and whatever ultimate more substantive understanding of 'national interest' might be aspired to.

Notwithstanding the above, as a concept, national interest has attracted relatively little psychological interest, and has (perhaps as a consequence) little if any technical psychological meaning. Psychologists are of course well versed in understanding issues to do with individual interest, and national interest might be regarded in some sense as the aggregate of a lot of individual interests. Viewing it in this way might in turn relate to broader collective concepts such as public interest (in contributing, for example, in some sense to 'public good') that might have psychological resonance. Social psychologists do talk about collective activity and there are a number of tools with which to explore collective decision-making, for example, or collective action in crowd behaviour, areas where it might be thought there is some, perhaps tangential, relevance. Work on attitudinal and identity change and development, as noted earlier, might approach closer in this sense to what might be meant by national interest, particularly if there is an assumed correlation between the expression of attitudinal qualities and a sense of identity – which is questionable (van Doorn et al. 2007).

Indeed, much of the attitudinal work in this area has been criticised as being limited and simplistic, and essentially rhetorical in quality. Condor, Gibson and Abell (2006) for example identify how national surveys which ask respondents to indicate the extent to which they identify as British and/or English tend to underestimate the extent to which such attitudes are much more complex and nuanced than the headline accounts suggest, particularly in the way these terms are used in everyday language.

Another related collective approach might be when the expression of national interest is seen as analogous to some kind of actuarial aggregate of aspiration or need. Leaving aside the problem referred to earlier of aggregating what and who, this has certain attractions in that it seems to offer a possibility of some kind of numerical evidence on which to base a sense of interest – a potential democratic operational definition even. However Trivers (2011) has effectively criticised this approach, characterising it as describing a non-existent individual (or collection of individuals) that has pejoratively been termed 'actuarial man'. Such an actuarial sense of national interest, as well as being essentially fictional (descriptions of central tendency necessarily homogenise difference), also necessarily looks back towards what has been, rather than forward to what should be for the future; and as the concept of national interest tends to be used, future looking seems to be an important element.

The rhetorical use of the concept of national interest to generate support for essentially partisan political policies, which we noted earlier as an element in the construction of national identity, has been illustrated by Dickerson (1998) in his analysis of televised political discussion. In this study, he noted that,

> the concept of National Interest was used as a rhetorical device by politicians to both construct social realities around particular ideological positions (supporting of course their own position), and to engage in activities such as blaming or exonerating to support and argue for essentially local partisan positions. National Interest used in this way therefore becomes a resource to position arguments – to positively construct privileged political realities, and negatively position

contrary political perspectives. It becomes an end or objective with which conflicting views might be contrasted, but remains essentially a tool rather than something abstract and absolute – a form in a sense of the 'rules'-based process approach identified above.

The best that seems possible to conclude from this brief survey of psychological context is that 'national interest' as used seems to be a slippery concept with little substance other than as an element in political rhetoric. Indeed, from an evidence-based perspective, notions like 'idealist' and 'realist' that occur in discussions of national interest appear to be not much more than theoretical descriptions of processes, and seem to reflect little either on end states or individual action in the terms we have identified here.

Indeed idealist and realist notions can be subjected to a further, quite substantial criticism. In a worrying way, they draw on what Lewis (1994) has termed 'folk psychology' explanations – psychological theory constituted by the platitudes about the mind that the man or woman in the street might be inclined to endorse. As a means of organising our everyday lives, folk psychology (or as some would term it, a 'theory of mind') suffices. We get around our world adequately, and we generally manage to adjust to our environments using broad 'rules of thumb'. But serious questions must be asked if this form of naive psychologising is a substitute for evidence-based understanding. Although they don't make reference to notions of folk psychology, Shleifer and Treisman's (2011) critical analysis of Russian international behaviour illustrate this point. They note the prevalence of what are essentially folk psychology concepts like 'impulsivity', 'childishness' and 'wounded ego' in accounts of the underlying motivations behind Russian policy. Attractive and simple as these concepts might be, Schleifer and Treisman note they offer little to progress analysis, and have limited evidential support. A further substantive weakness associated with a dependence on folk psychology explanations is the tendency to attribute individual or collective mental states based on the observer's view, rather than the evidence. This is an example of how the ideology of the observer becomes imported into our understanding of the actions of other people, thus both distorting our understanding and privileging the observer's view. Interestingly, Schleifer and Treisman offer essentially an ecologically based account as a corrective to what they describe as the flawed 'psychology' accounts; they locate the determinants of Russian policy in the context of choices made in the immediate geographical and internal and external political environment.

An evolutionary and ecological perspective

Perhaps, however, the above discussion explores the concept of national interest from the wrong psychological perspective. There are other psychological ways of thinking that might reflect on the problem, and offer a way of moving the debate forward, taking us away from both individualist and ideological perspectives, and furthermore grounding our understanding within that of the natural sciences. The title of this chapter makes reference to an ecologically grounded approach; if the discussion is located within an evolutionary and ecological perspective, we may be able to progress the debate. In the following, taking an evolutionary psychology approach we will first explore what an ecologically grounded understanding of national interest might consist of, exploring both context and process, and how that might apply to the general concept of national interest, as distinct from a particular country or nation's sense of national interest. We will then explore what this might mean within a UK context.[4]

Evolutionary psychology locates our understanding of behaviour in the relationship between our environment and, essentially, our evolved biological *adaptation* to that environment. Central to this is the notion that our evolved brain structures (and therefore our cognitive and behavioural capacities) underpin and essentially determine our ability to respond and adapt to the environment. For example, Johnson (2009) explores our understanding of asymmetric conflict from this perspective, discussing why notions of adaptation help us understand why the weaker element of a conflict (weaker from the perspective of less military power) paradoxically often seems to have the advantage over a militarily stronger adversary (Johnson 2009). He notes, for example, that weaker sides have more diverse combatants, increasing the 'trait-pool' leading to a high level of innovation; adaptation in weaker sides is enhanced through military pressure; and weaker sides, through longer exposure to conflict gain experience and learning, in contrast to more powerful combatants who rotate soldiers on combat tours. Clearly, situational and cultural factors are also relevant in particular examples, but it remains an uncomfortable feature of contemporary irregular warfare (as we have seen in Iraq and Afghanistan) that weaker sides in asymmetric conflict paradoxically seem to have the advantage. Perhaps, as Johnson suggests this is because 'Weaker sides adapt faster and more effectively' (p. 89).

The emphasis on adaptation does not necessarily mean, however, that the time frames we need to consider are glacial – in a sense we live in a short-term world, and through natural selection we have acquired the capacity to function in that world. As a result of changes in the new technologies as we discussed in the introduction, timescales may even be further shortening.

In summary, from an evolutionary psychology perspective, it is natural selection that has provided us both individually and collectively with adaptations to the environment in which we have evolved and in which we continue to evolve. The emphasis on the link between biological and psychological adaptation is what really distinguishes evolutionary psychology from other approaches to understanding behaviour. But one of the great challenges in understanding behaviour from these perspectives is how we link individual factors that control behaviour (for which we may see a rather obvious evolutionary context which essentially operates at an individual level), with large-scale social factors that seem to influence behaviour in aggregate (into which category we might place national interest).

Clearly big social processes influence us, but how do these translate into individual action and how do we understand the effects of differences in timescales between big social movements and individual directed behaviour; how can individual forces that are frequently idiosyncratic (and arguably because of that have potential evolutionary benefits through contributing to variance) co-exist, aggregate and interact with big social processes? An example of a big social process can be seen in what Rapoport (2002) has described as 'waves of terrorism', a powerful way of understanding terrorist behaviour in which 'waves' extend over periods of decades and at one level do seem to characterise the shifting focus and qualities of terrorist activity. Yet terrorist action is made up of individuals doing things. However compelling Rapoport's analysis is, we are no clearer about what determines the waves, nor do we understand how individual behaviour (which is primarily determined by local factors) relates to such large-scale proximate factors. This analysis applies to notions of national interest as much as terrorism.

Schelling (1971), in his paper 'On the ecology of micromotives', goes some way to exploring that conceptual gap by drawing our attention to the significance of both process and the perspective from which we look at that process and its consequences. To begin our analysis, we might assert that one potential problem in analysis is the widely held assumption that we should conceptualise big social processes as something from which individual behaviour derives meaning; from an ecological perspective we might in fact invert that relationship and suggest that the social processes we observe are fundamentally the aggregate of responses of individuals 'each going about his own business, most of them... without the slightest idea that they are engaged together in selective adaptation.... The results are statistical, collective and aggregate; the process is molecular and individual' (p. 89).

If we disturb a flock of migratory geese, they take flight; the observer on the ground sees not a random mellée but an organised flight of birds that rapidly settle into a 'V' formation. When closely observed the individual bird's behaviour is more diverse, and individual geese change places, move around and break away, to return; odd outliers seem to persist, and occasionally smaller 'V' formations break off and return. But the overwhelming impression is of an organised structure, with direction and purpose, because that is what a 'statistical, collective and aggregate' perspective looks like to an observer at a distance. But to the participant birds, we need ascribe no future planning, no particular purpose other than to escape, reflecting the genetic and morphological possibilities each bird has, the particular environment they find themselves in and an inherent sensitivity to positive feedback. Put more generally, as Schelling notes (p. 89) there need be 'no universal teleology relating individual adaptations to collective results, neither a beneficent teleology nor a pernicious one'. And what of course follows from that is that 'some adaptive processes work out fine and some do not'. This is natural selection in action.

Using the example of a flock of migratory geese might seem an odd basis on which to draw conclusions about national interest. Its significance for our purpose is that it illustrates complex organised behaviour which has origins in one sense in an immediate issue (threat or escape from a perceived threat) but which is expressed through complex structured biological systems, tempered by morphological constraints that, critically, require no assumed teleology. It can be thought of as a form of complex system[5] – a series of interacting components asymmetrically organised. We might take other examples of complex systems that draw on evolutionary contexts which more obviously apply to thinking about national interest. Johnson and Thayer (2013) for example explore how we might understand contemporary warfare in terms of our evolutionary past. They note that if we have regard to the broader context of the emergence of aggressive behaviour,

> We... need to amend Clausewitz. Humans do indeed wage war for political purposes, but long before war for raison d'etat there was war for resources. International politics is therefore not the root of war but merely an example of it – the continuation of seeking access to valuable resources by other means.

In their terms, 'war is one of Mother Nature's solutions to compete successfully for resources'. And as resource, identity and availability changes, so we see ebb and flow of pressures, the dynamic of change.

Ferguson (2010) reflects on how processes of international relations might be thought of in terms of complex systems. He argues that minor changes (analogous to the perceived threat experienced by our flock of geese, perhaps the local source of a conflict, or a sudden innovative discovery) might give rise to unanticipated, and potentially catastrophic, changes without any necessary teleological quality, or without necessarily even self-knowledge on the part of the participants in the larger events of which those minor changes form a part. Whether there is a direction or deterministic quality to such change (as for example Oswald Spengler might suggest in terms of the decline of the West [Spengler 1932] or in the equally apocalyptic future envisaged by Girard [2010]) or whether they are merely random occurrences dependent on chance, or indeed whether instead they reflect emergent properties of complex systems is a more difficult question; but our fleeing goose, our soldier fighting a war or our innovator are all generally unaware of the broader import of action, and, importantly, need not necessarily be aware for the action to have significance.

When observing a large-scale social process, we are not seeing an end product, but rather a part of a dynamic and changing process. We, the observers, may see an organised whole (and the gestalt psychologists have explored how we see structure in complex visual and cognitive arrays) because we draw inferences from only one array of elements of a complex temporal sequence, but we may have no knowledge of its aetiology or likely outcome. For the immediate participant in such a process, there may be no necessary sense of awareness, purpose or direction. Given that circumstances may diminish behavioural options open to the individual, this will further limit choice and flexibility.

What links the big and little accounts? In the sense we have used here, one central concept that might help us to understand the mediation between the ecological environment and behaviour, and between large and small issues, is the concept of *affordance*. This concept is grounded in the perceptual psychology of J.J. Gibson (1977, 1986), who argued that visual stimuli in our environment suggest how we should interact with them. More recently the concept has been extended to include not just visual stimuli, but a much broader range of social qualities and engagements that might be characterised as 'actionable properties between the world and an actor' (Norman 1999) in both an individual and a social and societal sense. Extending the utility of the concept, Taylor and Currie (2012) have explored how ideas about affordance might be of value in better understanding terrorism and political violence.

Three fundamental properties of affordances can be identified. First, that an affordance exists relative to the action capabilities of a particular actor. Second, that the existence of an affordance is independent of the actor's ability to perceive it. Finally, that an affordance does not change as the needs and goals of the actor change. In my earlier discussion of the concept of affordance (Taylor 2012) I explored how the essentially perceptual qualities of an affordance might play a role in facilitating the expression of particular kinds of behaviour. The central point to emphasise is 'the essential "complementarity" between organism and environment' (Scarantino 2003) that determines how we resolve the behavioural choices confronting us, either at a local proximal level or at a more complex distal level. As with rational choice perspectives on decision-making, with which this approach shares many assumptions, the idea of affordance emphasises the significance of factors determining choice. But it recognises, as Simon (1991) did with the concept of 'bounded rationality' in the context of rational choice theory, that the determinants of choice, whilst rational, are limited not by mathematics or logic, but by the information the individual has available to him. In many cases this may be essentially perceptual (or at least sensory) dependant, and furthermore can be usefully conceptualised in terms of affordance qualities.

The concept of affordance is grounded in an ecological approach, and is in many respects a core quality on which other ecological processes draw. In the sense used here, ecology is that branch of biology that deals with the relations of organisms to one another and to their physical surroundings. It also refers to the study of the interaction of people with their environment. Affordance implies a world where we interact with opportunities and choices – affordance makes some things more likely than others, but in particular and at times idiosyncratic ways. We can influence those choices by the way we design things, or by what we have done in the past, but ultimately biology and ecology determine how and what choices are made. In the sense used here then, ecologies are self-organising, interactive, adaptive and thrive on variance and redundancy: in the terms used above, they are complex systems. In this sense therefore the Darwinian notion of survival of the fittest understands the fittest as those best able to adapt to change in the environment, and to adapt the environment itself, rather than, in a more conventional sense, survival of the strongest (Williams 2012) – a very important distinction in the context of national interest. What is important to stress in this chapter is that structuring our understanding of choice and opportunity in this way at both an individual and collective level does not simply imply passivity in the face of events. Affordances are not *in* the environment, but in the *interaction* with the environment.

The concept of affordance has particular resonance in the contemporary digitally networked environment. With the globalisation of information flow, and the ability of the internet to influence behaviour through social networking, it represents a useful tool, given our analysis here, in understanding how forces which affect national interest might emerge in future. Knor-Cetina (2005) has explored the implications of this in terms of microstructures, stressing the significance of 'flat' network structures, and the emergent qualities that facilitate choice and adaptation.

Adaptation (as a consequence of choice) lies at the very heart of any sense of political change, and a necessary element of a process of adaptation is innovation. Innovation in this sense refers to the expression of variance in behaviour between similar actors in similar circumstances. Such variance also lies at the very heart of evolutionary change at an individual level, and we can assume a similar process to lie at the core of relationships between countries and societies. Variance creates new possibilities for structuring the world, and for interacting with it, creating the capacity for the emergence of advantage and adaptation. Our social context has always offered this, but contemporary digitised society provides a rapid and hitherto unprecedented capacity to rapidly generate such variation, interaction and access to information. This lies at the heart of the changing international context in which we might see a changed sense of national interest. The speed of technical innovation in recent years has advanced this process.

Before moving to consider what this might mean in terms of our understanding of British national interest, we must raise one further issue, related to the tendency in this area to privilege one explanation over another to meet an author's *post hoc* ideological perspective or political agenda. This is not denying a political context to national interest, nor a social or collective context. But debates about national interest tend to be characterised by a sense of what things should be, rather than what they are, and are often characterised by *post hoc propter hoc* arguments. This seems to suggest a need for conceptual clarity; it also strongly suggests a need for 'non-theoretical' reference points to act as benchmarks. If the kind of analysis presented here is at all meaningful, it has profound potential consequences, in that it challenges Weberian assumptions of organisation and order which we often assume to be a 'given' in understanding social structure. In Knorr-Cetina's words, 'the texture of the global world becomes articulated through microstructural patterns that develop in the shadow of (but liberated from) national and local institutional patterns' (Knorr-Cetina 2005, p. 214).

The above discussion of affordance, and its ecological context, has pointed us towards a different set of concepts for understanding how we might conceptualise national interest from those conventionally employed; perhaps these are best seen as concepts which enable us to identify how we get to a sense of national interest, rather than an assertion of what national interest actually is. In other words, in the terms described here we can see national interest as a dynamic ecological process rather than its product. The challenge for policymakers is therefore to recognise this, and to harness it in such a way that nature must not win.

Implications for a sense of British national interest

In the grounds of Jervaulx Abbey, North Yorkshire, is a commemorative bench. Like others there that identify and commemorate loved ones, this carries a commemorative engraving with the words,

> It is upon the Navy under the providence of God that the safety and welfare of this Empire depend.

This is a variant of the preamble to the original Articles of War of the British navy written in Charles II's reign (1660–1685). It is a quotation that frequently appears in one form or another, but unlike the original quotation, which makes reference to 'realm', or the similar reference in the Navy Discipline Act 1866, which makes reference to 'Kingdom', this usage refers to 'Empire'. The bench is not particularly old, but shows some weathering – perhaps it is 80 or 90 years old.[6]

About 80 or 90 years ago, reference to empire would not have seemed especially out of place. In 2013, at the time of writing, it is inconceivable that such a reference would now be made. Times have changed. Then, the British navy was a force to be reckoned with and to be celebrated as the guardian of an empire that seemed to our parents and grandparents something real and tangible; now the British navy has been emasculated to the point of near irrelevance (Blackham and Prins 2010), and the empire no longer exists. The significance of this is that it illustrates how, in a relatively short period of time, what might have seemed like a fundamental quality and order of life has simply disappeared.[7] The decline of the British Empire was extraordinarily rapid; as Ferguson (2010) notes 'the United Kingdom's age of hegemony was effectively over less than a dozen years after its victories over Germany and Japan' ended the Second World War.

Ferguson suggests this rapid decline reflects the tendency for complex adaptive systems to suddenly move from stability to instability. British society has changed, continues to change rapidly, and at least from inside seems to be changing in unpredictable directions. Indeed, current economic and social circumstances might lead to a suspicion that the period of instability is not yet complete. The challenge for policymakers seeking to optimise possible choices in this complex unstable world is to recognise the potential of unpredictability, the role of self-corrective and feedback systems, and to at least seek to better understand the self-organising, interactive, adaptive and affordance opportunities of a world that thrives on variance and redundancy. For a nation, such as the UK, that has lost economic and military power this might be the best mechanism for the expression of national interest that we can achieve.

The nature of some of the forces leading to unpredictability has been discussed above, and perhaps the most important element relates to technological changes over which a country like Britain can exercise little if any influence. These changes are also necessarily bound up with economic change.

Whilst it is of course important not to over-emphasise the significance of this at the expense of more traditional ways of thinking about the world, it is also important to recognise our poor ability to anticipate the consequences of technical change, and to recognise that change can generate unintended consequences in timescales that are unpredictable, but probably rapid (as Ferguson 2010, noted). In terms of our local experience the new technologies illustrate this, but are not necessarily unique in this respect. If an element of national interest is to maximise for the UK the social and economic benefits of the contemporary world, the analysis offered here presents an important window of opportunity, and seems to imply a need for openness to the possibility of change and an effort to develop useful lenses of the kind identified in this chapter through which to view the world. What also follows, given this, is that modelling outcomes based on assumptions about optimisation, for example, are unlikely to be useful; nor are models of future change based on actuarial assessment likely to be helpful.

Undoubtedly, there is the need for a holistic approach drawing on not just official structures, but civil society agencies (including commercial organisations) to identify priorities and opportunities. The evidence suggests that governments in the modern world do not produce innovation; nor do they generate change. To place this in the ecological and evolutionary psychology context developed in this chapter, as suggested earlier, survival of the fittest in this sense means having the fitness to adapt to change in the environment, and to adapt the environment itself; the structures that might be put in place to do this are important, but follow from an understanding of the structure of the environment (particularly its physical, ecological, psychological and social affordance qualities). It also follows that we need to explore ways that will allow such flexibility to emerge, and the implication of this chapter is that this will not necessarily lie exclusively (or indeed at all) within governments or politics, but with an understanding of the accelerating ecological and evolutionary context in which we live. This represents a very real challenge for understanding how we might in the future engage with the process whereby national interest is identified.

Where does this lead? The first step is to recognise the issues that are of concern and how they can be addressed, and how they relate to the social and psychological environment. We also need to systematically explore what affordance opportunities the environment offers, and the ways in which our environment interacts with opportunity to enable and facilitate effective choice. There is clearly a sense of demand (what people want) and supply (what is available or possible to meet those demands); and a challenge for any policymaker is to adapt to changes in the environment to achieve these ends, or at least to limit negative consequences, and perhaps also where possible to adapt the environment itself. This in turn implies mechanisms that balance the potential costs of alternative decisions, in other words balancing risk and minimising the cost of error in a world of uncertainty and complexity. An important element of this is may be the recognition that decisional biases which are often regarded as inevitable limitations to effective decision-making may paradoxically represent adaptive solutions to *evolutionary* decisional challenges, and the development of strategies that maximise fitness to adapt to change (Williams 2012). Strategies to achieve this can be found, for example, in error management theory (Johnson et al. 2013).

Opportunities for public diplomacy and opinion formation are one obvious simple area for further exploration, in relation to the new communication technologies, of the ideas presented in this chapter. The Pew Research Center report on social networking[8] systematically explored the extent of social network usage and noted, for example, that 'Expressing opinions about politics, community issues and religion is particularly common in the Arab world' (p. 2), and is a more general feature of social networking in low and middle-income nations. In contrast, more economically developed nations seem less enthusiastic in their adoption of social networking. This offers an opportunity for persuasive access to areas of the world that are difficult for the UK to influence, and for Western nations more generally (Garzone and Degano 2010), based not on intuition, but on a more systematic assessment of possibilities, affordances, choices and constraints.

Such 'soft power' initiatives seem particularly appropriate for the reduced state of the British capacity to influence world affairs. But more generally, the implication of the analysis presented here is that there needs to be, in the terms described above, a systematic exploration of the potential and the capacity the UK has to engage with and optimise the benefits to the UK from the changing world environment, identifying affordance qualities and beneficial adaptation. A further implication of this analysis is that whilst ecological and evolutionary psychology insights may identify a 'lens' through which we might view national interest and our approach to strategy, the critical issue is the sense of what an environment affords for the observer at a particular time.

Notes

1. Ecology is used here to refer to the relations and interactions between individuals (and states) and their environment.
2. Social media is used here to refer to means of interactions among people in which they create, share and/or exchange information and ideas using virtual communities and networks.
3. http://www.internetworldstats.com/emarketing.htm
4. This chapter was written before the referendum on Scottish independence.
5. Complex systems refers to a field of science studying how parts of a system give rise to the collective behaviours of the system, and how that system interacts with its environment.
6. The author wishes to thank Mr Ian Burdon of Jervaulx Abbey for information on this.
7. Indeed, even the unitary nature of the UK is questioned by the Scottish referendum on independence in 2014.
8. Pew Research Center (2012) Global Attitudes Project, 'Social Networking Popular across Globe'.

12
Britain's Strategic Culture in Context: A Typology of National Security Strategies

Tim Oliver and Austin Knuppe

Britain's development of its first National Security Strategy (NSS) in 2008 (Cabinet Office 2008) was a welcome step forward in efforts to organise the ways, means and ends of the UK's international affairs. Two years later, the Conservative – Liberal Democrat coalition government published a new NSS (Cabinet Office 2010a) and a Strategic Defence and Security Review (SDSR) (Cabinet Office 2010b). The SDSR was controversial for reasons that are outlined below. It was notable, however, for its use of a risk-based approach to structure its analysis, which allowed policymakers to view threats in terms of their estimated probability and impact, instead of providing a simple laundry list of concerns. At the same time, the review and consequent developments reveal the problems Whitehall faces in its attempt to balance concerns about security risks with the concomitant goals of economic growth and deficit reduction.

That Britain today has an NSS, and a national security council to oversee it, hardly seems unusual given that an increasing number of states have adopted such documents. Across Europe states have dedicated varying amounts of time, energy and resources to national security planning and risk assessments. Regardless, the continent as a whole is strategically adrift, characterised in the words of de France and Witney (2013) as 'Europe's strategic cacophony'. This has created a pan-European situation in which, as de France and Witney (2013 p. 2) argue,

> Europe's failure to develop a shared strategic culture has not just undermined its ambition to be a more credible and effective actor,

and therefore one that carries greater political weight, on the international scene – it has also hamstrung its efforts to maintain its defence capabilities in the wake of the financial crisis gripping the continent.

The aim of this chapter is to employ an ideal-type framework of national security strategies to examine dynamics of British strategic culture through the lens of the NSS and SDSR. To accomplish this task we introduce a typology of national security strategies and discuss the relative merits and drawbacks of each approach. This typology functions as a proof of concept (see Ray 1999) for the relative utility of using ideal types to conduct cross-national reviews of national security. In doing so, it forms part of a wider research agenda which investigates Europe's strategic incoherence through the lens of how various security strategies interact under collective security.

Our goal in this chapter, however, is to introduce the typology as a means of assessing the comparative advantages and weaknesses of British national security planning. Through this exercise, we hope to address how future innovations can improve the policy planning process in the UK, as well as in continental Europe. While our approach is limited to ideal types, the overall typology is not intended to point to a single strategy as paramount. As will become clear, each of the various types has its pros and cons. Nor is it intended to argue that a specific security strategy is wholly of one type or another.

We focus on British strategic culture not simply because of the topic of this book. For all its faults, the UK's approach to national security planning has been at the forefront of efforts to come to terms with the contemporary security environment. The UK has used novel methods of risk assessments, published a variety of documents connected to the topic and pushed efforts to reform strategic thinking amongst its allies. While faced with considerable economic and budgetary difficulties, it has used its still considerable range of military, humanitarian, diplomatic and other tools to lead efforts to minimise risks ranging from climate change through to traditional state threats.

Defining national security and strategy

Strategy is the process of balancing ends (foreign policy goals), ways (operational and tactical concepts) and means (capabilities). It demands that policymakers set priorities among competing objectives and weigh the risks and rewards of various courses of action by anticipating their outcomes. As Andrew Krepinevich (2012) explains, 'At its core, strategy should provide a guide for using available resources to achieve realistic objectives.'

Policymaking occurs in a complex and interdependent environment, demanding that strategies engage in a dynamic process of constant reassessment, adjustment and innovation. As Murray and Grimsley observe, 'strategy is a process, a constant adaptation to shifting conditions and circumstances in a world where chance, uncertainty, and ambiguity dominate' (1994, p. 1). In the international arena, strategy involves the interaction of multiple actors (state and non-state) under conditions of uncertainty, chance and imperfect information. Domestically, strategy evolves out of a dialogue between political and military leaders. Regardless of the framework, all strategists seek to mitigate uncertainty by providing clarity as to how a country can accomplish its stated goals.

National security is a particular variant of strategic thinking concerned with the protection of a state's people, interests and way of life. In a prescient analysis of US foreign policy after the Second World War, George Kennan reminded policymakers that national security is 'the continued ability of the country to pursue the development of its internal life without serious interference, or threat of interference, from foreign powers' (Gaddis 2005, p. 26). Regardless of how national security planning is conducted, policy planning never occurs in a political vacuum. Policymakers at all levels of government must consider the interests and preferences of different domestic audiences – including voters, media and 'the marketplace of ideas' – while keeping in mind how a strategy will affect the international audience's view of a state.

For our purposes, we frame national security as an institutional process rooted in material sources of power and shaped by policy elites. As such, we are concerned with strategic culture – how policymakers identify the requirements necessary to maintain the survival of the state through the use of political, economic and military power. We define an NSS as 'a nation's plan for the coordinated use of all the instruments of state power – nonmilitary as well as military – to pursue objectives that defend and advance the national interest' (Doyle 2007, pp. 624–628).

A typology of national security strategies

The post-Cold War period saw renewed interest in comparative studies of national security strategies. Only a handful of these projects, however, provide a concrete framework for analysing policy planning between countries. Our goal in adopting a typology is to capture the range and scope of existing strategies. As stated previously, however, an ideal-type conception of national security planning rests on generalisations that describe constantly changing strategies. A typology can therefore allow us a general understanding of national security strategies, but each approach must be understood in the specific political, security and strategic circumstances of the particular state.

The framework in this chapter grew out of Cornish and Dorman's work on UK approaches to national strategy and defence reviews. Seeking to place the current NSS and SDSR in historical context, the authors classify previous national strategy and defence reviews under the following rubrics: threat-oriented, capabilities-driven, effects-based, Treasury-constrained and foreign policy-led (Cornish and Dorman 2011, p. 345).

Our theoretical contribution expands on Cornish and Dorman's classification by adapting it to analyse cross-national security strategies. This comparative perspective requires that we balance our ideal-typical framework of national security strategies with the empirical nuances of each particular approach in context. In general, we contend that security for a given state can be characterised by how that state's values are to be secured, the specific values being addressed, the degree of the security to be attained, the kinds of threats the security must direct itself to, the means for coping with such threats, the costs for doing so and the relevant time period (Stolberg 2012, p. 9). In sum, generalising Cornish and Dorman's contribution provides extended analytical leverage by which to orient our comparative theoretical framework.

Foreign policy led

In an ideal world, national interests – those things deemed by the state to be desired goals – provide metrics for policymakers to evaluate necessary operational and tactical concepts, as well as the necessary finances. Thus foreign-policy-led national security strategies serve as 'a unifying document for the executive branch...designed to create an internal consensus on foreign, defence, diplomatic, economic, and homeland security strategy' (Stohlberg 2012, p. 3).

Foreign-policy-led strategies focus more on goals and potential opportunities than on assessing risk, eliminating threats and mitigating uncertainty. They often contain a strategic vision that provides 'a conceptual framework that describes how the world is, envisions how it ought be, and specifies a set of policies that can achieve that ordering' (Stohlberg 2012, p. 3). Due to their goal-oriented nature, these security strategies are often led by the executive branch and implemented by policy planners in the state's central bureaucracy.

By their very nature, all strategies contain an element of foreign policy, even if competing factors such as budgets or capabilities overrule them. As a result, foreign-policy-led strategies are often labelled 'grand strategy' or 'national strategy', something that is all encompassing and by its nature impossible to capture completely.

Threat-orientated

While foreign policy goals should not be overlooked, in practice, strategies often deal with pressing domestic and foreign threats. A threat-oriented approach to national security has to calculate the capabilities (political, economic and military) of a state's opponents, their geographical proximity and their perceived intentions (Walt 1987, p. vi).

It should come as no surprise that threat-oriented national security strategies tend to emerge when a state faces aggressive and capable opponents. Indeed, Posen (1984) observes that policy planning is more innovative and less prone to bureaucratic infighting when a state faces a high-threat environment. Clear threats provide policymakers with clear guidelines for ranking strategic priorities, as well as managing public opinion.

Moreover, material capabilities are often easier to assess than an opponent's motives. Even when the world is relatively peaceful, however, the logic of the security dilemma reminds us that the complexity of the present and uncertainty about the future means even highly capable states with benign intentions can be misperceived as threatening, producing arms races and crisis escalation (Jervis 1978, pp. 167–214). Additionally, interpreting intentions is not only a function of the material world, but also a constitutive element of how actors think and talk about international politics (Wendt 1992, pp. 391–425).

As several analyses have shown (Leffler 1992, pp. 48–49), threat-oriented national security planning risks politicians or policymakers engaging in threat inflation by issuing claims that go beyond the range of ambiguity that disinterested experts would credit as plausible (Kaufmann 2004). Threat inflation clouds strategic priorities, turning strategy into a tool for political posturing at best, and violating the civil liberties of private citizens at worst. The post-9/11 environment has produced its fair share of these pathologies (see Mueller 2006, 2011). Consider the controversy arising out of discoveries that the National Security Agency (NSA)'s PRISM surveillance programme was not only monitoring thousands of US citizens without warrants, but also foreign heads of state, such as the German chancellor, Angela Merkel (Mazetti 2013).

Viewed through a theoretical lens, threat-oriented policy planning favours state and non-state actors too heavily. As a result, it provides fewer tools for diagnosing systematic challenges to national security such as economic turbulence, environmental threats and political change. Unsurprisingly, with the demise of the USSR, threat-oriented national security strategies appear to be relics of a bygone era.

Capabilities driven

A capabilities-driven approach ranks strategic priorities based on the resources at a state's disposal. In this context, capabilities are best conceived as bundles of skills, assets (especially, but not only, military ones) and technologies capable of delivering a specified outcome. As a result, capabilities-driven policies seek to maximise a state's comparative advantage in material and ideational resources.

Net assessment – an objective analysis of the strengths and weaknesses of each actor's capabilities with an eye towards identifying how these might interact in a conflict – is the principle framework for capabilities-driven strategies. As such, this strategy aims to mitigate uncertainty by developing forces, and other state-managed instruments, capable of mitigating an opponent's capabilities. In the absence of a clear opponent, the goal is to develop adaptable, flexible capabilities, useful across a wide range of military roles and potential security challenges (Fasana 2011, pp. 143–146).

One of the strengths of a capabilities-driven approach is that it allows policy planners to analyse a state's comparative advantage vis-à-vis allies and opponents. It is thus a popular lens of analysis as policy-makers consider a state's role in collective security organisations or military alliances. The introduction of NATO's 'smart defense' doctrine represents one contemporary example of policy planning coordinated around the relative material capabilities of each ally.

Budget constrained

All strategies face budget constraints. Here, a budget-constrained NSS is one driven by a single-minded determination to achieve economic stability, reconstruction and international competitiveness (Cornish and Dorman 2011, p. 348). It sets policy by ranking strategic interests based on the division of financial resources. As a result, the state's economic vitality becomes – to borrow from Clausewitz – the 'centre of gravity' for national security planning.

Budget-constrained strategies are the result of a myriad of factors. Facing the risk of financial insolvency as a result of mounting entitlement costs combined with declining tax revenue due to demographic decline, social welfare democracies must prioritise spending. In situations where states face no major threats to their survival, it is commonplace for central government to shift spending from defence to social welfare, tax cuts, unfunded liabilities or servicing sovereign debt. These domestic trade-offs are often exacerbated by turbulence in the world economy. The 2008 global financial crisis, in particular, demonstrated how exogenous economic shocks, ones amplified by globalised economic interdependence, can force states to reassess their national interests.

Negative externalities are not the only exogenous factors that shape budget-constrained policymaking. In addition to providing collective security benefits, alliances can also introduce a moral hazard problem by providing perverse incentives for states to free-ride on the capabilities and funds provided by more powerful members (see Olson 1971; Sandler 1993). Unsurprisingly, alliance entrapment grows out of a security environment where alliance members face few serious contenders or external threats. In the post-Cold War period, US military hegemony has afforded Europe the opportunity of curtailing defence spending without significantly modifying their foreign interests. Indeed, free-riding has been a problem for NATO since its founding in 1949 and has become an even more pressing problem since the end of the Cold War, with US Defense Secretary Robert Gates (2011) warning of the growing divide within the alliance 'between those willing and able to pay the price and bear the burden of commitments, and those who enjoy the benefits of NATO membership but don't want to share the risks and costs'.

Public opinion plays a role in the construction and revision of budget-constrained planning. Public pressure is often strongest in economies with high levels of social welfare spending, where the electorate is especially sensitive to shifts in the provision of public goods from social programmes to defence. Indeed, the logic of the post-Cold War 'peace dividend' predicted long-term economic benefits as savings from defence spending were redirected to welfare programmes and reduced tax rates. Empirical evidence for the phenomenon, however, is still hotly contested.

Budget-constrained strategies offer a mixture of strengths and weaknesses. They have the advantage of forcing policymakers to conduct a sobering financial assessment of a state's national security interests. As such, they have the potential to clarify the process whereby policymakers rank priorities among competing objectives and weigh the risks and rewards of various courses of action. To accomplish this task, policymakers often rely on quantitative methodologies, such as cost–benefit analysis, to critically examine the expected utility of particular details in a security strategy.

Interestingly enough, by limiting freedom of choice at the domestic level, decision-makers can turn budgetary and material weakness into negotiating strength (Schelling 1960, pp. 22–23). For example, in states where public opinion is deeply opposed to increases in defence spending, leaders can credibly argue that their hands are tied. If they were to agree to commit more resources to an alliance, the shift in spending at home runs the risk of creating a political backlash threatening the political survival of the ruling coalition. In other words, the risk of electoral punishment provides political cover for states to continue free-riding on their more powerful allies. In the context of our previous discussion about NATO, this translates to many European allies limiting military contributions in combat zones to tasks such as humanitarian relief, development and peacekeeping. While the US has incentives to monitor and enforce the contributions of alliance members, it is unlikely that Washington will take drastic action to exclude free-riders, because the alliance provides more net benefits than costs.

The disadvantages of a budget-constrained approach are more intuitive. Because threats to the national interest can appear quickly, states that under-invest in security run the risk of being unable to protect themselves in a crisis. Traditional security dilemma logic (Jervis 1978) dictates that states that under-invest in defence may actually be more secure than their more capable neighbours, because their lack of military capabilities signals peaceful intensions as well as allaying other states' concerns about maintaining power parity. As Schweller (1996) and others have noted, however, the security dilemma only addresses situations where all states are genuine security-seekers. In scenarios where a rising military power has revisionist intentions, under-investing in defence can be dangerous. Unable to respond to revisionist threats, such states will be reliant on the goodwill and capabilities of their allies. Moreover, when policymakers do decide to reinvest in national security, the inevitable delays in bureaucracy, industry and society will slow a new strategy from being implemented. As a result, developments in the strategic environment can outpace national security strategies.

Risk-based

In a risk-based approach to national security, policymakers calculate the perceived likelihood of an event multiplied by the estimated impact. Because risk is the effect of uncertainty on policy objectives, risk-based strategies emphasise potentiality rather than imminent danger (Edmunds 2012, p. 267). Risks include threats from sentient actors like rival states and non-state actors, as well as 'inanimate' risks like climate change. This comprehensive approach to risk assessment has grown in the post-Cold War period, where the majority of Western states face few external threats from rival powers (Edmunds 2012, p. 265).

In a vein similar to other rational choice models, risk-based strategies conceive of uncertainty in two dimensions. First, there is the uncertainty inherent to making decisions under incomplete information in a complex environment. Second, uncertainty also characterises policymakers' limited ability to foresee future events. Both structural limitations compel actors to identify risks to the national interest behind the veil of ambiguous information (see Stein 1999).

Policymakers implementing a risk-based approach rely on two primary tools. The first, risk assessment, involves a sequential process of identifying, classifying and ranking potential risks to a state's interests. Policymakers then assign a risk tolerance, or the degree of variability in outcomes that fits within the confines of the strategy. The most critical stage of risk assessment involves the assessment of the likelihood and impact of potential risks.

In quantitative risk assessment, policymakers construct a risk matrix by calculating the probability that harm occurs multiplied by the severity of that harm. This simple mechanism allows policymakers to increase the visibility of risks and develop appropriate mitigation strategies. In practice, incomplete information about potential low probability/high impact – 'Black Swan' – events limits the accuracy of risk estimates (Taleb 2010). For example, the UK's 2008 National Risk Register (Cabinet Office 2008b, p. 5 and p. 28) noted how rare examples are of 'non-conventional attacks' – use of a chemical, biological, radiological and nuclear materials – but that there was still a need to plan for them.

The second tool, risk management, involves the coordination and application of resources to monitor, minimise and augment the probability and/or impact of unforeseen events. There is a range of four strategies available. On one end of the spectrum stands risk avoidance, or the elimination of risk by augmenting interests or end goals. One example would be the worry-prone traveller who decides to stop flying completely to avoid plane hijackings. Risk avoidance is the only strategy for completely removing risk, but for policymakers is untenable because it also means losing any potential gains that said risk may involve.

The middle of the spectrum comprises risk reduction and sharing strategies. Risk reduction involves the investment of resources to reduce either the probability or the impact of an event. By far the most popular technique, risk reduction is intimately related to the net of assessment in the defence community. Moreover, risk reduction strategies throughout all tiers of the public sector define how resources are allocated to implement policy. Policymakers can also devise risk-sharing strategies with the goal of transferring the burden of loss or benefits to third parties, for example through an alliance such as NATO.

Finally, policymakers can retain the possibility of certain risks by accepting and budgeting for their occurrence in their strategy. All risks that are not avoided, reduced or transferred are retained by default. Risk retention is the primary strategy for low probability events regardless of their perceived impact on strategic interests. Low probability/low impact events are of limited concern because they can be addressed with pre-existing resources. More troublesome, however, are Black Swan events, where uncertainty on both axes (likelihood and impact) prevents the implementation of avoidance, reduction or sharing strategies. Despite recent innovations in political forecasting methods, predicting Black Swans remains extremely difficult.

A strength of risk-based strategies is their ability to anticipate threats before they fully materialise. This framework also allows policymakers to recognise challenges to national security that go beyond state or non-state actors. Britain's 2010 NSS, for example, identified climate change and demographic trends as posing various degrees of risk to the national interest. However, risk assessments can complicate the process of ranking strategic priorities by allowing overzealous policymakers to draw up 'laundry lists' of every potential risk to the state's national security.

Britain's approach to national security strategy

Gordon Brown's commissioning in October 2008 of an NSS was greeted as a step-change in the way the UK approached national security. But Britain's experiences in security strategies started long before 2008; the Committee of Imperial Defence (1902–1939) was an early British attempt to provide much needed coordination between the various armed forces and administrations of the empire. Nor was the 2008

NSS the first British attempt at a strategic security review. The 1959 'Future Policy Study, 1960–1970' (Cabinet Office 1959), commissioned by Harold Macmillan, was both wide ranging (covering everything from the Commonwealth to Britain's economic problems) and candid in its assessments. It was so candid that Macmillan blocked it from discussion in cabinet. While the UK might have subsequently avoided undertaking any further comprehensive reviews, it has undertaken numerous reviews focused on defence, along with several on the UK's overseas representation (see Oliver 2011). Cornish and Dorman (2011, p. 345) provide an overview of those strategies – often named after the secretaries of state for defence who oversaw them – from which part of the idea for this chapter's typology is drawn. Before the 1959 review, the 1957 review by Duncan Sandys provided a more traditionally focused defence review. Sandys focused on the changing threat from developments in nuclear missiles, and as such was a threat-orientated review. John Nott's 1981 review was capabilities driven thanks to a focus on cutting the UK's expeditionary warfare capabilities in favour of capabilities to support NATO operations in Europe and the North Atlantic. The 1974 review by Roy Mason and the 1994 review by Malcolm Rifkind were both driven by demands from the Treasury for cuts in defence spending to fit wider economic changes, making them budget-constrained reviews. Finally, the 1998 Strategic Defence Review (SDR) was a foreign-policy-led strategy, embracing as it did the idea – one especially pushed and redefined by New Labour – of the UK as a force for good. It was later extended by reviews in 2001 and 2003–2004 that focused more on capabilities.

By 2007 there was growing demand for a wide-ranging review of Britain's national security. This was in part a reflection of a growing trend amongst Britain's allies to adopt national security strategies. Several think tanks, academics and commentators began to call for the UK to adopt such a document, moving it away from the more pragmatic, *ad hoc* approach which has meant the UK is 'tactical rather than strategic' (Cornish 2013, p. 384). As touched on earlier, a powerful background factor was the perception that the UK – in common with other Western states – lacked a sense of direction in facing new security challenges. Added to this was a feeling that British foreign, security and defence policy had been defined mainly by the personality of Tony Blair. When Brown's strategy (Cabinet Office 2008) was issued it was therefore heralded as a break from the Blair era. However the strategy took some time to draft and was only published after protracted negotiations within government.

For the Brown government the document reinforced the need for joined-up government, a long sought after objective which was now to be applied on a much grander scale to deal with a panoply of international and domestic challenges. To deliver this a national security secretariat was established in the Cabinet Office. Serving the prime minister and cabinet it would take a national viewpoint and so avoid a narrow departmental outlook. The NSS succeeded in cataloguing many of the interconnected risks facing the UK, and went beyond traditional concerns to encompass risks such as transnational organised crime and influenza pandemics. Yet, at 61 pages, it was hardly a popular read. A bigger problem lay in how, by going beyond traditional concerns, it broadened the scope of security concerns too much. This might not have been a problem had the document not lacked the prioritisation that could give credence to it being called a strategy. Without this it became less a strategy and more a laundry list of security concerns.

Some derided the strategy as a means of avoiding a review of the Iraq War, or as a way of furthering anti-terrorist legislation that would further erode civil liberties. It was also criticised for offering little on big issues such as relations with the EU and US. Peter Hennessy (2008) critiqued the strategy's underlying assumptions:

> last week's document, subtitled 'Security in an interdependent world', is very Gordon – a mixture of Lord Curzon (we Brits still have a chunk of high-quality armed forces at our disposal so Johnny Foreigner had better watch out) and Blue Peter (we Brits can lead the world to relieving poverty in Africa and then, next week, to alleviating climate change).

The 2010 NSS and SDSR

It was hardly surprising that the Conservative–Liberal Democrat coalition agreement (Cabinet Office 2010c) announced the establishment of a national security council along with an overhaul of the NSS and an SDSR. It would have been close to impossible to delay a review by a few months given the budgetary and political pressures then facing the Ministry of Defence (MoD), the wider security community and the UK.

The coalition agreement also reflected the work both parties had undertaken in opposition, both urging a review, and one focused on security and defence (RUSI 2010; Cornish 2010). Here they were not entirely playing party politics. The British military was in a state of crisis after more than a decade of continuous operations and insufficient budgets (Cornish and Dorman 2009). The clearest demonstration of this had been the experiences in Basra – where the British army suffered what many considered a 'strategic defeat' – and the weaknesses they exposed in British army counter-insurgency doctrine, along with strained efforts by the British army to rebuild its reputation in Afghanistan (see Oliver 2012). To make matters worse, there had been no comprehensive review of defence since the 1998 SDR. The 2010 review would need to take into account the dire state of the nation's finances after the 2007 Great Recession, the wider economic situation in the Western world, the emergence of new powers, and the US's moves to bolster its defence commitments in the Asia-Pacific region. With the start of a defence review being made in early 2010 (MoD 2010), the then Labour government had itself recognised the situation was unsustainable.

The NSS, and to a lesser extent the SDSR, were to be overseen by the new National Security Council, meeting weekly under the leadership of the prime minister. This was to be a body with the political weight to provide the direction the 2008 NSS had lacked. As with the 2008 strategy, drafting of the documents involved contributions from across government and thus went beyond the MoD, although the MoD remained the dominant actor in developing the SDSR. Good central coordination was essential to not only meet high political expectations, but also to ensure it was concluded before 20 October 2010, the date the chancellor was to announce the government's first comprehensive spending review (CSR).

The NSS was published on 18 October, followed the next day by the SDSR, when the prime minister spoke about both in the House of Commons. The following day the CSR confirmed the cuts in spending the SDSR had outlined. Their separate publication helped clarify their different purposes. The NSS outlined what it termed the 'strategic context' in which the UK found itself. In doing so it drew on many of the ideas outlined in the 2008 strategy, such as environmental challenges and international terrorism. Unlike the 2008 strategy, however, the 2010 revision provided a prioritisation of the risks the UK would face over the next 20 years, thanks to a risk assessment methodology – termed the National Security Risk Assessment (NSRA) (Cabinet Office 2010e). Dividing the risks the UK faced into three tiers, the strategy presented those in tier one as assessed to pose both the highest likelihood and highest impact. By prioritising risks and identifying the type of international norms the UK would seek to uphold, the NSS therefore outlined the ends the UK would seek to achieve. The ways and means of achieving these ends were then set out in the SDSR. This outlined how Britain's defence, security and, to a more limited extent, other international capabilities were to be restructured to provide the means for achieving those ends. It was also announced that the Cabinet Office and National Security Council would regularly review both the NSS and NSRA. Annual reports were to be presented to the Joint Parliamentary Committee on the NSS. An aim was also set down to publish a new NSS and SDSR every five years.

The NSS and SDSR have been subject to considerable analysis and criticism, and some praise (see Watt 2010; JCNSS 2012a,b,c). They were praised for retaining a wide sense of risks such as cyber security and terrorism. But they were criticised for prescribing two new aircraft carriers as the means to tackle this, while decommissioning the UK's ability to deploy an aircraft carrier with a fixed wing capability. The NSS was also praised for offering a foreign policy vision which it sought to implement. However, questions were asked whether the British government had lost the ability to undertake 'grand (or national) strategy', limiting the thinking behind the documents and their implementation (PASC 2010). For those concerned with strategy, the key criteria for judging success or failure lay in whether the ends of the NSS fitted with the SDSR's ways and means.

The UK 2010 NSS and SDSR in the typology

As this brief overview demonstrates, the UK's 2010 NSS and SDSR were shaped by budgetary pressures, risks assessments, capabilities reviews and the foreign policy aims of both governing parties. But which type does the strategy therefore best fit? And what can the British experience tell us about our typology more generally?

Foreign-policy led

The NSS was foreign-policy led in the sense that it prioritised foreign-policy goals, as well as identifying future opportunities for British foreign affairs. This was hardly surprising given both coalition parties supported, as the SDSR put it, that, 'Britain's national interest requires us to reject any notion of the shrinkage of our influence' (Cabinet Office 2010, p. 10). While there were differences over Iraq, both parties have generally supported the UK's involvement in conflicts such as Kosovo or Afghanistan. The decision by David Cameron to commit his party to a foreign-policy agenda of 'liberal conservatism' (Beech 2011), and to mirror the Liberal Democrats commitment to spending 0.7 per cent of gross national income (GNI) on international aid, meant both parties found a degree of cooperation on international issues which is often overlooked when the focus is on divisions over the replacement of Trident or UK–EU relations. Despite talk of a 'fundamental reappraisal of Britain's place in the world' (Hague 2010), the fundamental foreign-policy priorities of the UK have remained in place, with neither the NSS nor the SDSR changing the UK's relations with the US, NATO and the EU. While both parties were keen not to appear 'slavish' to US interests, the UK's military remained configured to operating with the US, so as to serve as a force multiplier, as well as secure British influence in Washington. Here the strategy continued the long-standing aim of retaining a place for the UK at the top tables of international affairs. The NSS and SDSR then were not short on foreign-policy aims, but the overarching goal was about maintaining the status quo.

Threat-oriented

While identifying, assessing and responding to threats remains a mainstay of any security strategy, this approach has declined thanks to a lack of clear and present external threats. The difficulty in using a threat-oriented approach to confront systemic risks such as climate change has also limited the appeal of this type of strategy. Unsurprisingly, the 2010 NSS and SDSR continued the trend away from threat prioritisation. The NSS did not overlook these challenges, but external threats were given lower priority compared to the more pressing domestic threats of terrorism and organised crime.

Capabilities driven

If the 2010 NSS and SDSR were primarily capabilities driven, they would have focused attention on the material and ideational resources at Whitehall's disposal for pursuing foreign-policy goals. Such a strategy would be concerned more with operations and tactics than strategy. The NSS and SDSR were not short of controversial decisions about capabilities. From the start, the review was shaped by a decision to bracket capabilities required for operations in Afghanistan. The SDSR cancelled the £14 billion defence training rationalisation project, amongst a long list of decisions that also included scrapping the Nimrod MRA4 maritime patrol aircraft shortly before it was due to enter service, withdrawing the Type 22 frigates, reducing the fast jet fleet, withdrawing UK forces from Germany by 2020, cutting the numbers of main battle tanks and self-propelled guns, and reducing personnel across all branches (Evans 2010).

At the same time, the SDSR exercised foresight in modernising capabilities to contribute to a new force structure known as Future Force 2020. Designed to face the challenges the NSS predicted Britain would confront beyond 2020, the primarily expeditionary-capable force will support a revised set of defence planning assumptions which outline the type, intensity and number of military operations the government believes the armed forces should be able to mount (see Cabinet Office 2010d). Defence planning assumptions are not a new innovation – the 1998 SDR contained plenty of them. But these were soon breached thanks to events after 9/11 and a political willingness to use the armed forces without reviewing the force structures or resources necessary for maintaining them. As Hew Strachan (see Edmunds 2012, p. 270) argues, such a capabilities-driven approach risks becoming more about, 'how armed forces should fight rather than what they should be fighting for'. The 2010 defence planning assumptions run this risk, but have been located within a strategy which, through prioritising certain risks, provides some guidance as to what they will be fighting for.

One of the SDSR's most controversial decisions was to gap Britain's aircraft carrier capability until the introduction of new, more capable carrier capabilities around 2020. This was based on an assessment that the UK would not need carrier support in Afghanistan, with other possible operations having air-support provided from ground bases or by allies. The commissioning of two new carriers by 2020 means the UK will then have the capabilities the NSS believes will be necessary beyond 2020. While many defence analysts rejected this proposal out of hand – and while inter-service rivalry, bureaucratic politics and employment issues in certain parliamentary constituencies all played a role – the decision was based in part on a risk-based assessment, rather than one based purely on capabilities.

Risk based

If there is one thing the 2010 strategy is praised for – albeit with some strong caveats – it is that 'for the first time in a public document, a risk assessment and management methodology was placed at the heart of British security and defence policy' (Cornish and Dorman 2011, p. 339). The UK's approach fits with the broader trend noted earlier of Western states using risk assessments to manage and guide their security policy (Edmunds 2012, p. 272). The UK's 2010 approach also made up for previous reviews where planning assumptions turned out to have been overly optimistic and so failed to tailor forces to the risks the UK faced (Edmunds 2012, p. 271).

The development of a classified National Security Risk Assessment – based on existing government assessments of the risks facing the UK – allowed the National Security Council to compare, assesses and prioritise the risks facing UK security. Looking ahead 20 years, the risks can be plotted onto a graph. One axis measures the likely impact in terms of the economy, casualties and social and structural factors. The other axis measures the likelihood. From here three levels of priority risks were identified, with those most likely and with high impact forming the highest priority risks (see Cabinet Office 2010a, p. 27). Tier one included international terrorism, cyber security, major accident or natural hazards, and an international military crisis drawing in the UK and its allies. Tier two included an attack on a UK overseas territory, instability/civil war overseas that terrorists would exploit, organised crime, and disruption to satellite communication. Tier three, the lowest of the priority risks, was also the longest of the three, listing a conventional attack on the UK, its overseas territories or its allies, concerns over border security, disruption to energy and resource supplies, and a civil-nuclear emergency.

Edmunds (2012 p. 272) has argued the NSS and SDSR demonstrated six features that they share with other risk assessment approaches. First, they deal with the generalities so common of risk rather than the specifics of threats. Second, they provide a hierarchy of risks, more so than previous attempts, allowing capabilities to be better tailored. Third, they are precautionary because they emphasise the need to prevent risks becoming threats. Fourth, they presume the UK will work with allies in facing common risks. Fifth, they emphasise a hierarchy of readiness for the UK's force structure, meaning capabilities that can deal with the more pressing risks and threats are held at high readiness, with others held ready to be reactivated or recreated when needed. Sixth, the review will be reviewed regularly, allowing changes such as recreation of certain capabilities to face new risks as they emerge.

Budget constrained

There can be no denying that the economic turbulence confronting the UK heavily shaped the 2010 NSS and SDSR. All three main British parties campaigned in the 2010 general election on varying promises to bring the country's debts under control. With the exception of the NHS and the Department for International Development (DFID), and to a certain extent operations in Afghanistan, all government departments were told to expect cuts, with figures of over 25 per cent being touted (Prince 2010). In this the MoD was expected to meet two challenges: first, to contribute to government-wide spending cuts; second, to fill an unfunded liability for the next ten years of around £38 billion (Chalmers 2011, p. 3). This financial 'black hole' had developed through commitments to projects the MoD would lack the necessary future funding to pay for. Having started before the recession, the hole showed how even if the UK had not faced tough economic times, the MoD would still have faced painful spending choices. The MoD's budget now also includes the cost of replacing Britain's nuclear deterrent and, as announced in the 2013 spending review, paying around half the cost of operational deployments, both of which were previously financed centrally by the Treasury (Cornish and Dorman 2013, p. 1187). Talk of defence spending being cut by 8 per cent therefore hid much larger cuts, both brought in at the time and in the following few years. If we exclude the reductions that followed the end of the world wars, for Cornish and Dorman (2013, p. 341): 'When taken together, the cuts are actually far greater than those that were imposed by any previous UK defence review.'

For the coalition government, the greatest threat or risk facing the UK was economic uncertainty. As the prime minister and deputy prime minister made clear in the SDSR's foreword (Cabinet Office 2010, p. 3):

> The difficult legacy we have inherited has necessitated tough decisions to get our economy back on track. Our national security depends on our economic security and vice versa. So bringing the defence budget back to balance is a vital part of how we tackle the deficit and protect this country's national security.

Cuts were also imposed on the BBC World Service, the Foreign and Commonwealth Office and the Home Office. DFID funding might have been ring-fenced, and a commitment made to spending 0.7 per cent of the UK's GNI on aid, but it has come under pressure to spend more of this on areas deemed essential to British national security (BBC 2013).

The focus of cuts in security and defence spending was always likely to fall heavily on the defence budget. The Institute of Economic Affairs, a free-market think tank, put the economy first when it called for cuts in defence spending of around 50 per cent (Robinson 2011). For Robinson, if defence planners stopped conflating vital and secondary interests, then they 'would have had to admit that Britain's vital interests are not threatened by the sort of danger for which military force is an appropriate response. Much of today's armed forces is entirely inappropriate to the country's security needs and can be safely dismantled.'

Failure to do so now meant sapping Britain's financial resources, undermining its ability to recover from the economic crisis of the time and thus weakening its long-term ability to afford the type of defence capability it might need to confront future crises. As Paul Cornish (2010, p. 1) summarised the dilemma: was it to be a healthy economy or national security and defence? While cuts of 50 per cent were never likely, the review did see the Treasury putting substantial pressure on the MoD. As a leaked letter from Liam Fox (Telegraph 2010) argued: 'Frankly this process is looking less and less defensible as a proper SDSR and more like a "super-Comprehensive Spending Review."' Fox's efforts might have paid off, with what could have ended up being even more severe cuts being limited.

In the face of such leaks it becomes clear that the only actor in government who had any clear programme was the Treasury with its austerity agenda. This may in part reflect how the MoD is in a state of 'organizational, bureaucratic and intellectual decay' (Cornish and Dorman 2009, p. 261). Making the situation worse was a disconnect between the public and the security policymaking elite. While the general public have shown strong concerns about soldiers' welfare, terrorism and jobs connected to defence, they have remained somewhat indifferent to the wider debates about the security risks and threats facing the UK. In the absence of the clear threats of the Cold War, policymakers have struggled to connect their decisions and discussions about security to a general public whose perceptions of threats and risks remain distant to that of the security policy elite (Edmunds 2012). For Cornish (2010, p. 26), the NSS and SDSR were a clear example of 'muddling through' – instead of, 'seeking a balance between effective defence and healthy economy, muddling through is what happens when the balance is tipped in favour of the economy and defence is required to "make do" as best it can'.

Conclusion

Analysis of national security strategies remains largely focused on the experiences of individual states. The strategic incoherence that plagues European thinking, however, has renewed interest in transnational comparisons of national security strategies. The typology outlined in this chapter provides a 'proof of concept' for theorising national security. While each approach – foreign-policy led, threat oriented, capabilities driven, budget constrained, and risk based – consists of ideal types, they provide analysts with a rational basis by which to compare strategies and evaluate the effectiveness of policy planning.

224   *Strategy and Planning*

The UK's experience with managing national security planning has not been without its problems. The 2010 review, in particular, increasingly appears to have been a budget-constrained review. In an effort driven by the Treasury, the budget hawks within Whitehall's bureaucracy were able to successfully play on divisions and weaknesses within the MoD to ensure that defence cuts played a prominent role in the coalition government's wider austerity programme. Nevertheless, the 2010 NSS and SDSR stand as boundary markers for a strategic culture that has evolved from threat-oriented towards risk-based policy planning. It is likely the UK will maintain this approach when it next undertakes a large-scale review, widely expected after the 2015 general election.

The extent to which the 2010 NSS and SDSR should be understood as budget-constrained strategies is also to some degree relative to how the British experience compares with that of its European and transatlantic allies. Despite the size of defence cuts, the UK has demonstrated a determination to maintain capabilities able to confront a wide-range of risks and threats. As previously discussed, this is largely due to a strategic approach that sought to match risks with capabilities under a limited budget. When studied in a regional context, the NSS and SDSR stand as commendable examples of risk-based policy planning.

As is the case with many theory-driven analyses, our typology provides plenty of avenues for additional research. Perhaps the most pressing task is to test the external validity of our theory by classifying the national security strategies of major NATO allies, such as the US, France and Germany. In addition to strengthening the theoretical foundations of the typology, this comparison would provide clues as to how various strategies interact under an alliance framework. Moreover, while the origins of each type are largely exogenous to this treatment, a valuable contribution could investigate whether there is a causal relationship between the various approaches. Examining the evolution of European strategic culture through the lens of our typology may also elucidate previously unexplored points of variation.

Conclusion: A Return to the National Interest?

Timothy Edmunds, Jamie Gaskarth and Robin Porter

This book examines the concept of the British national interest in the contemporary global policy environment. It does so against the background of a sustained academic and popular critique of British foreign and security policy since the 9/11 terrorist attacks in New York, and a resurgence of debate around the meaning and utility of the national interest in response to this. The character of this debate has been diverse, and reflected perspectives from across the political spectrum and academic community. However, throughout, it has, in various ways, addressed a series of interconnected questions relating to the nature of the 'national' political community, the role of the state and government in reflecting and representing a form of common good derived from this, and the manner in which such collective interests, however they may be defined, can be translated into effective action in the policy arena.

The chapters in this volume offer theoretical, historical, empirical and policy-orientated perspectives on these questions. They are united in their understanding of the national interest as less an enduring and fundamental property of the contemporary national state and more a constitutive framework through which foreign policy goals are identified, contested and pursued. Such an approach is important for three reasons. First, because it draws attention to the manner in which political communities privilege particular national goals as important and come to decisions about how these should best be advanced and resourced. Second, because it highlights the means–ends logics implicit in such claims, and so provides a basis against which such policies can be evaluated and critiqued. Finally, because it introduces questions of public and collective good into such calculations, and, crucially, suggests that the legitimacy and sustainability of particular foreign policy actions may be linked to the robustness of these claims.

Interpreting the British national interest

All contributors to this volume share a scepticism towards the notion of an enduring and objectively knowable 'national interest'. As Max Taylor observes so powerfully in Chapter 11, changes in both international and domestic environments mean that UK national interests have shifted over time, sometimes dramatically. Taylor points to the decline of the British Empire in the decades after the end of the Second World War to illustrate how swiftly apparently core national interests can evaporate. In fact, narratives of empire, Atlanticism, Europeanism, internationalism and isolationism have ebbed and flowed in the discourse of UK national interest over the years, as have the driving forces of British foreign policy. Former state adversaries such as the Soviet Union have disappeared, while others, albeit of a different scale and character, have emerged. Previously all-consuming and nascently existential threats such as the nuclear confrontation of the Cold War have likewise dissipated, to be replaced by challenges of sometimes radically different character, such as climate change or international terrorism. Even such apparently irreducible interests as national survival and territorial integrity have been profoundly challenged by – arguably – closer integration into the EU and – indisputably – the 2014 referendum on Scottish independence.

These changes have impacted significantly on the UK's engagement in the international arena, with different conceptions of interest and priority emerging over time. For Jamie Gaskarth, national interests are 'specific and historically contingent', and determined by a combination of national values and political circumstance. He employs role theory to examine how differing or changing conceptions of UK identity lead to specific interpretations of national interest, which in turn foster (and legitimate) particular kinds of action in the foreign policy arena. Helen Parr reaches similar conclusions through her examination of British conceptions of interest during the Falklands War. For Parr, the British government responded the way it did to the Falklands crisis in large part due to a logic of appropriateness. Appropriateness in this case was rooted in an identity and role conception that posited Britain as a global power, whose 'national' interests were global in nature, and included an active commitment to upholding both the sovereignty of its overseas territories, but also international law and the principle of non-intervention.

Jonathan Gilmore also explores the role of values and political agency in shaping the national interest. He argues that foreign policy under the

Blair/Brown Labour governments and the subsequent Con–Lib coalition was influenced by a more or less explicit merger of values and interests. Specifically, 'traditional objectives of national [self] interest' were accompanied by 'an "ethical dimension" that...attempted to improve the wellbeing of vulnerable non-citizens'. However, he also observes that these centralised attempts to craft such unified, normatively ambitious approaches to the national interest risked foundering as they came into tension with other imperatives, promoting trade or sustaining relations with allies. Indeed, his verdict that New Labour's self-consciously 'ethical' approach to the national interest led ultimately to 'a highly moralistic and militarised foreign policy, that when combined with the polarising rhetoric of the war on terror, left little room for diversity in international relations', is a damning one. More widely, Gilmore's analysis indicates both the intrinsic mutability of the national interest concept, but also the way in which it can be riven by tensions and contradictions in practice.

This is not to say that continuities in British foreign policy over the years have been entirely absent. Certain partnerships and ambitions have persisted, though their character has shifted over time. In his contribution to this volume, Robin Porter examines the UK's 'special relationship' with the US. Porter's position is a critical one, and he questions the extent to which the UK's closeness to the US has really been able to deliver an aggregate benefit to the British national interest. Even so, his analysis highlights, albeit with some frustration, the tenacious manner in which successive UK governments have prioritised their relationship with the US, even where the two countries' foreign policy objectives have been apparently at odds. Pelopidas and Weldes' discussion of UK nuclear interests likewise demonstrates the manner in which Britain's commitment to retaining a nuclear capability has remained remarkably consistent, and adapted to shifting discourses of interest, security and resilience. Parr too shows that the desire to maintain influence and status in global affairs has long been an important driver of UK policy.

Even so, the sense of a consistent, dominant and purposive idea of the national interest as an underlying determinant of strategy and foreign policy has largely been absent. Instead, the UK has had enduring relationships, broad aspirations and multiple interests; interests that have been multifaceted, changing, shaped by political context and preference, and often contested. Indeed, as a number of contributors to this volume have argued, the entire notion of a single, unified 'national' interest or even interests may be problematic because it carries with it the twofold – though often unspoken – assumption that, first, the nation state is the most appropriate and legitimate lens through which to understand and articulate collective interest, and that, second, by extension, the nation state's interest(s) necessarily represent and reflect those of the political community as a whole.

David Wearing challenges these assumptions, arguing that British foreign policy in the Middle East has been driven more by the economic interests of a global corporate elite than by any real notion of collective or public 'national' interest. Similarly, Nick Ritchie argues that the interests of the state are not in themselves unified, and do not necessarily or even generally represent the individual or community interests of the citizenry as a whole. Drawing on the concept of human security and using the examples of the 2008 financial crisis and British participation in the so-called 'war on terror' he contends that these were all actions that served ultimately to undermine, rather than to advance, the public good. As such, he argues, it is crucial to ask whose interests are being talked about when the national interest is invoked, and to recognise that 'defining interests in terms of practical and aspirational ends, appropriate and legitimate means, and associated allocation of resources is a political project... especially so when the reproduction of national role conceptions and elite systems of social and political control are at stake'.

Despite his ultimately critical approach, Ritchie's contribution points to the importance of some notion of the collective good in underpinning any meaningful claim to the national interest in contemporary foreign policy. The nature of that collective may be disputed and contestable. However, it is striking that much recent criticism of UK foreign policy has concerned the failure of successive governments to sustain public support for, or even engagement with, foreign policy actions whose relevance to the national interest has been widely perceived to be tenuous, indirect or non-existent. While the proposed solutions have varied – from calls for more effective public diplomacy to a reinvigoration of UK strategic capacities, and more radical responses such as those by the Occupy movement – the issue of contention has been perhaps less about significance of the national interest claim in and of itself, and more about the extent to which such claims legitimately and effectively represent the interests of the political communities from which they derive.

This link to the collective good highlights a further fundamental point about the notion of the national interest. Specifically, that if the concept of the national interest is to have any meaning then it must necessarily be linked to some form of means–ends reasoning in foreign policy. Interests in this sense represent the subjectively legitimate goals (or ends) of the political community. Foreign policy actions are the means by which such goals are achieved, or not, and it is on this basis that they are likely to be evaluated. Without some wider concept of the collective interest in which to ground these judgments, such debates would remain politically empty. In this context, and given that the British state is a nationally constituted and legitimised political community, the notion of the *national* interest (albeit a national interest that is ultimately subjective and probably contested) has continuing rhetorical, analytical and substantive relevance. Rhetorically, claims to the national interest (or their obverse) function as a powerful legitimising (or delegitimising) mechanism in political discourse. Analytically, the notion of a national interest or interests provides us with a measure against which foreign policy actions taken in the name of the political community can be evaluated and critiqued. Substantively, it provides the goals to which foreign policy is set, and so functions as an important guide to action – whether implicit or explicit – in the process of strategy making. And it is to the question of strategy – the manner in which interests are translated into action – that this chapter now turns.

From interest to action

Strategy is widely understood to be the manner in which means and resources are purposively linked to achieve particular ends. It is best understood as a theory of action, and the strategy making process itself as an institution through which actors attempt to exert agency in the achievement political goals. Strategy as a concept is used in multiple contexts and at many different levels, from the boardroom to the battlefield. However, in the context of this book, we are especially interested in the notion of 'grand' or 'national' strategy. Grand strategy is the substantive articulation of national interest; it is the mechanism through which national goals are prioritised and resources are allocated and applied to further their realisation.

For Gaskarth, the UK's determination of interest and range of strategic choice is shaped by the collective self-identity of the British state and people. He develops his analysis through a model of UK ideal-type role orientations, alongside the range of strategic action such subject positions engender. In so doing, he provides a heuristic framework through which the costs, benefits and trade-offs of particular national goals can be assessed, and against which policy can be devised and directed. In the

UK case, he argues that a range of different national role conceptions and potentially viable avenues of strategic choice remain extant in the public and political consciousness. These in turn suggest that UK policymakers retain significant scope for strategic agency in the international arena, while at the same time reflecting values that are sustainably rooted in existing notions of collective identity. Interestingly, he concludes by arguing that the national resonance of the 'great power' role has faded in recent years. This is important, not just because it indicates a decline in the traditional significance of great power identities amongst British policymakers and the general public, but also because it suggests the subject position of the UK as a collective whole may be in the process of a significant shift away from historical patterns.

Certainly the changing nature of the international environment, and the UK's position within it, retains a pressing influence on British strategy making. It has become nearly ubiquitous to describe the contemporary global security environment as 'complex and uncertain'. However, taking complexity seriously means moving beyond rhetorical cliché. Drawing on formal complexity theory, Edmunds argues that the international environment is systemically dynamic and adaptive, and not necessarily subject to straightforward relationships of cause and effect. For Edmunds, monolithic notions of the national interest are unhelpful as a guide to action under such circumstances. More relevant are adaptive responses that are able to cross traditional policy boundaries and necessarily involve a multiple range of actors both within and outside government.

Taylor draws similar conclusions. He too employs insights from formal complexity theory to examine the global ecology in which UK interests and actions are located. He argues that the recent proliferation of global connectivities – through the rapid spread of social media, internet access and so on – is transforming the landscape of state action and agency. In particular, he highlights the relative speed with which global events can propagate, their potentially cascading nature and the unanticipated consequences of their effects. For Taylor, the challenge for policymakers is to recognise the inherently dynamic and unpredictable nature of this environment and to develop flexible and holistic strategic capacities to deal with them.

Oliver and Knuppe examine the manner in which the UK National Security Strategy (NSS) and Strategic Defence and Security Review (SDSR) of 2010 have conceptualised these challenges. They do so against a typology derived from a historical and comparative analysis of British and European security review processes (and building on earlier work by

Cornish and Dorman [2011]). In so doing, they identify a series of 'ideal type' methodologies for such exercises, incorporating foreign-policy-led, threat-orientated, capabilities-driven, budget-constrained and risk-based approaches. They argue that the NSS and particularly the SDSR were heavily influenced by budgetary austerity, and ultimately flawed and strategically problematic documents as a consequence.[1] Even so, they suggest that the two documents were significant because they introduced new ways of thinking into the British strategic policy process. Specifically, that they 'stand as boundary markers for a strategic culture that has evolved from threat-orientated towards risk-based policy planning', and in so doing reflect an increasing shift from viewing the global environment as an essentially knowable and fixed arena for action, to one characterised by uncertainty and change.

Indeed, for Edmunds, the British strategic policy community has been the site of considerable innovation since 2010, in large part in response to the perceived failures of the NSS and SDSR. He points to the range of novel methodologies that have matured and proliferated across the strategic policy community in this period – from formal risk assessment to horizon scanning and scenario planning – the aims of which are 'to provide a detailed sense of context through which strategic risk and opportunity can be judged and against which decision-making can take place'. He argues that such developments are indicative of an emergent, and distinctively British, theory of action; one that favours strategic adaptivity bounded by futures-orientated analysis over grand hegemonic notions of the national interest. This dissipated and iterative approach, he concludes, 'accords well not only with historically grounded notions of incrementalism in British policymaking, but also with the nuanced and conditional position of the British general public in relation to core questions of national interest'.

It would, of course, be wrong to assume that such developments represent a completely new dawn for British strategy making or finally draw a line under debates about the national interest. Where innovations have taken place they have been nascent in their efficacy and influence, and significant challenges of strategic practice remain. As Alex Evans argues in his contribution to this volume, many of the thorniest aspects of strategic planning are also the most enduring and have been familiar to foreign policymakers for decades. In particular, the tensions between long-term planning and the immediate demands of everyday policy are endemic and, to some degree, unavoidable. The danger, he implies, is that what may appear to be flexibility and adaptivity in a nation's strategic posture may actually mask a more pathological bias towards short-termism, reactive pragmatism and what he calls 'recentism' – a focus on the immediate past rather than the long view – in the policymaking process.

Evans examines attempts to address these issues in the British Foreign and Commonwealth Office (FCO) and US State Department over the years. He concludes that the ability to foster strategic, anticipatory and innovative thinking in government is crucial for effective foreign policymaking. However, he also suggests that the source of these faculties lies less in strategic planning methodologies or institutional reforms, but more in the organisational culture of the strategic policy community itself. In effect, individuals matter more than systems. In the UK case, he argues that more could be done to build such capacities in the FCO and elsewhere, including by creating protected space in which policymakers are encouraged to think strategically, fostering engagement with expert communities outside government, and promoting the institutional value of imagination and dissent in the policy planning process.

Whither the national interest?

The concept of the national interest is 'about how putative national goals are pursued under particular conditions' (Humphreys forthcoming). Yet recognising and embracing its political and politicised nature is precisely what gives the concept its utility and meaning. Conceived in this way, the contributions to this book highlight at least three components of the national interest debate that require further exploration. The first of these is the issue of contestation. A central thrust of this volume has been that the UK has multiple interests, and these in turn are both subjective and to some degree politically conditioned. The manner in which particularly notions of the national interest become dominant is thus key to understanding which interests are important and why. Dynamics of contestation are played out at numerous levels in the policy process. They exist both within and amongst different groups in government, as well as between different sections of the political community more widely. The process by which particular interpretations of interest prevail and become determinant to policy in what is an increasingly variegated and distributed strategic policy community is thus key to understanding how the national interest is practically articulated and why.

A second and related point pertains to the issue of legitimacy. If the national interest is necessarily representative of some wider, albeit abstract, conceptualisation of the collective good, then the question arises of who is able to make such claims and how these claims should be assessed. Such an issue is not simply one of academic interest. After all, the UK government struggled to maintain public legitimacy for its actions in Iraq and Afghanistan, despite repeated elite claims that they were in the national interest. Likewise, the 2013 controversy over the *Guardian's* decision to publish leaked documents on UK and US surveillance practices revolved around competing – and in this case diametrically opposed – claims to the public interest. In this respect, we echo the call of the Public Administration Select Committee, in 2010 and 2013, for a more open and transparent debate on contemporary British values and the interests that derive from these, as well as the implications of such a debate for strategy and policy in practice. Significantly, and as a number of chapters in this volume suggest, we believe that this cannot simply take place amongst established strategic and foreign policy elites – whether they be drawn from government, the military or academia – but must involve civil society and the general public more widely.

The final point relates to the utility of the national interest. There are at least two aspects to this question. The first is resolutely practical and relates to the means–ends reasonings that underpin particular policies in the foreign policy arena and elsewhere. How and in what ways is government policy expected to advance the collective good? What are the trade-offs and potential vulnerabilities inherent in such logics? Making these questions explicit not only provides a measure against which to gauge the efficacy of policy in strategic terms, but also a means through which debates about public legitimacy can be articulated and structured. The second question is perhaps a deeper one and concerns the issue of who benefits from actions taken in the name of the national interest and how. This brings us back again to wider questions about values: about how wide or narrow our conception of the political community should be; about what, if any, interests and responsibilities this engenders for non-citizens; and about how these might legitimately be advanced through government policy.

Whatever insights future research may bring to these questions, we are clear that the relevance of the national interest concept remains. Far from being a relic of a bygone era of traditional diplomacy and great power politics, it retains its rhetorical, analytical and substantive significance for both policymakers and academics. Even in the complex, uncertain and interconnected environment of contemporary global affairs, the notion of the national interest endures.

Note

1. It should be noted however, that these budgetary pressures were themselves grounded in a government view that the future health of the British economy was the overwhelming national interest at the time, and that austerity was the best way to achieve this.

Bibliography

Achcar, G. (2004) *Eastern Cauldron: Islam, Afghanistan, Palestine and Iraq in a Marxist Mirror* (London: Pluto Press).
Achcar, G. (2011) 'Libya: A legitimate and necessary debate from an anti-imperialist perspective', *ZNet* 25 March, http://www.zcommunications.org/libya-a-legitimate-and-necessary-debate-from-an-anti-imperialist-perspective-by-gilbert-achcar, accessed 21 June 2013.
Achcar, G. and Chomsky, N. (2007) *Perilous Power: The Middle East and US Foreign Policy* (London: Hamish Hamilton).
Aggestam, L. (2006) 'Role theory and European foreign policy: A framework of analysis' in Elgstrom, O. and Smith, M. (eds.), *The European Union's Roles in International Politics* (London: Routledge), pp.11–29.
Al Arabiya News (2012) 'Bahrain and Britain sign defence treaty to increase military co-operation,' 12 October, http://english.alarabiya.net/articles/2012/10/12/243298.html, accessed 3 March 2013.
Allison, G. T. and Zelikow, P. (1999) *Essence of Decision: Explaining the Cuban Missile Crisis* (2nd edn.) (Harlow: Longman).
Amin, S. and Luckin, D. (1996) 'The challenge of globalization', *Review of International Political Economy*, 2: 216–259.
Amnesty International, (2003) *Bahrain: 'Freedom Has a Price': Two Years After Bahrain's Uprising*, 14 February, http://www.amnesty.org/en/library/info/MDE11/005/2013/en, accessed 3 March 2013.
Ancram, M. (2006) *Hansard, HC Deb.* 20 July, c541.
Anderson, P. (2002) 'Force and consent', *New Left Review*, 17 (September–October): 5–30.
Andrew, C. (2004) 'Intelligence analysis needs to look backwards before looking forward', *History & Policy*, pp. 1900–1960.
Arendt, H. (1958) *The Human Condition* (Chicago: University of Chicago Press).
Arms Control Association (2013) 'The European phased adaptive approach at a glance', May.
Arrighi, G. (1994) *The Long Twentieth Century: Money, Power, and the Origins of Our Times* (London: Verso).
Arrighi, G. and Silver, B. J. (2003) 'Polanyi's "Double Movement": The Belle Epoques of British and US Hegemony compared', *Politics and Society*, 3: 325–355.
Atkins, J. (2013) 'A renewed social democracy for an "age of internationalism": An interpretivist account of New Labour's foreign policy', *British Journal of Politics and International Relations*, 15:2, 175–191.
Atkinson, W. (2013) 'Everyday crisis and classed everyday life: Hysteresis, positional suffering and symbolic violence', in Atkinson, W., Roberts, S. and Savage, M. (eds.) *Class Inequality in Austerity Britain* (Basingstoke: Palgrave).
Bailes, A. (2005) 'Reflections on 30 years in the diplomatic service', in Johnson, G. (ed.) *The Foreign Office and British Diplomacy in the Twentieth Century* (London: Routledge).

Baldwin, D. (1997) 'The concept of security', *Review of International Studies*, 23:5, 5–26.
Barnett A. (1982) *Iron Britannia: Why Parliament Waged its Falklands War* (London: Allison and Busby).
Baylis, J. (ed.) (1997) *Anglo-American Relations Since 1939: The Enduring Alliance* (Manchester: Manchester University Press).
BBC (2011) 'Iraq war in figures', http://www.bbc.co.uk/news/world-middle-east-11107739, accessed 14 December 2011.
BBC News (2013) 'Aid money could go to defence – David Cameron'http://www.bbc.co.uk/news/uk-politics-21528464, accessed 21 February 2013.
Beard, C. (1977) *The Idea of the National Interest* (Chicago: Greenwood Press).
Beck, P. (1992) 'The policy relevance of the Falklands/Malvinas past', in Alex Danchev (ed.) *International Perspectives on the Falklands Conflict: A Matter of Life and Death* (New York: St. Martin's Press), pp. 12–46.
Beck, U. (1990) *World Risk Society* (Cambridge: Polity).
Beck, U. (1992) *Risk Society: Towards a New Modernity* (London: Sage).
Beech, M. (2011) 'British conservatism and foreign policy: Traditions and ideas shaping Cameron's global view', *British Journal of Politics and International Relations*, 13:1, 348–363.
Beyerchen, A. (1992–1993) 'Clausewitz, nonlinearity, and the unpredictability of war', *International Security*, 17:3, 59–90.
Billig, M. (1995) *Banal Nationalism* (London: Sage).
Blackham, J. and Prins, G. (2010) 'Why things don't happen. Silent principles of national security', *RUSI Journal*, August/September, 155, 123–158.
Blair, T. (1997) Speech to the Lord Mayor's Banquet, Guildhall, London, 10 November, http://webarchive.nationalarchives.gov.uk/20070701080624/http://www.pm.gov.uk/output/Page1070.asp accessed 11 September 2013.
Blair, T. (1998) Speech on foreign affairs, London, 15 December.
Blair, T. (1999) 'Doctrine of the international community', speech at The Economic Club, Chicago, 24 April,http://www.britishpoliticalspeech.org/speech-archive.htm?speech=279 accessed 11 September 2013.
Blair, T. (2000) Speech at the Mansion House, London, 13 November.
Blair, T. (2001) Speech at the Lord Mayor's Banquet, London, 13 November.
Blair, T. (2002) Speech at the George Bush Presidential Library, Texas, 7 April.
Blair, T. (2003) 'Motion for war' 18 March, http://www.publications.parliament.uk/pa/cm200203/cmhansrd/vo030318/debtext/30318-06.htm.
Blair, T. (2003) Speech at the foreign office, London, 7 January.
Blair, T. (2004) 'Full text: Blair's Mansion House Speech'. *Guardian*, 16 November.
Blair, T. (2004) 'Speech delivered in Sedgefield', 5 March http://www.britishpoliticalspeech.org/speech-archive.htm?speech=282 accessed 11 September 2013.
Blair, T. (2006) 'PM's foreign policy speech – Third in a series of three', Georgetown University, 26 May.
Blair, Tony. (2006) 'Not a clash between civilisations, but a clash about civilisation', speech to the Foreign Policy Centre, London, 21 March.
Blair, T. (2007) 'Defending the UK and its interests',speech at the Royal United Services Institute, 12 January, http://fora.tv/2007/01/12/Tony_Blair_Defense_of_the_UK_and_Its_Interests, accessed 24 June 2013.

Blair, T. (2007) 'Our nation's future – defence', speech aboard HMS Albion, Portsmouth, 12 January.
Blair, T. (2010) *A Journey* (London: Hutchinson).
Blakeley, R. (2009) *State Terrorism and Neoliberalism: The North in the South* (Abingdon: Routledge).
Bluth, C. (1992) 'Anglo-American relations and the Falklands conflict', in Danchev, A. (ed.), *International Perspectives on the Falklands Conflict* (Basingstoke: Palgrave Macmillan) pp. 203–223.
Booth, K. (2007) *Theory of World Security* (Cambridge: Cambridge University Press).
Boyce, D. G. (2005) *The Falklands War* (Basingstoke: Palgrave).
Boyle, R. B. (2007) 'The US national security strategy: policy, process, problems' *Public Administration Review*, 67:4, 624–629.
Braithwaite, Sir R. (2003) 'End of the affair'. *Prospect*, May.
Brewer, A. (1990) *Marxist Theories of Imperialism: A Critical Survey* (London: Routledge).
Brewer, P. R. (2006) 'National interest frames and public opinion about world affairs', *The Harvard International Journal of Press/Politics*, 11:4, 89–102.
Bright, J. (1858) 'Principles of foreign policy' reproduced in Jones, E. (ed.), *Selected Speeches on British Foreign Policy 1738 to 1914* (UK: Kessinger Publishing), pp. 186–204.
Brighton, S. (2007) 'British Muslims, multiculturalism and UK foreign policy: "Integration" and "cohesion" in and beyond the state', *International Affairs*, 83:1, 1–17.
British Conservative Party (2010) 'A resilient nation: National security green paper', Policy paper no. 13,http://www.conservatives.com/news/news_stories/2010/01/~/media/30D1AC669FE746E5ABCE8EB7C5E068D4.ashx, accessed 16 October 2013.
Brown, G. (2007) Speech to the Lord Mayor's Banquet, London, 12 November.
Brown, G. (2008a) Speech delivered at the Kennedy presidential library and museum, Boston, 18 April, in Brown (2010b), pp. 17–29.
Brown, G. (2008b) Speech to the Lord Mayor's Banquet, Guildhall, London, 10 November, in Brown (2010b), pp. 32–40.
Brown, G. (2009a) Speech at department for international development, London, 9 March http://webarchive.nationalarchives.gov.uk/20100429125008/http://www.number10.gov.uk/news/speeches-and-transcripts/2009/03/speech-to-dfid-conference-on-eliminating-world-poverty-18554 accessed 11 September 2013.
Brown, G. (2009b) Speech to the UN General Assembly, New York, 23 September, in Brown (2010b), pp. 43–47.
Brown, G. (2009c) Speech to the Lord Mayor's Banquet, Guildhall, London, 16 November, in Brown (2010b), pp. 49–57.
Brown, G. (2009d) Speech to the UN climate change conference, Copenhagen, 17 December, in Brown (2010b), pp. 81–83.
Brown, G. (2010a) Remarks at the foreign press association, London, 19 March http://webarchive.nationalarchives.gov.uk/20100429125008/http://www.number10.gov.uk/news/speeches-and-transcripts/2010/03/opening-remarks-at-fpa-event-22876 accessed 11 September 2013.

Brown, G. (2010b) *The Change We Choose: Speeches 2007–2009* (Edinburgh: Mainstream).
Bull, H. (2002 [1977]) *The Anarchical Society: A Study of Order in World Politics* (3rd edn.) (Basingstoke: Palgrave).
Burall, S., Donnelly, B. and Weir, S. (2006) *Not in Our Name: Democracy and Foreign Policy in the UK* (London: Politico's).
Burchill, S. (2005) *The National Interest in International Relations Theory* (Basingstoke: Palgrave Macmillan).
Burke, A. (2007) 'What makes security possible? Some thoughts on critical security studies', Working Paper 2007/1 (Canberra: Department of International Relations, Australian National University).
Buzan, B. (2010) 'China in international society', *Chinese Journal of International Politics*, 3:1, 5–36.
Cabinet Office Papers (National Archives): CAB128/75; CAB148/211; CAB148/212.
Cabinet Office (1959) *Study of Future Policy*, 1960–1970. National Archives: PREM 11/3432.
Cabinet Office (2008) *The National Security Strategy of the UK: Security in an Interdependent World*, Cmd. 7291(London: HMSO).
Cabinet Office(2008b) *National Risk Register*.
Cabinet Office (2009) *The National Security Strategy: Security for the Next Generation*, Cm 7590 (London: HMSO).
Cabinet Office (2010a) *A Strong Britain in an Age of Uncertainty: National Security Strategy of the UK*, Cmd. 7953 (London: HMSO).
Cabinet Office (2010b) *Securing Britain in an Age of Uncertainty: The Strategic Defence and Security Review*. Cmd. 7948 (London: HMSO).
Cabinet Office (2010c) 'The coalition: Our programme for government', May.
Cabinet Office (2010d) *Fact Sheet 5: Future Force 2020 – Summary of Size, Shape and Structure*, https://www.gov.uk/government/uploads/system/uploads/attachment_data/file/62487/Factsheet5-Future-Force-2020.pdf
Cabinet Office (2010e) *Fact Sheet 2. National Security Risk Assessment* https://www.gov.uk/government/uploads/system/uploads/attachment_data/file/62484/Factsheet2-National-Security-Risk-Assessment.pdf
Cabinet Office (2012) *National Risk Register of Civil Emergencies* (2012 edn.), February, https://www.gov.uk/government/uploads/system/uploads/attachment_data/file/61929/CO_NationalRiskRegister_2012_acc.pdf, accessed 18 June 2013.
Cabinet Office (2013) 'The Coalition: Together in the national interest. A Mid-term Review', January.
Cabinet Office (2013a) 'Preparation and planning for emergencies: The national resilience capabilities programme,' 20 February, https://www.gov.uk/preparation-and-planning-for-emergencies-the-capabilities-programme#national-resilience-capabilities-programme-nrcp, accessed 29 June 2013.
Cabinet Office (2013b) *Trident Alternatives Review*, 16 July, https://www.gov.uk/government/publications/trident-alternatives-review, accessed 8 November 2013.
Cabinet Office (2013c) *National Risk Register of Civil Emergencies* (2013 edn.) https://www.gov.uk/government/uploads/system/uploads/attachment_

data/file/211867/NationalRiskRegister2013_amended.pdf, accessed 21 October 2013.
Cable, J. (1981) 'The useful art of international relations', *International Affairs*, 57: 2, 301–314.
Cable, J. (1994) 'Foreign policy-making: Planning or reflex', in Beshoff, P. and Hill, C. (eds.) *Two Worlds of International Relations: Academics, Practitioners and the Trade in Ideas* (London: Routledge).
Callinicos, A. (2009) *Imperialism and Global Political Economy* (Cambridge: Polity).
Camerer, C. and Kunreuther, H. (1989) 'Decision processes for low probability events: Policy implications', *Journal of Policy Analysis and Management*, 8: 4, 565–592.
Cameron, D. (2006) Speech to the British American project, 11 September http://www.conservatives.com/News/Speeches/2006/09/Cameron_A_new_approach_to_foreign_affairs__liberal_conservatism.aspx accessed 11 September 2013.
Cameron, D. (2009) 'The age of austerity', speech to the Conservative Party Forum, Cheltenham, 26 April.
Cameron, D. (2010) 'Why Britain matters in the world', London, 6 November.
Cameron, David (2010) 'Oral evidence to House of Commons Liaison Committee', 18 November.
Cameron, D. (2011) 'Statement on UN resolution' 18 March, http://www.bbc.co.uk/news/uk-politics-12786225.
Cameron, D. (2012) 'Address to the UN General Assembly', 26 September.
Cameron, D. and Clegg, N. (2010) 'Foreword', in *A Strong Britain in an Age of Uncertainty: The National Security Strategy* (London: UK Cabinet Office) 3–6, https://www.gov.uk/government/uploads/system/uploads/attachment_data/file/61936/national-security-strategy.pdf, accessed 16 October 2013.
Cantir, C. and Kaarbo, J. (2012) 'Contested roles and domestic politics: Reflections on role theory in foreign policy analysis and IR theory' *Foreign Policy Analysis*, 8, 5–24.
Carnoy, M. (1984) *The State and Political Theory* (Princeton: Princeton University Press).
Central Policy Review Staff (1977) *Review of Overseas Representation: Report* (London: HMSO).
Chalmers, Malcolm. (2011) *Looking into the Black Hole: Is the UK Defence Budget Crisis Really Over?* (RUSI:RUSI).
Chandler, D. (2002) *From Kosovo to Kabul: Human Rights and International Intervention* (London: Pluto Press).
Charlton, M. (1989) *The Little Platoon: Diplomacy and the Falklands Dispute* (Oxford: Basil Blackwell).
Chatham House-YouGov. (2010) 'British attitudes towards the UK's international priorities', *Chatham House Survey*, 2 July.
Chomsky, N. (1991) *Deterring Democracy* (London: Vintage).
Chomsky, N. (2006) *Failed States* (London: Hamish Hamilton).
Christopher, A. (2004) 'Intelligence analysis needs to look backwards before looking forward', *History & Policy*, June.

Clark, I. (2009) 'Towards an English school theory of hegemony', *European Journal of International Relations* 15:2, 203–228.
Clarke, L. (1999) *Mission Improbable: Using Fantasy Documents to Tame Disaster* (Chicago: University of Chicago Press).
Clarke, M., Stansfield, G. and Kelly, S. (April 2013) 'A return to east of Suez: UK military deployment to the Gulf', *Royal United Services Institute Briefing Paper* http://www.rusi.org/downloads/assets/East_of_Suez_Return_042013.pdf, accessed 30 September 2013.
Clinton, W. D. (1991) 'The national interest: normative foundations' in Little, R. and Smith, M. *Perspectives on World Politics* (2nd edn.) (London: Routledge), pp. 47–58.
Cobain, I. (2012) 'MoD pays out millions to Iraqi torture victims', *Guardian*, 20 December, http://www.guardian.co.uk/law/2012/dec/20/mod-iraqi-torture-victims, accessed 20 December 2012.
Cobden, R. (1886) 'England', in Bright, J. (ed.) *Political Writings of Richard Cobden* (London: Cassell & Co. Ltd).
Cohn, C. (1987) 'Sex and death in the rational world of defense intellectuals', *Signs* 12:4, 687–718.
Coker, C. (2002) *Globalisation and Insecurity in the Twenty-First Century: NATO and the Management of Risk*, Adelphi Paper 345 (London: International Institute for Strategic Studies).
Coles, J. (2000) *Making Foreign Policy: A Certain Idea of Britain* (London: John Murray).
Colley, L. (1994) *Britons: Forging the Nation, 1707–1837* (London: Pimlico).
Collier, P. (2008) *The Bottom Billion* (Oxford: Oxford University Press).
Committee on Representational Services Overseas (1964) *Report of the Committee on Representational Services Overseas* (London: HMSO).
Committees on Arms Export Controls (2013) *First Joint Report of the Business, Innovation and Skills, Defence, Foreign Affairs and International Development Committees of Session 2013–2014: Volume I* (London: TSO).
Condor, S., Gibson, S. and Abell, J. (2006) 'English identity and ethnic diversity in the context of UK constitutional change', *Ethnicities*, 6,123–158.
Connelly, M. (2004) *We Can Take It: Britain and the Memory of the Second World War* (London: Pearson Longman).
Conservative Party (2010) *A Resilient Nation: National Security Green*, Paper, Policy Green Paper No. 13.
Conservative Party (2010) *Invitation to Join the Government of Britain: The Conservative Manifesto 2010* (London: Conservative Research Department).
Cook, R. (1997a) Speech delivered at the FCO, London, 12 May http://www.britishpoliticalspeech.org/speech-archive.htm?speech=292 accessed 11 September 2013.
Cook, R. (1997b) 'Human rights into a new century', speech given on 17 July. In Royal United Services Institute (eds.) (2003) *Documents on British Foreign and Security Policy, Volume II: 1997–1998* (London: TSO).
Cook, R. (1998) 'BBC radio interview', 14 May. In Royal United Services Institute (eds.) (2003) *Documents on British Foreign and Security Policy, Volume II: 1997–1998* (London: TSO).
Cook, R. (2003) 'Resignation speech', 17 March, http://www.publications.parliament.uk/pa/cm200203/cmhansrd/vo030317/debtext/30317-33.htm.

Cornish, P. (2010) *Strategy in Austerity: The Security and Defence of the United Kingdom* (London: Chatham House).
Cornish, P. (2013) 'United Kingdom' in Biehl, H. et al. (eds.) *Strategic Cultures in Europe: Security and Defence Policies Across the Continent*, Springer VS.
Cornish, P. and Dorman, A. (2009) 'Blair's wars and Brown's budgets: From strategic defence review to strategic decay in less than a decade', *International Affairs*, 85:2, 247–261.
Cornish P. and Dorman, A. (2010) 'Breaking the mould: the United Kingdom strategic defence and security review of 2010', *International Affairs*, 86:2, 395–410.
Cornish, P. and Dorman, A. (2011) 'Dr Fox and the philosopher's stone: The alchemy of national defence in the age of austerity', *International Affairs*, 87:2, 335–353.
Cornish, P. and Dorman, A.M. (2013) 'Fifty shades of purple? A risk sharing approach to the 2015 strategic defence and security review', *International Affairs*, 89: 5, 1183–1202.
Cox, M. (1998) 'Rebels without a cause? Radical theorists and the world system after the cold war', *New Political Economy*, 3:3, 445–460.
Cox, R. (1986) 'Social forces, states and world orders: Beyond international relations theory', in Keohane, R. (ed.) *Neorealism and Its Critics* (Chichester: Columbia University Press), pp. 204–254.
Crocker, C.A. (2008) 'Reflections on strategic surprise' in Cronin, P. (ed.) *The Impenetrable Fog of War: Reflections on Modern Warfare and Strategic Surprise* (Westport, CT: Praeger Security International), pp. 177–185.
Crowe, E. (1907) 'Memorandum on the Present State of British Relations with France and Germany' in Gooch, G.P. and Temperley, H. (1928) *British Documents on the Origins of the War, 1898-1914'* (London: HMSO), Appendix A, pp. 397–420.
Curtis, M. (2003) *Web of Deceit: Britain's Real Role in the World* (London: Vintage).
Curtis, M. (2004) *Unpeople: Britain's Secret Human Rights Abuses* (London: Vintage).
Curtis, M. (2010) *Secret Affairs* (London: Serpent's Tail).
Daddow, O. (2011) 'Conclusion', in Daddow and Gaskarth (2011) *British Foreign Policy*, (London: Palgrave Macmillan), pp. 221–235.
Daddow, O. and Gaskarth, J. (eds.) (2011) *British Foreign Policy: The New Labour Years* (Basingstoke: Palgrave Macmillan).
Dalyell, T. (1983) *Thatcher's Torpedo: The Sinking of the Belgrano* (London: Cecil Woolf).
Danchev, A. (1998) *On Specialness: Essays in Anglo-American relations* (London: Macmillan).
Development, Concepts and Doctrine Centre (DCDC) (2013) 'Setting the strategic context for defence and security: method', *Global Insecurities Centre consultation*, University of Bristol, 26 September.
de France, Olivier and Witney, Nick. (2013) *Europe's Strategic Cacophony*. European Council on Foreign Relations.
Defense Update (2013) 'British destroyer to participate in US missile defense trials', 7 March, http://defense-update.com/20130307_british-destroyer-to-participate-in-u-s-missile-defense-trials.html, accessed 16 October 2013.
Department of Defense (DoD) (2010) *Quadrennial Defense Review* (Washington: DoD).

Dickerson, P. (1998) "'I did it for the nation": Repertoires of intent in televised political discourse' *British Journal of Social Psychology*, 37: 477–494.
Dixit, A. and Nalebuff, B. (1998) *The Art of Strategy* (New York: Norton).
Doig, A. and Phythian, M. (2005) 'The national interest and the politics of threat exaggeration: The Blair government's case for war against Iraq', *Political Quarterly*, 76 (3), pp. 368–376.
Doorn, J. van Verhoef, P.C. and Bijmolt, T.H.A. (2007) 'The importance of non-linear relationships between attitude and behaviour in policy research', *Journal of Consumer Policy*, 30: 75–90.
Downer, J. (2011) '737 Cabriolet: The limits of knowledge and the sociology of inevitable failure', *American Journal of Sociology*, 117:3, 725–762.
Doyle, R.B. (2007) 'The U.S. National Security Strategy: Policy, Process, Problems', *Public Administration Review*, January–February 624–629.
Drezner, D. (ed.) (2009) *Avoiding Trivia: The Role of Strategic Planning in American Foreign Policy* (Washington: Brookings Institution).
Duffy, S. (Director, Centre for Welfare Reform) (2013) 'It's clear who is the hardest hit – disabled people', *The Huffington Post UK*, 9 May.
Dumbrell, J. (2001) *A Special Relationship: Anglo-American Relations in the Cold War and After* (Basingstoke: Macmillan).
Dunleavy, P. and O'Leary, B. (1987) *Theories of the State: The Politics of Liberal Democracy* (Basingstoke: MacMillan).
Dunn, D. H. (2008) 'The double interregnum: UK–US relations beyond Blair and Bush'. *International Affairs* 84: 1131–1143.
Dunning, D., Johnson, K., Ehrlinger, J. and Kruger, J. (2003) 'Why people fail to recognize their own incompetence', *Current Directions in Psychological Science*, 12: June.
Dyson, S. B. (2011) 'New labour, leadership, and foreign policy-making after 1997', in Daddow and Gaskarth (2011) *British Foreign Policy*, pp. 63–83.
Eckstein, H. (1975) 'Case studies and theory in political science' in Fred Greenstein and Nelson Polsby (eds.) *Handbook of Political Science*, Volume 7. (Reading, Mass: Addison-Wesley).
Edmunds, T. (2010) 'The defence dilemma in Britain', *International Affairs*, 86:2, 377–394.
Edmunds, T. (2012) 'British civil-military relations and the problem of risk', *International Affairs*, 88:2, 265–282.
Elgstrom, O. and Smith, M. (2006) 'Introduction' in Elgstrom and Smith *The European Union's Roles*, pp. 1–10.
Ellerby, C. (1992) 'The role of the Falklands lobby', in Danchev, *International Perspectives*, pp. 85–108.
Ellis, P. (2010) 'A nation's resilience as a deterrence factor', in Schneider, B. and Ellis, P. (eds.) *Tailored Deterrence: Influencing States and Groups of Concern* (Maxwell Air Force Base, Alabama: USAF Counterproliferation Center), pp. 372–407.
Evans, A. (2010) Remarks in Evans, Steven and Niblett, *UK and the World: Governing in an Age of Uncertainty*, 9 June http://www.chathamhouse.org/sites/default/files/public/Meetings/Meeting%20Transcripts/09062010alexevansetal.pdf.
Evans, A. and Steven, D. (2010) *Organizing for Influence: UK Foreign Policy in an Age of Uncertainty*, June http://www.chathamhouse.org/sites/default/files/public/Research/Europe/r0610_stevens_evans.pdf.

Evans, B. and Reid, J. (2013) 'Dangerously exposed', *Resilience*, 1: 2, 83–93.
Evans, B. and Reid, J. (2014) *Resilient Life: The Art of Living Dangerously* (London: Polity).
Evans, E. (2013) (3rd edn.) *Thatcher and Thatcherism* (London: Routledge).
Evans, G. (1990) 'Foreign policy and good international citizenship', speech given in Canberra, 6 March.
Evans, L. (2010) 'Defence review: See the list of cuts in full', *Guardian*, 19 October 2010. http://www.theguardian.com/news/datablog/2010/oct/19/defence-review-cuts-list
Fasana, K. G. (2011) 'Using capabilities to drive military transformation: An alternative framework' *ArmedForces and Society*, 37:1, 141–162.
Fawcett Society (2012) *The Impact of Austerity on Women*, March.
Foreign and Commonwealth Office (2012) *Annual Report 2011–2012*, HC 59 (London: The Stationery Office), https://www.gov.uk/government/uploads/system/uploads/attachment_data/file/32880/annual-report-accounts-2011-12.pdf.
Foreign and Commonwealth Office (2013a) 'William Hague and Angelina Jolie visit eastern DRC', press release, 25 March, http://www.politicshome.com/uk/article/75120/fco_william_hague_and_angelina_jolie_visit_eastern_drc.html.
Foreign and Commonwealth Office (2013b) 'G8 foreign ministers' meeting statement', 11 April, https://www.gov.uk/government/news/g8-foreign-ministers-meeting-statement.
Foreign and Commonwealth Office (2013c) *Human Rights and Democracy: The 2012 FCO Report* (London: TSO).
Feaver, P. D. and Sharp, K. T. (2010) 'The United States', in Born, H., Gill B. and Hanggi, H. (eds.), *Governing the Bomb: Civilian Control and Democratic Accountability of Nuclear Weapons* (Oxford: Oxford University Press).
Ferguson, N. (2010) 'Complexity and collapse. Empires on the edge of chaos', *Foreign Affairs*, March/April.
Fisher, D. and Biggar, N. (2011) 'Was Iraq an unjust war? A debate on the Iraq war and reflections on Libya', *International Affairs*, 87:3, 687–707.
Fontaine, R. and Burton, B. (2010) *Eye to the Future: Refocusing State Department Policy Planning* (Washington: Center for a New American Security – CNAS) Policy Brief, August.
Foreign Affairs Committee (2011) *The Role of the FCO in Government: Volume I* (London: TSO), also (2010/11) at http:// www.publications.parliament.uk/pa/201012/cmselect/cmfaff/665/66506.htm, accessed 19.06.13.
Foreign Affairs Committee (2012a) 'Developments in UK foreign policy: Oral and written evidence', *House of Commons*, 18 September.
Foreign Affairs Committee (2012b) *British Foreign Policy and the 'Arab Spring'* (London: TSO).
Foreign Affairs Committee of the House of Commons (2010) 'FCO Priorities', *The Role of the FCO in UK Government – Foreign Affairs Committee*. www.publications.parliament.uk/pa/201012/cmselect/cmfaff/665/66506.htm, accessed 19 June 2013.
Foreign and Commonwealth Office (FCO) (2003) *UK International Priorities: A Strategy for the FCO*. Cmd. 6052.
Foreign and Commonwealth Office (2006) *Active Diplomacy for a Changing World: The UK's International Priorities*. Cmd. 6762.

Foreign and Commonwealth Office (2007) 'Foreign and Commonwealth Office objectives for spending review period 2005–2008.' *FCO Aims and Objectives*, http://www.fco.gov.ukaccessed 19 June 2013.

Foreign and Commonwealth Office (2010) *UK Government Strategy on the Protection of Civilians in Armed Conflict* (London: FCO).

Foreign and Commonwealth Office (2012a) *Business Plan 2012–2015* (London: FCO).

Foreign and Commonwealth Office (2012b) *Human Rights and Democracy: The 2011 FCO Report* (London: TSO).

Forster, A. and Blair, A. (2002) *The Making of Britain's European Foreign Policy* (London: Longman Political Dynamics of the European Union Series).

Frankel, J. (1970) *National Interest* (London: Praeger).

Franks, O. (1954) 'Britain and the tide of world affairs' Reith Lectures, Home Service, 7 November, http://downloads.bbc.co.uk/rmhttp/radio4/transcripts/1954_reith1.pdf.

Freedman, L. (2005) (Kindle edn.) *The Official History of the Falklands War: Volume 2, War and Diplomacy* (London: Routledge).

Freedman, L. (2006) 'The special relationship: Then and now', *Foreign Affairs* 85: May/June, 61–73.

Freedman, L. and Gamba-Stonehouse, V. (1990) *Signals of War: The Falklands Conflict of 1982* (London: Faber and Faber).

Frost, Mervyn. (1999) 'Putting the world to rights: Britain's ethical foreign policy', *Cambridge Review of International Affairs*, 12:2, 80–89.

Gaddis, J. L. (2005) *Origins of Containment* (2nd edn.) (New York: Oxford University Press).

Galtung, J. (1990) 'Cultural violence', *Journal of Peace Research*, 27:3, 291–305.

Garrison, D. (2006) *Bracing for Armageddon: Why Civil Defence Never Worked* (Oxford: Oxford University Press).

Garton Ash, T. (2000) 'Is Britain European?', *International Affairs*, 77:1, 1–13.

Garzone, G. and Degano, C. (2010) 'Public diplomacy, multimodality and the world wide web', in Overton, G. T. (ed.) *Foreign Policy in an Interconnected World* (Hauppauge, New York: Nova Science Publishers).

Gaskarth, J. (2001) 'Entangling alliances? The UK's complicity in torture in the global war on terrorism' *International Affairs*, 87, 945–964.

Gaskarth, J. (2006) 'Discourses and ethics: The social construction of British foreign policy', *Foreign Policy Analysis*, 2:4, 325–341.

Gaskarth, J. (2011) 'Identity and new labour's strategic foreign policy thinking', in Daddow and Gaskarth (2011) *British Foreign Policy: The New Labour Years* (Basingstoke: Palgrave Macmillan), pp. 84–99.

Gaskarth, J. (2013) *British Foreign Policy* (Cambridge: Polity Press).

Gaskarth, J. (2013) 'Interpreting ethical foreign policy: Traditions and dilemmas for policymakers', *British Journal of Politics and International Relations*, 15:2, 192–209.

Gaskarth, J. (2014) 'Strategizing Britain's role in the world', *International Affairs*, 90:3, 559–581.

Gates, Robert. (2011) The Security and Defense Agenda (Future of NATO),speech delivered, Brussels, Belgium.http://www.defense.gov/speeches/speech.aspx?speechid=1581.

George, A. (2006) *On Foreign Policy: Unfinished Business* (Boulder, CO: Paradigm).

Gibson, J. J. (1977) 'The theory of affordances' in Shaw, R. and Bransford, J. (eds.) *Perceiving, Acting, and Knowing: Toward an Ecological Psychology* (Hillsdale, NJ: Lawrence Erlbaum), pp. 67–82.
Gibson, J. J. (1986) *The Ecological Approach to Visual Perception* (Hillsdale, NJ: Erlbaum).
Girard, R. (2010) *Battling to the End; Conversations with Benoît Chantre*, translated by Mary Baker. (East Lansing, Michigan: Michigan State University Press).
Good, R. C. (1960) 'The national interest and political realism: Niebuhr's "debate" with Morgenthau and Kennan', *Journal of Politics*, 22:4, November, 597–619.
Gowan, Peter (2003) 'US:UN', *New Left Review* 24, November–December 2003.
Tickell *Workshop: Latin America, the United States and the Rise of the New Imperialism* (NewYork: Metropolitan Books).
Gray, C. (2010) 'Strategic thoughts for defence planners', *Survival*, 52:3, 159–178.
Gray, C. (2011) 'Conclusion', in Olsen, J. A. and Gray, C. S. (eds.) *The Practice of Strategy: from Alexander the Great to the Present* (Oxford: Oxford University Press).
Greenwald, G. (2013) 'Washington gets explicit: its "war on terror" is permanent', *Guardian*, 17 May, http://www.guardian.co.uk/commentisfree/2013/may/17/endless-war-on-terror-obama.
Guardian (2004) 'Full text: Blair's Mansion House Speech', 16 November.
Guardian (2012) 'MoD signs £500m missile defence deal', 30 January, http://www.theguardian.com/business/2012/jan/30/air-defence-seaceptor-missile-contract, accessed 17 October 2013.
Guldi, J. (2006) 'The uses of planning and the decay of strategy', *Contemporary Security Policy*, 27:2, 209–236.
Haas, E. B. (1953) 'The balance of power as a guide to policy-making', *The Journal of Politics*, 15:3, 370–398.
Haddad, M. (2012) *The Perfect Storm* (Oxford: Oxfam).
Hague, W. (2009) 'The future of British foreign policy', speech to the Institute for Strategic Studies, London, 21 July.
Hague, W. (2010) 'Britain's foreign policy in a networked world', speech at the Foreign and Commonwealth Office, London, 1 July, http://www.conservatives.com/News/Speeches/2010/07/William_Hague_Britains_Foreign_Policy_in_a_Networked_World.aspx accessed 11 September 2013.
Hague, W. (2010) 'Britain's values in a networked world', speech given at Lincolns Inn, London, 15 September.
Hague, W. (2010) Speech delivered at the Royal United Services Institute, London, 10 March, http://www.conservatives.com/News/Speeches/2010/03/William_Hague_The_biggest_risk_for_Britain_is_five_more_years_of_Brown.aspx accessed 11 September 2013.
Hague, W. (2011) Speech delivered at the FCO, London, 8 September https://www.gov.uk/government/speeches/the-best-diplomatic-service-in-the-world-strengthening-the-foreign-and-commonwealth-office-as-an-institution accessed 11 September 2013.
Hague, W. (2013) 'A safer future is within our grasp – We will not rest until we have secured it', Huffington Post Blog, 13 February, http://www.huffingtonpost.co.uk/william-hague/arms-trade-treaty-safer-future-within-our-grasp_b_2669081.html accessed 24 February 2013.
Hain, P. (2001) *The End of Foreign Policy?* (London: Fabian Society/RIIA).

Hall, I. and Rengger, N. (2005) 'The right that failed? The ambiguities of conservative thought and the dilemmas of conservative practice in international affairs', *International Affairs*, 81:1, 69–82.
Hammerstad, A. and Boas, I. (2012) 'National security risks? The language of risk in the formulation of the UK's national security strategy', paper presented at the annual conference of the International Studies Association, San Diego, April.
Hanieh, A. (2011) 'Finance, oil and the Arab uprisings', *Socialist Register*, 48, 1–24
Hardest Hit Coalition. (2012) *The Tipping Point: The Human and Economic Costs of Cutting Disabled People's Support*, October, http://www.thehardesthit.wordpress.com.
Hardt, M. and Negri, A. (2000) *Empire* (London: Harvard University Press).
Harnisch, S. (2012) 'Conceptualizing in the minefield: Role theory and foreign policy learning' *Foreign Policy Analysis*, 8, 47–69.
Hartley, K. (2010) 'The economics of the defence review', *The RUSI Journal*, 155:6, 4–8.
Harvey, D. (2005) *The New Imperialism* (Oxford: Oxford University Press).
Harvey, M. (2011) 'Perspectives on Britain's place in the world', *Europe Programme Paper 2011/01* (London: RIIA).
Hay, C. (2008) '(What's Marxist about) Marxist state theory?', in Lister, M. and Marsh, D. (eds.) *The State: Theories and Ideas* (Basingstoke: Palgrave Macmillan), pp. 39–58.
Hehir, Aidan. (2007) 'The myth of the failed state and the war on terror: A challenge to the conventional wisdom', *Journal of Intervention and Statebuilding*, 1:3, 307–332.
Henderson, N. (1995) *Mandarin: The Diaries of an Ambassador, 1969–1982* (London: Weidenfeld and Nicolson).
Hennessy, P. (2000) *Prime Ministers: The Office and its Holders Since 1945* (Harmondsworth: Penguin).
Hennessy, P., Rayment, S. and Amoore, M. (2009) 'Afghanistan offensive "shows signs of success" says Gordon Brown', *Daily Telegraph*, 12 July.
Hennessy, P. (2008) 'Blink and you'd miss it. Brown said sorry', *Independent*, 23 March.
Hermann, M. G. (1987) 'Foreign policy role orientations and the quality of foreign policy decisions' in Walker, S.G. (ed.) *Role Theory and Foreign Policy Analysis* (Durham N. C.: Duke University Press), 123–140.
Herring, E. and Rangwala, G. (2005) 'Iraq, imperialism and global governance' *Third World Quarterly*, 26:4/5, 667–683.
Herring, E. (2002) 'Between Iraq and a hard place: A critique of the British government's case for economic sanctions', *Review of International Studies*, 28:1, 39–56.
Hersh, S. M. (2004) 'Torture at Abu Ghraib', *The New Yorker*, 10 May, http://www.newyorker.com/archive/2004/05/10/040510fa_fact, accessed 6 January 2013.
Hill, C. (1979) 'Britain's elusive role in world politics', *British Journal of International Studies*, 5:3, October, 248–259.
Hill, C. (2010) 'Tough choices', *The World Today*, April.
HM Government (2007) 'Foreign and Commonwealth Office Objectives for Spending Review Period 2005–2008', in *FCO Aims and Objectives* (London:

HMSO) HM Government (2008) *The National Security Strategy of the United Kingdom: Security in an Interdependent World* (London: TSO).
HM Government (2009) *The National Security Strategy of the United Kingdom: update 2009 – Security for the Next Generation* (London: TSO).
HM Government (2010) *A Strong Britain in an Age of Uncertainty: The National Security Strategy* (London: TSO).
HM Government (2011) *Building Overseas Stability Strategy* (London: FCO, MoD & DFID Joint Publication).
HM Government (2013) *United Kingdom Strategic Export Controls Annual Report* (London: TSO).
HM Treasury (2010) *Budget 2010*, HC 61 (London: HMSO).
HM Treasury (2010) *Spending Review 2010*, Cmd. 7942. (London: HMSO).
Hobsbawm, E. (1983) 'Falklands fallout', in Hall, S. and Jacques, M. (eds.) *The Politics of Thatcherism*. (London: Lawrence and Wishart), pp. 257–270. First published in *Marxism Today*, January.
Hobsbawm, E. (1987) *Age of Empire* (London: Abacus).
Hobson, J. A. (1938) *Imperialism: A Study* (London: George Allen & Unwin).
Hoffman, D. E. (2009) *The Dead Hand: the Untold Story of the Cold War Arms Race and its Dangerous Legacy* (New York: Doubleday).
Hollis, M. and Smith, S. (1986) 'Roles and reasons in foreign policy decision making' *British Journal of Political Science*, 16:3, July, 269–286.
Hollis, R. (2010) *Britain and the Middle East in the 9/11 Era* (Chichester: Wiley Blackwell).
Holsti, K. (1970) 'National role conceptions in the study of foreign policy' *International Studies Quarterly*, 14:3, September, 233–309.
House of Commons Debates (1982), various debates (April–May) accessed via http://hansard.millbanksystems.com/commons/1982/apr/03/falkland-islands
House of Commons Library (2008) 'British foreign policy since 1997' *House of Commons Library Research Paper 08–56*, 23 June, http://www.parliament.uk/briefing-papers/rp08-56.pdf, accessed 19 June 2013.
House of Lords/House of Commons, Joint Committee on the National Security Strategy (2012) *First Review of the National Security Strategy 2010* (27 February 2012) HC 1384 http://www.publications.parliament.uk/pa/jt201012/jtselect/jtnatsec/265/265.pdf.http://www.isj.org.uk/index.php4?id=824, accessed 21 June 2013.
Hughes, T. (1969) 'The fate of facts in the world of men', *Proceedings of the American Society of International Law at Its Annual Meeting (1921–1969)* Volume 63, *Perspectives for International Legal Development*, April, 233–245.
Humphreys, A. (2013), 'Gordon Brown's "Global Society": From National Interest to Global Order', paper presented to conference on British Foreign Policy and the National Interest, Chatham House, London, 12 July 2013, p.1.
Human Security Report Project (2010) *Human Security Report 2009/2010: The Causes of Peace and the Shrinking Costs of War*, Simon Fraser University, Canada (Oxford: Oxford University Press).
Huntington, S. P. (1997) 'The erosion of American national interests' *Foreign Affairs*, 76:5, 28–49.
Huntington, S. P. (2003) 'America in the world', *The Hedgehog Review*, 5: 7–19.
Hurd, D. (1997) *The Search for Peace* (London: Little, Brown and Company).

Hurd, D. and Young, E. (2010) *Choose Your Weapons* (London: Weidenfeld & Nicolson).
Hurrell, A. (1983) 'The politics of South Atlantic security: A survey of the proposals for a South Atlantic treaty organisation'. *International Affairs*, 59: 179–93.
Hutton, W. (1992) 'Britain in a cold climate: The economic aims of foreign policy in the 1990s', *International Affairs*, 68:4, 619–632.
Institute of Contemporary British History Witness Seminar (2005) *The Falklands War* (London: King's College Institute of Contemporary British History) http://www.kcl.ac.uk/sspp/departments/icbh/witness
IPPR (2009) *Shared Responsibilities. A National Security Strategy for the UK*, 30 June.
Janis, I. (1972) *Victims of Groupthink: A Psychological Study of Foreign-Policy Decisions and Fiascoes* (Boston MA: Houghton Mifflin).
JCNSS (2012a) 'First review of the national security strategy 2010', *Joint Committee on the National Security Strategy HC1384* (London: TSO).
JCNSS (2012b) *Government Response to the Committee's First Report of the Session 2012–2013* (London: TSO).
JCNSS (2012c) 'The work of the joint committee on the national security strategy in 2012', *Joint Committee on the National Security Strategy HC984* (London: TSO).
Jenkins, S. (2010) 'Does Britain really need the military?', *Guardian*, 5 November.
Jermy, S. (2011) *Strategy for Action* (London: Knightstone).
Jervis, R. (1978) 'Cooperation under the security dilemma' *World Politics*, 30:2, 167–214.
Johnson, D. (2009) 'Darwinian selection in asymmetric warfare: The natural advantage of insurgents and terrorists', *Washington Academy of Sciences,* Fall: 80–112.
Johnson, D. and Thayer, B. A. (2013) 'What our primate relatives say about war', *National Interest*, 29 January.
Johnson, D. D. P., Blumstein, D. T., Fowler, J. H. and Haselton, M. G. (2013) 'The evolution of error: error management, cognitive constraints, and adaptive decision-making biases', *Trends in Ecology & Evolution*, August, 28: 8, 474–481.
Johnson, S. (2002) *Emergence: The Connected Lives of Ants, Brains, Cities and Software* (Harmondsworth: Penguin Books).
Joint Committee on the National Security Strategy, *First Review of the National Security Strategy 2010*, HL Paper 265/HC1384, The Stationery Office, 2012. http://www.publications.parliament.uk/pa/jt201012/jtselect/jtnatsec/265/265.pdf
Joyce, C., Stevenson, C. and Muldoon, O. (2013) 'Claiming and displaying national identity: Irish travellers' and students' strategic use of "banal" and "hot" national identity in talk', *British Journal of Social Psychology*, 52: 450–468
Jung, C.G. (1967) *Alchemical Studies (CW 13)*, translated by Hull, R. F. C. (Princeton: Princeton University Press).
Kampfner, J. (2004) *Blair's Wars* (New York: Free Press/Simon and Schuster).
Katzenstein, P. J. (ed.) (1996) *The Culture of National Security: Norms and Identity in World Politics*. (New York: Columbia University Press).
Kaufmann, C. (2004) 'Threat inflation and the marketplace of ideas' *International Security*, 29:1, 5–48.
Kelleher, C., Dombrowski, P. and Auner, E. (2013) 'Demystifying iron dome', *The National Interest*, July/August, http://nationalinterest.org/article/ demystifying-iron-dome-8649 accessed 16 October 2013.

Kennedy, P. M. (1976) 'The tradition of appeasement in British foreign policy 1865–1939', *British Journal of International Studies*, 2:3, 195–215.
Kettle, M. (2007) 'Iraq's future now depends on how it plays in Omaha', *The Guardian*, 14 July.
Kettel, S. (2013) 'Dilemmas of discourse: Legitimising Britain's war on terror', *British Journal of Politics and International Relations*, 15:2, 263–279.
King, A. (2011) 'Having brigades will never deliver the same punch as a division' *Parliamentary Brief Online*, 27 October http://www.parliamentarybrief.com/2011/10/having-brigades-will-never-deliver-the-same-punch-as-a.
Kirkup, J. (2011) 'Saudi troops sent to crush Bahrain protests "had British training"', *Daily Telegraph*, 25 May, http://www.telegraph.co.uk/news/worldnews/middleeast/saudiarabia/8536037/Saudi-troops-sent-to-crush-Bahrain-protests-had-British-training.html, accessed 3 March 2013.
Kissinger, H. (1994) *Diplomacy* (New York: Simon and Schuster).
Kitchen, C. and Vickers, R. (2013) 'Labour traditions of international order and the dilemma of action towards Iran', *British Journal of Politics and International Relations*, 15:2, 299–316.
Kitchen, N. (2010) *The Future of UK Foreign Policy*, LSE IDEAS, October, http://www.lse.ac.uk/ideas/publications/reports/SR006 accessed 16 December 2013.
Klein, N. (2008) *The Shock Doctrine* (London: Penguin).
Knorr-Cetina, K. (2005) 'Complex global microstructures: The new terrorist societies'. *Theory, Culture and Society*, 22: 213–234.
Krahmann, E. (2011) 'Beck and beyond: Selling security in a world risk society', *Review of International Studies*, 37:1, 349–372.
Kratochwil, F. (1982) 'On the notion of "interest" in international relations', *International Organization*, 36:1, 1–30.
Krepinevich, Andrew F. (2012) 'Strategy in a time of austerity: Why the pentagon should focus on assuring access', *Foreign Affairs*, November.
Kristol, W. and Kagan, R. (1996) 'Toward a neo-Reaganite foreign policy', *Foreign Affairs*, July/August, 75:4.
Lai, M. H. C., Ren, M. Y. W., Wu, A. M. S. and Hung, E. P. W. (2013) 'Motivation as mediator between national identity and intention to volunteer', *Journal of Community and Applied Psychology*, 23: 128–142.
Laski, H. (1931) *The Limitations of the Expert* (London: Fabian Society).
Layton, P. (2012) 'The idea of grand strategy', *RUSI Journal*, 157: 4.
Le Pestre, P. G. (ed.) (1997) *Role Quests in the Post-Cold War Era: Foreign Policies in Transition* (London: McGill-Queen's University Press).
Leffler, Melvyn P. (1992) *A Preponderance of Power: National Security, the Truman Administration* (Palo Alto: Stanford University Press).
Levene, P. et al. (2011) *Defence reform: An Independent Report into the Structure and Management of the Ministry of Defence* (London: TSO).
Lewis, D. (1994) 'Reduction of mind', in Guttenplan, S. (ed.), *A Companion to Philosophy of Mind*, (Oxford: Blackwell).
Limnios, M., Alexandra, E., Mazzarol, T., Ghadouani, A. and Schilizzi, S. G. M. (2012) 'The resilient architecture framework: Four organizational archetypes', *European Management Journal*, early online publication December, http://dx.doi.org/10.1016/j.emj.2012.11.007accessed 18 June 2013.
Linklater, A. (2005) 'Marxism', in Burchill, S. (ed.), *Theories of International Relations* (Basingstoke: Palgrave Macmillan), pp. 129–154.

Mabey, N. (2010) *The UK and the world: Session 4*, 13 July (London: Chatham House).
Macleod, A. (1997) 'Great Britain: Still searching for status?' in Le Pestre (ed.), *Role Quests in the Post-Cold War Era*, pp. 161–186.
Mangold, P. (2001) *Success and Failure in British Foreign Policy* (Basingstoke: Palgrave)
Mann, M. (2005) *Incoherent Empire* (London: Verso).
Manningham-Buller, E. (2010) 'Testimony to the Iraq inquiry', 20 July, http://www.iraqinquiry.org.uk/media/48331/20100720am-manningham-buller.pdf.
Marshall, M. and Cole, B. (2011) *Global Report 2011: Conflict, Governance and State Fragility*, Center for Systemic Peace, December.
Martinson, J. (2012) 'Women paying the price for Osborne's austerity package', *Guardian*, 30 March.
Marx, K. and Engels, F. (2004) *The Communist Manifesto* (London: Penguin).
Mason, P. (2012) *Why It's Kicking Off Everywhere: The New Global Revolutions* (London, Verso).
Maunder, J. (2012) 'The Syrian crucible', *International Socialism*, 28 June.
May, P. (1992) 'Policy learning and failure', *Journal of Public Policy*, pp. 331–354.
Mazetti, M. (2013) 'Tap on Merkel provides peek at vast spy net', *New York Times*, 30 October, accessed at http://www.nytimes.com/2013/10/31/world/europe/tap-on-merkel-provides-peek-at-vast-spy-net.html.
MccGwire, M. (2006) 'Comfort blanket or weapon of war', *International Affairs*, 82:4, 639–650.
McCormack, T. (2011) 'From "ethical foreign policy" to national security strategy: Exporting domestic incoherence', in Daddow and Gaskarth (eds.) *British Foreign Policy*, 103–122.
McCourt, D. (2011) 'Role playing and identity affirmation in international politics: Britain's reinvasion of the Falklands, 1982', *Review of International Studies*, 37:4, 1599–1621.
McCourt, D. (2011) 'The New Labour governments and Britain's role in the world', in Daddow, O. and Gaskarth, J. (eds.) (2011) *British Foreign Policy: The New Labour Years* (Basingstoke: Palgrave Macmillan), pp. 31–47.
McGuire, S. and Werth, C. (2009) 'Forget the great in Britain' *Newsweek International*, Monday, 17 August.
Mearsheimer, J. (2003) *The Tragedy of Great Power Politics* (New York: Norton).
Miliband, R. (1969) *The State in Capitalist Society* (London: Quartet Books).
Miliband, R. (1982) *Capitalist Democracy in Britain* (Oxford: Oxford University Press).
Miliband, D. (2007) 'New diplomacy: Challenges for foreign policy', speech at Chatham House, 19 July, http://www.davidmiliband.net/speech/new-diplomacy-challenges-for-foreign-policy, accessed 21 June 2013.
Miller, Benjamin. (2010) 'Democracy promotion: Offensive liberalism versus the rest (of IR Theory)', *Millennium*, 38:3, 561–591.
Milne, S. (2012a) 'Intervention is now driving Syria's descent into darkness', *Guardian*, 7 August http://www.guardian.co.uk/commentisfree/2012/aug/07/intervention-syria-descent-into-darkness, accessed 7 August 2012.
Milne, S. (2012b) *The Revenge of History: the Battle for the 21st Century* (London: Verso).
Ministry of Defence (1998) *Strategic Defence Review*, Cm 3999 (London: HMSO).

Ministry of Defence (2003) *Delivering Security in a Changing World*, Cm 6041-I (London: HMSO).
Ministry of Defence (2010) *Adaptability and Partnership: Issues for the Strategic Defence Review*, Cm 7794 (London: HMSO).
Ministry of Defence (2010a) *Strategic Defence and Security Review*, (London: MoD).
Ministry of Defence (2010b) *A guide to Joint Doctrine Publication 3–40: Security and Stabilisation, the Military Contribution* (London: MoD).
Monaghan, D. (1998) *The Falklands War: Myth and Countermyth* (Basingstoke: Macmillan).
Moore, C. (2013) *Margaret Thatcher: The Authorised Biography. Volume One: Not for Turning* (London: Allen Lane).
Morgenthau, H. (1993) *Politics Among Nations: The Struggle for Power and Peace* (New York: McGraw Hill).
Morgenthau, H. J. (1950) 'The mainsprings of American foreign policy: The national interest vs. moral', *American Political Science Review*, 44: 4, 833–854.
Morgenthau, H. J. (1952) 'Another "Great Debate": The national interest of the United States', *American Political Science Review*, 46:4, 961–988.
Morris, J. (2011) 'How great is Britain? Power, responsibility and Britain's future global role' *British Journal of Politics and International Reltions*, 13:3, 326–347.
Mueller, J. (2006) *Overblown: How Politicians and the Terrorism Industry Inflate National Security Threats, and Why we Believe Them* (New York: Free Press).
Mueller, J. and Stewart, M. (2011) *Terror, Security, and Money: Balancing the Risks, Benefits, and Costs of Homeland Security* (Oxford: Oxford University Press).
Murray, W. and Grimsley, M. (1994) 'Introduction: On Strategy', in W. Murray, M. Knox and A. Bernstein, *The Making of Strategy: Rules, states and war* (Cambridge: Cambridge University Press), pp.1–23.
Muttitt, G. (2012) *Fuel on the Fire: Oil and Politics in Occupied Iraq* (2nd edn.) (London: Vintage Books).
Myers, K. (2006) 'Bush routinely ignoring Blair', interview with BBC News Channel, 30 November, http://news.bbc.co.uk/1/hi/uk/6158435.stm, accessed 21 June 2013.
Neocleous, M. (2013) 'Resisting resilience', *Radical Philosophy*, 178: 6, 2–7.
Niblett, R. (2006) 'Islamic extremism in Europe', testimony to the Senate Foreign Relations Committee, Subcommittee on European Affairs, 5 April, cited in Armitage, D. 'The European Union: Measuring Counter-terrorism Cooperation', *Strategic Forum*, September 2007.
Niblett, R. (2010) *Playing to its Strengths: Rethinking the UK's Role in a Changing World* (London: Chatham House).
National Intelligence Council (NIC) (2008) *Global Trends, 2025: A Transformed World* (Washington, DC: US Government Printing Office) http://www.dni.gov/nic/NIC_2025_project.html.
Noakes, L. (1998) *War and the British: Gender, Memory and National Identity* (London: IB Tauris).
Norman, D. A. (1999) 'Affordance, conventions, and design', *Interactions*, 6: 38–43.
Norton Taylor, R. (2013) 'Afghanistan war has cost Britain more than £37bn, new book claims' *Guardian*, 30 May, http://www.guardian.co.uk/world/2013/may/30/afghanistan-war-cost-britain-37bn-book.

Nott, J. (2002) *Here Today: Gone Tomorrow: Memoirs of an Errant Politician* (London: Politicos).
Nuechterlein, D. (1976) 'National interests and foreign policy: A conceptual framework for analysis and decision-making', *British Journal of International Studies*, 2:3, 246–266.
Nye Jr. J. S. (1999) 'Redefining the national interest' *Foreign Affairs*, 78:4, 22–35.
Nye, J. S. (2002) 'The American national interest and global public goods', *International Affairs*, 78:2, 233–244.
Oliver, T. (2011) *The British State and the World*, Ph.D. thesis (London :London School of Economics).
Oliver, T. (2012) 'Why has Britain been in Afghanistan?' in Oppermann, K. (ed.) *British Foreign and Security Policy: Historical Legacies and Current Challenges* (Augsburg: Wissner-Verlag).
Olson, M. (1971) *The Logic of Collective Action: Public Goods and The Theory of Groups* (Cambridge: Harvard University Press).
Omand, D. (2004) 'National resilience priorities for UK government,' *RUSI Analysis*, 1 July, http://www.rusi.org/analysis/commentary/ref:C40AB913E66BA2/#.Ul56k1BeZ8F, accessed 16 October 2013.
Omand, D. (2005) 'Developing national resilience', *RUSI Journal* 150: 4, 14–18.
Omand, D. (2010) *Securing the State* (London: Hurst & Company), http://www.armscontrol.org/factsheets/Phasedadaptiveapproach,accessed 8 November 2013.
Osborne, G. (2010) 'Emergency budget speech, House of Commons', 22 June, http://www.guardian.co.uk/uk/2010/jun/22/emergency-budget-full-speech-text.
Panitch, L. and Gindin, S. (2005) 'Superintending global capital', *New Left Review*, 35 (September–October), 101–123.
Parekh, A., MacInnes, T. and Kenway, P. (2010) *Monitoring Poverty and Social Exclusion 2010* (York: Joseph Rowntree Foundation), http://www.poverty.org.uk/reports/mpse%202010%20findings.pdf.
Parsons, A. (1983) 'The Falklands crisis in the United Nations', *International Affairs*, 59, 169–178.
Pelopidas. B. (2011) 'The oracles of proliferation: How experts maintain a biased historical reading that limits policy innovation', *Nonproliferation Review*, 18:1, 297–314.
Pelopidas, B. (2013a) 'Avoir la bombe. Repenser la puissance dans un contexte de vulnérabilité nucléaire globale' [Having the bomb: Rethinking power in a context of global nuclear vulnerability], *CERIscope*, November, http://ceriscope.sciences-po.fr/puissance/content/part1/avoir-la-bombe-repenser-la-puissance-dans-un-contexte-de-vulnerabilite-nucleaire-globale, accessed 17 October 2013.
Pelopidas, B. (2013b) 'Why nuclear realism is unrealistic', *Bulletin of the Atomic Scientists*, 26 September, http://thebulletin.org/why-nuclear-realism-unrealistic, accessed 17 October 2013.
Pelopidas, B. (2013c) 'Innovation in nuclear thinking: Incompetent, dangerous or futile,' paper presented at the seminar of the program on science and global security, Princeton University, 10 April.
Pelopidas, B. and Weldes, J. (in progress) 'Re-narrating the Cold War', manuscript.

Pérez de Cuéllar, J. (1997) *Pilgrimage for Peace: A Secretary General's Memoir* (Basingstoke: Macmillan).
Perrigo, S. (2010) 'Undermining international humanitarian law and the politics of liberal democracies', in Whitman, J. and Perrigo, S. (eds.) *The Geneva Conventions Under Assault* (London: Pluto Press), pp. 222–247.
Perrow, C. (1999) *Normal Accidents: Living with High Risk Technologies* (Princeton: Princeton University Press).
Peters, R. S. (1958) *The Concept of Motivation* (London: Routledge and Kegan Paul).
Pin-Fat, V. (2005) 'The metaphysics of the national interest and the "mysticism" of the nation-state: Reading Hans J. Morgenthau', *Review of International Studies*, 31, 217–236.
Platt, D. C. M. (1968) *Finance, Trade, and Politics in British Foreign Policy, 1815–1914* (Oxford: Clarendon Press).
Podvig, P. (2013) 'Unexpected dangers', *Bulletin of Atomic Scientists*, 7 October, http://thebulletin.org/unexpected-dangers, accessed 17 October 2013.
Porter, P. (2010) 'Last charge of the knights? Iraq, Afghanistan, and the special relationship', *International Affairs*, 86, 355–375.
Porter, P. (2010) 'The maps are too small: Geography, strategy and the national interest', *World Today*, 66, 4–6.
Porter, P. (2010b) 'Why Britain doesn't do grand strategy', *RUSI Journal*, 155: 4–6.
Porter, R. (2008) 'Interfacing China: Note on the conduct of Britain's relations with China', *Journal of Asian Public Policy*, 1:1, March, 104–114.
Posen, B. (1984) *The Sources of Military Doctrine* (Ithaca: Cornell University Press).
Prashad, V. (2012) *Arab Spring, Libyan Winter* (Edinburgh: AK Press UK).
Press Association (11 September 2003) 'PM warned of heightened terror risk', *Guardian*, http://www.guardian.co.uk/politics/2003/sep/11/iraq.iraq1, accessed 21 June 2013.
Price, S. and Sanders, D. (1993) 'Modelling government popularity in postwar Britain: A methodological example'. *American Journal of Political Science*, 37, 317–334.
Prince, R. (2010) 'Budget 2010: Whitehall departments braced for 25 per cent cuts' *Telegraph*, 22 June 2010. http://www.telegraph.co.uk/news/politics/7847238/Budget-2010-Whitehall-departments-braced-for-25-per-cent-cuts.html
Project for a New American Century (1997) 'Statement of principles', 3 June. http://www.newamericancentury.org/statementofprinciples.htm accessed 25 February 2013.
Pry, P. (1999) *War Scare: Russia and America and the Nuclear Brink* (Westport, CT: Praeger).
Public Accounts Committee (2011) *Who Does UK National Strategy? Further Report* (25 January), http://www.publications.parliament.uk/pa/cm201011/cmselect/cmpubadm/713/71303.htm.
Public Administration Select Committee (2010) *Who Does UK National Strategy?* House of Commons, HC 435, http://www.publications.parliament.uk/pa/cm201011/cmselect/cmpubadm/435/435.pdf.

Public Administration Select Committee (PASC) (2012) 'Strategic thinking in government: Without national strategy, can viable government strategy emerge?' *Public Administration Select Committee, HC1625* (London: TSO).

Public Administration Select Committee (2013) *Engaging the Public in National Strategy*, HC435 (London: TSO).

Pym, F. (1984) *The Politics of Consent* (London: Hamish Hamilton).

Ralph, J. (2011) 'A difficult relationship: Britain's "doctrine of international community" and America's "war on terror"', in Daddow, O. and Gaskarth, J. (eds.) (2011) *British Foreign Policy: The New Labour Years* (Basingstoke: Palgrave Macmillan), 123–138.

Rapoport, D. C. (2002) 'The four waves of rebel terror and September 11' *Anthropoetics*, 8:1 (http://www.anthropoetics.ucla.edu/ap0801/terror.htm#n1)

Rasmussen, M. V. (2006) *The Risk Society at War: Terror, Technology and Strategy in the Twenty-First Century* (Cambridge: Cambridge University Press).

Ray, L. J. (1999) *Theorizing Classical Sociology* (Buckingham: Open University Press).

Rayment, S. (2004) 'US tactics condemned by British officers', *Daily Telegraph*, 11 April, http://www.telegraph.co.uk/news/worldnews/middleeast/iraq/1459048/US-tactics-condemned-by-British-officers.html?mobile=true, accessed 6 January 2013.

Rayment, S. (2005) 'Secret MoD poll: Iraqis support attacks on British troops', *Daily Telegraph*, 23 October, http://www.telegraph.co.uk/news/worldnews/middleeast/iraq/1501319/Secret-MoD-poll-Iraqis-support-attacks-on-British-troops.html, accessed 6 January 2013.

Reagan, R. (1983) 'Address to the nation on national security', 23 March, http://www.fas.org/spp/starwars/offdocs/rrspch.htm, accessed 16 October 2013.

Reed, H. (2012) 'In the eye of the storm: Britain's forgotten children and families', Research report for the NSPCC, The Children's Society and Action for Children, June.

Rhodes, R. 'Everyday life in a ministry: public administration as anthropology', *American Review of Public Administration*, 35:1, 2005, 3–25.

Reicher, S. D. and Hopkins, N. (2001) *Self and Nation* (London: Sage).

Reicher, S. D., Hopkins, N. and Condor, S. (1997) 'Stereotype construction as a strategy of influence', in Spears, R., Oakes, P. J., Ellemers, N. and Haslam, S. A. (eds.) *The Social Psychology of Stereotyping and Group Life* (Oxford: Blackwell).

Rice, C. (2000) 'Promoting the national interest', *Foreign Affairs*, 79:1, January/February, 45–62.

Richardson, D. (2013) 'MBDA wins sea ceptor production contract', *HIS Jane's Missiles & Rockets*, 25 September, http://www.janes.com/article/27471/mbda-wins-sea-ceptor-production-contract accessed 16 October 2013.

Ritchie, N. (2011) 'Rethinking security: A critical analysis of the strategic defence and security review', *International Affairs*, 87:2, 355–376.

Robinson, P. (2005) *Doing Less with Less: Making Britain More Secure* (Exeter: Imprint Academic).

Robinson, P. (2011) 'Substantial cuts in the defence budget should be a priority'. *Institute of Economic Affairs*, 22 July. http://www.iea.org.uk/blog/substantial-cuts-in-the-defence-budget-should-be-a-priority

Robinson, W. I. (2006) 'What to expect from US "democracy promotion" in Iraq', *New Political Science*, 26:3, 441–447.
Rogers, P. (2002) 'A never-ending war? Consequences of 11 September', Oxford Research Group Briefing Paper, March.
Rogers, P. (2007) 'A necessary war?' *Political Studies Review*, 5, 25–31.
Rogers, P. (2007) *Global Security and the War on Terror: Elite Power and the Illusion of Control* (Abingdon: Routledge).
Rogers, P. (2013) 'A decade's war: Legacy and lesson', *OpenDemocracy*, 4 April, http://www.opendemocracy.net/paul-rogers/decades-war-legacy-and-lesson.
Rosenau, J. G. (1984) 'A pre-theory revisited: World politics in an era of cascading interdependence' *International Studies Quarterly*, 28:3, September, 245–305.
Rosenfeld, D. (2009) 'National missile defense', *Defense and Security Analysis*, 25: 2, 205–213.
Rothschild, E. and Sen, A. (2006) 'Adam Smith on justice, rights, and law,' in Haakonssen, K. (ed.), *The Cambridge Companion to Adam Smith* (Cambridge: Cambridge University Press) pp. 319–365.
Rühle, M. (2013) 'The future of the transatlantic security relationship' *American Foreign Policy Interests*, 35, 283–287.
RUSI (2010) 'Defence perspectives,'*RUSI Journal*, 155:2, 6–12.
Ryan, A. (2009) 'The foundation for an adaptive approach: insights from the science of complex systems', *Australian Army Journal*, 6:3, 69–90.
Sagan, S. D. (1993) *The Limits of Safety: Organizations, Accidents, and Nuclear Weapons* (Princeton: Princeton University Press).
Sagan, S. D. (2004) 'The problem of redundancy problem: Why more nuclear security forces may produce less nuclear security', *Risk Analysis*, 24:4, 935–946.
Sandler, T. (1993) 'The economic theory of alliances – A survey', *Journal of Conflict Resolution*, 37:3, 446–383.
Scarantino, A. (2003) 'Affordances explained', *Philosophy of Science*, 70, 949–961.
Schelling, T. (1960) *The Strategy of Conflict* (Cambridge: Harvard University Press).
Schelling, T. (1966) *Arms and Influence* (New Haven: Yale University Press).
Schelling, T. C. (1971) 'On the ecology of micromotives', *National Interest*, Fall, 25, 61–98.
Schleifer, A. P. and Treismans, D. (2011) 'Why Moscow says no.: A question of Russian interests, not psychology', *Foreign Affairs*, 90:1. January/February.
Schlosser, E. (2013a) 'Nuclear weapons: An accident waiting to happen', *Guardian*, 14 September, http://www.theguardian.com/world/2013/sep/14/nuclear-weapons-accident-waiting-to-happen, accessed 8 November 2013.
Schlosser, E. (2013b) *Command and Control* (London: Lane).
Schweller, R. L. (1996) 'Neorealism's status quo bias — What security dilemma?'*Security Studies*, 5:3, 90–121.
Seldon, A. and Lodge, G. (2010) *Brown at 10* (London: Biteback).
Sharp, P. (1997) *Thatcher's Diplomacy: The Revival of British Foreign Policy* (Basingstoke: Macmillan).
Shaw, J. (2013) 'Whitehall's strategic deficit and its threat to overseas operations', speech to the Global Strategy Forum at the National Liberal Club, March 2013, http://www.guardian.co.uk/politics/defence-and-security-blog/2013/mar/06/defence-security-strategy.
Shaw, M. (2005) *The New Western Way of War* (Cambridge: Polity Press).

Sherman, D. and Cohen, G. (2002) 'Accepting threatening information: Self-Affirmation and the reduction of defensive biases', *Current Directions in Psychological Science*, 11: 4,119–123.
Shih, Chih-yu, (1998) 'National role conception as foreign policy motivation: The psychocultural bases of Chinese diplomacy', *Political Psychology*, 9:4, 599–631.
Simon, H. (1991) 'Bounded rationality and organizational learning', *Organization Science* 2:1, 125–134.
Slackman, M. and Audi, N. (2011) 'Bahrain police use force to crack down on protests', *New York Times*, 16 February, http://www.nytimes.com/2011/02/17/world/middleeast/17bahrain.html?pagewanted=all&_r=1&, accessed 3 March 2013.
Smith, A. (1776a (1999 edn.) *The Wealth of Nations, Books I – III* (London: Penguin).
Smith, A. (1776b (1999 edn.) *The Wealth of Nations, Books IV – V* (London: Penguin).
Smith, M. (1988) 'Britain and the United States: Beyond the "Special Relationship"', in Peter Byrd. (ed.) *British Foreign Policy Under Thatcher* (New York: St. Martin's Press), 8–19.
Smith, A. (1999a) *Wealth of Nations* Vol I (Penguin Classics Edition).
Smith, A. (1999b) *Wealth of Nations* Vol II (Penguin Classics Edition).
Smith, A. (1999c) *Wealth of Nations* Vol III (Penguin Classics Edition).
Smith, R. (2006) *The Utility of Force: The Art of War in the Modern World* (London: Penguin Books).
Smith, S. (2005) 'The contested concept of security', in Booth, K. (ed.), *Critical Security Studies and World Politics* (London: Lynne Rienner), pp. 27–62.
Spengler, O. (1932) *Man and Technics. A Contribution to a Philosophy of Life*, translated from German by Atkinson, C.E. (London: G. Allen and Unwin).
Spectator, 'Not-so-special relationship' 5 January 2013.
Stavridis, S. and Hill, C. (1996) *Domestic Sources of Foreign Policy: West European Reactions to the Falklands Conflict* (London: Berg).
Steele, J. and Jamail, D. (2005) 'This is our Guernica', *Guardian*, 27 April, http://www.guardian.co.uk/world/2005/apr/27/iraq.iraq5, accessed 6 January 2013.
Stein, A. A. (1999) 'The limits of strategic choice: Constrained rationality and incomplete explanation' Lake, D. A. and Powell, R. (eds.) *Strategic Choice and International Relations* (Princeton, New Jersey: Princeton University Press).
Steiner, Z. (1969) *The Foreign Office and Foreign Policy, 1898–1914* (Cambridge: Cambridge University Press).
Stimson Center (2011) *Forging a 21st-Century Diplomatic Service for the United States through Professional Education and Training* (Washington: Stimson Center/American Academy of Diplomacy).
Stocker, J. (2004) *Britain's Role in US Missile Defense* (Carlisle, PA: Strategic Studies Institute, US Army War College).
Stokes, D. (2005) 'The heart of empire? Theorising US empire in an era of transnational capitalism', *Third World Quarterly*, 26:2, 217–236.
Stolberg, Alan. (2012) *How Nation-States Craft National Security Strategy Documents* (Carlisle, Pennsylvania: Strategic Studies Institute, US Army War College).
Strachan, H. (2005) 'The lost meaning of strategy', *Survival*, 47:3, 33–54.

Strachan, H. (2006) 'Making strategy: Civil-military relations after Iraq,' *Survival*, 48:3, 59–82.
Strachan, H. (2009) 'The strategic gap in British defence policy', *Survival*, 51:4, 49–70.
Strachan, H. (2011) 'Strategy and contingency', *International Affairs*, 87:6, 1281–1296.
Strachan, H. (2013) 'British national strategy: who does it?' *Parameters* 43: 2, Summer 2013, 49–50.
Straw, J. (2001) 'Pursuing an active and engaged foreign policy', speech in the House of Commons, London, Friday 22 June.
Straw, J. (2003) 'Speech to the Labour Party conference, Bournemouth', 1 October, http://www.theguardian.com/politics/oct/01/labourconference.labour2.
Straw, J. (2012) *Last Man Standing* (Basingstoke: Macmillan).
Sylvan, D. and Majeski, S. (2009) *US Foreign Policy in Perspective: Clients, Enemies and Empire* (London: Routledge).
Taleb, Nassim N. (2010) *The Black Swan: The Impact of the Highly Improbable* (New York: Random House).
Taylor, A. J. P. (1957) *The Troublemakers* (London: H. Hamilton).
Taylor, M. (2012) 'Introduction', in Taylor, M. and Currie, M. (eds.) *Terrorism and Affordance* (London: Continuum International Publishing Group).
Taylor, M. and Currie, M. (eds.) (2012) *Terrorism and Affordance* (London: Continuum International Publishing Group).
Telegraph (2010) 'Defence cuts: Liam Fox's leaked letter in full', 28 September 2010. http://www.telegraph.co.uk/news/uknews/defence/8031385/Defence-cuts-Liam-Foxs-leaked-letter-in-full.html.
Telegraph (2013) 'David Cameron: Trident "the best insurance policy you can have",' 4 April, video http://www.telegraph.co.uk/news/uknews/defence/9972136/David-Cameron-Trident-the-best-insurance-policy-you-can-have.html, accessed 16 October 2013.
Tetlock, P. (2005) *Expert Political Judgment: How Good is it? How can we Know?* (Princeton: Princeton University Press).
Thatcher, M. (1992) *The Downing Street Years* (London: Harper Collins).
Thies, C. (2009) 'Role theory and foreign policy', unpublished paper, May, http://myweb.uiowa.edu/bhlai/workshop/role.pdf.
Thies, C. G. (2012) 'International socialization processes vs. Israeli national role conceptions: Can role theory integrate IR theory and foreign policy analysis?'*Foreign Policy Analysis*, 8, 25–46.
Thompson, K. W. (1958) 'The limits of principle in international politics: Necessity and the new balance of power', *Journal of Politics*, 20:3, 437–467.
Tonra, B. (2001) 'Irish foreign policy', in Crotty, W. and Schmitt, D., *Ireland on the World Stage* (London: Routledge) 24–28.
Trivers, R. (2011) *The Folly of Fools: The Logic of Deceit and Self-Deception in Human Life* (New York: Basic Books).
US Department of Defense (2010) *Ballistic Missile Defense Review Report*, February, http://www.defense.gov/bmdr/docs/BMDR%20as%20of%2026JAN10%200630_for%20web.pdf, accessed 8 November 2013.
US Department of Homeland Security (2009) *National Infrastructure Protection Plan*, http://www.dhs.gov/xlibrary/assets/NIPP_Plan.pdf, accessed 20 May 2013.

UK Government, (n.d.) *Fact sheet 2: National Security Risk Assessment*, https://www.gov.uk/government/uploads/system/uploads/attachment_data/file/62484/Factsheet2-National-Security-Risk-Assessment.pdf, accessed 25 June 2013.

UK Ministry of Defence (2006) 'The future of the United Kingdom's nuclear deterrent,' White paper (Cm6994), https://www.gov.uk/government/uploads/system/uploads/attachment_data/file/27378/DefenceWhitePaper2006_Cm6994.pdf, accessed 23 June 2013.

UK Stabilisation Unit (2008) *The UK Approach to Stabilisation* (London: The Stabilisation Unit).

UN Department of Social and Economic Affairs (2010) *Rethinking Poverty: Report on the World Situation 2010* (New York: United Nations).

UN Development Programme (2011) *Human Development Report 2011: Sustainability and Equity* (New York: United Nations).

Verweij, M. (2011) *Clumsy Solutions for a Wicked World: How to Improve Global Governance* (Basingstoke: Palgrave Macmillan).

Vickers, R. (2003) *The Labour Party and the World, Volume1: The Evolution of Labour's ForeignPolicy 1900–1951* (Manchester: Manchester University Press).

Vinen, R. (2009) *Thatcher's Britain: The Politics and Social Upheavals of the 1980s* (London: Simon and Schuster).

Wæver O. (1995) '*Securitization and Desecuritization*', in Lipschutz, R. (ed.) *On Security* (New York: Columbia University Press), pp. 46–86.

Walker, J. and Cooper, M. (2011) 'Genealogies of resilience: From systems ecology to the political economy of crisis adaptation,' *Security Dialogue*, 42: 2, 143–160.

Walker, S. G. and Simon, S. W. (1987) 'Role sets and foreign policy analysis in Southeast Asia' in Walker, S. G. (ed.) *Role Theory and Foreign Policy Analysis* (Durham, N.C.: Duke University Press).

Walker, S. G. (ed.) (1987) *Role Theory and Foreign Policy Analysis* (Durham: Duke University Press).

Wall, S. (2011) 'Foreword', in Daddow and Gaskarth (2011) *British Foreign Policy: the New Labour Years'* (Basingstoke: Palgrave Macmillan), xii–xv.

Wallace, W. (1992) 'British foreign policy after the cold war', *International Affairs*, 68:3, 423–442.

Wallace, W. and Phillips, C. (2009) 'Reassessing the special relationship', *International Affairs* 85: 263–284.

Walt, S. (1987) *The Origin of Alliances* (New York: Cornell University Press).

Watt, N. (2010) 'Look away now if easily offended: Vacuous language of national security strategy will horrify many,' *Guardian*, 18 October http://www.theguardian.com/politics/blog/2010/oct/18/national-security-strategy-vacuous-language.

Weber, M. (2004 [1904]) 'The "objectivity" of knowledge in social science and social policy', in Whimster, S. (ed.), *The Essential Weber: A Reader* (London: Routledge), pp. 359–404.

Weldes, J. (1996) 'Constructing national interests' *European Journal of International Relations* 2:3, 275–318.

Wendt, A. (1992) 'Anarchy is what states make of it', *International Organization*, 46:2, Spring.

Wendt, A. (1999) *Social Theory of International Politics* (Cambridge: Cambridge University Press).
Wheeler, N. and Dunne, T. (2000) 'The Blair doctrine: Advancing the third way in the world', in Little, R. and Wickham-Jones, M. *New Labour's Foreign Policy: A New Moral Crusade?* (Manchester: Manchester University Press).
Wheeler, N. J. and Dunne, T. (1998) 'Good international citizenship: A third way for British foreign policy' *International Affairs*, 74:4, 847–870.
Wikileaks cables (2010) 'Conservatives promised to run "pro-American regime"', 4 December.
Wikileaks cables (2013) 'Britain should stay in European Union says Obama administration', 10 January.
Williams, M. (2008) '(In)security studies, reflexive modernization and the risk society', *Cooperation and Conflict*, 43:1, 57–79.
William, P. (2012) 'Affordances and the new political ecologies', in Taylor, M. and Currie, M. (eds.) *Terrorism and Affordance* (London: Continuum International Publishing Group).
Williams, M. C. (2004) 'Why ideas matter in international relations: Hans Morgenthau, classical realism, and the moral construction of power politics', *International Organization*, 58:4, 633–665.
Williams, M. C. (2005) 'What is the national interest? The neoconservative challenge in IR theory', *EJIR*, 11:3, 307–337.
Williams, P. (2010) *British Foreign Policy Under New Labour: 1997–2005* (Basingstoke: Palgrave-Macmillan).
Williams, S. A., Rear Admiral OBE(2012) *The Role of the National Interest in the National Security Debate*, Royal College of Defence Studies Seaford House Paper. (London: HMSO).
Williamson, M. and Grimsley, M., 'Introduction: On strategy' in Murray, W., Bernstein, A. and Knox, M. (1994) *The Making of Strategy: Rulers, States, and War* (Cambridge: Cambridge University Press).
Wish, N. B. (1987) 'National attributes as sources of national role conceptions' in Walker, S.G. (ed.) *Role Theory and Foreign Policy Analysis* (Durham: Duke University Press).
Wolfers, A. (1952) '"National Security" as an ambiguous symbol', *Political Science Quarterly*, LXVII: 4, 481–502.
Wolfers, A. (1962) *Discord and Collaboration: Essays on International Politics* (Baltimore: Johns Hopkins Press).
Wood, E. M. (1999) 'Unhappy families: Global capitalism in a world of nation states', *Monthly Review*, 51:3 http://monthlyreview.org/1999/07/01/unhappy-families, accessed 21 June 2013.
World Bank (2011) *World Development Report 2011: Conflict, Security and Development* (Washington DC: World Bank).
Wreford Brown, C. (2012) 'The Falklands war 30 years on', paper presented to University of Kent, 25 April.
Yarger, H. R. (2006) *Strategic Theory for the 21st Century: the Little Book of Big Strategy* (Carlisle: Strategic Studies Institute).
Yarger, H. R. (2006) *Strategic Theory for the 21st Century: The Little Book of Big Strategy* (Carlisle, PA: Strategic Studies Institute).
Young, H. (1989) *One of Us: A Biography of Margaret Thatcher* (London: Pan Books).
Young, H. (1999) This Blessed Plot (London: Macmillan).

Interviews

Ambassador Richard Boucher, telephone interview with the author, 7 Sept. 2012.
Ambassador Zal Khalilzad, telephone interview with the author, 2012.
Gallucci, R. L., telephone interview with the author, 3 Oct. 2012.
Gallucci 2012, Telephone interview with the author, October 2012.
George Percovitch, telephone interview with the author, Sept. 2012.
Hennessy, P., 'The horizon scanner's craft', Chatham House meeting transcript, 23 June 2011.
John Plender, conversation with the author, London, 2002.
Lord Jay, interview by Malcolm McBain, Churchill Archives Centre, British Diplomatic Oral History Programme, 4 Jan. 2007.
Lord Kerr of Kinlochard, interviewed by Malcolm McBain, Churchill Archives Centre, British Diplomatic Oral History Programme, 6 January, 2004.
Sir Brian Crowe, interview by Gwenda Scarlett, Churchill Archives Centre, British Diplomatic Oral History Programme, 15 Oct. 2003.
Sir Jeremy Greenstock, interview by Malcolm McBain, Churchill Archives Centre, British Diplomatic Oral History Programme, 22 June 2004.
Sir Michael Palliser, interview by John Hutson, Churchill Archives Centre, British Diplomatic Oral History Programme, 28 April 1999.
Sir Robert Wade-Gery, interview, Churchill Archives Centre, British Diplomatic Oral History Programme, 13 Feb. 2000.
Sir Rodric Braithwaite, British Diplomatic Oral History Programme, 1998.
Sir Sherard Cowper-Coles, interview by Malcolm McBain, Churchill Archives Centre, British Diplomatic Oral History Programme, 4 March 2011.
Tickell, interview by Malcolm McBain, Churchill Archives Centre, British Diplomatic Oral History Programme, 28 January 1999.
Wendy Chamberlin, former US Ambassador to Pakistan, telephone interview with the author, Oct. 2012.

Index

'7/7', 126, 180
'9/11', 10, 27, 93, 96, 98–100, 125–6, 180, 209, 220, 225

Accountability, 27–8, 87, 97, 182
Achcar, G., 108–9, 113–14, 117
Acheson, Dean, 121
Affordance, 19, 198
Afghanistan, 1, 2, 15, 28, 32–3, 39, 49–50, 64–5, 77, 93–5, 103, 126, 143, 172–3, 180, 184–5, 185, 195, 217–21, 233
Aggestam, Lisbeth, 44–5, 48, 64
America, *see* US, United States
Ancram, Michael, 134
Anderson, P., 108, 114
Arab uprisings, 103
Arendt, Hannah, 189
Argentina, 67–77, 82
armed humanitarian intervention, 25
arms exports, 13, 33–4, 36, 38–40
  and commercial interests, 5, 36–8
Arms Trade Treaty (2013), 30
Arrighi, G., 105
Atkinson, W., 99
Atlanticist (policy), Atlanticism, 29, 176–7, 226

Bahrain, 38, 118
Bailes, Alyson, 142
balance of power, 4–5, 105, 123, 191
Basra, 2, 131, 217
Billig, M., 192
Bismarck, Otto von, 54
'Black Swan events', 183, 214
Blair, Prime Minister Tony, 2, 10, 25–7, 59–60, 64, 97, 120, 124–6, 131–3, 215, 218
  on the ability to influence US policy, 131
  Blair 'Doctrine of the International Community', Chicago (1999), 23, 25, 93

justification of the Iraq War, 55
  on the merger of values and interests, 10, 23, 26, 31, 227
  on non-intervention and sovereignty, 60
Blakeley, R., 64, 108
Braithwaite, Sir Rodric, 133, 143, 145
Bright, John, 5, 49, 64
Brighton, Shane, 28
British Empire, 9, 124, 202
'British values', 3, 13, 23, 26, 28–33
Brown, Gordon, 11, 89, 95, 97, 120, 124, 214–16, 227

Cable, Sir James, 153
Callinicos, A., 103–4, 106–7, 109, 111, 113
Cameron, David, 30–3, 41, 55–6, 89, 97, 122, 124, 155, 158, 160, 163, 169, 218
Canning, George, 25
Capitalism, 3, 99, 103–9, 111
Carr, E.H., 5
Carrington, Lord Peter, 79, 143
Carter Doctrine (1980), 109
Castlereagh, Viscount Robert, 25
Chandler, David, 27–8
Chatham House, 29, 57, 60, 65, 142
China, 3, 43, 54–6, 61, 70, 109, 113, 127, 178, 189
Chomsky, N., 103, 107–9, 114, 116
City of London, 110–11
Clausewitz, Carl von, 190, 197, 211
climate change, 3, 58, 101, 127–8, 132, 175, 183, 206, 213–14, 216, 219, 226
Clinton, David W., 8, 42
Coalition (Conservative-Liberal Democrat), 3, 13, 23, 24, 28–40, 89, 92, 120, 205, 216, 218, 222, 224, 227
Coalition of forces (at war in Iraq), 113–16

261

262 Index

Coalition Provisional Authority (Iraq), 116
Cobden, Richard, 37, 49–51, 64
Cold War, 2, 10, 27, 52, 60, 62, 82, 95, 107–8, 121, 131, 158, 174, 177, 207, 211, 213, 226
Collier, P., 35
Commercial interests, 5, 36, 38
  in Iraq, 113
Commonwealth, 51, 129, 215
complexity (in international relations), 6, 164, 171–86
Comprehensive Spending Review, CSR, (2010), 217, 223
Condor, S., Gibson S., and Abell, J., 193
Congress of Vienna (1815), 123
Conservative-Liberal Democrat Coalition foreign policy, 28–40
  evidence to Foreign Affairs Committee (2011), 35
Conservative Party, 29–30, 67, 80, 87, 89, 155
Constructivists, 20
Cook, Robin, 2, 10, 23, 25, 36, 37, 61
Cornish, P., –16, 215, 223
Cornish, P. and Dorman, A., 1, 43, 171, 173, 180, 183, 208, 210, 215, 217, 220, 222–3, 231
corporate memory (FCO), 183
'cosmopolitanism' (in foreign policy), 26
Cowper-Coles, Sir Sherard, 142–4
Cox, Michael, 104
Cox, Robert, 105
Crowe, Sir Brian, 142, 144–5
Crowe, Sir Eyre, 54
Curtis, Mark, 60, 103, 111–12
cyber security, 180, 183, 218, 221

Declaration on Preventing Sexual Violence in Conflict, 58
Defence Board, 182
De France, O. and Witney, N., 205
Democracy, 25–7, 29, 31, 42, 47, 59, 62, 75, 81, 96, 103, 108, 113–14, 116, 118, 122, 124–5
Democratisation, 27, 117

Department for International Development (DfID), 25, 122, 221–2
Development, Concepts and Doctrine Centre (DCDC) of the MoD, 95, 181
Dickerson, P., 193
Diego Garcia, 131
Doctrine of the International Community, 23, 25, 93
Doig A. and Phythian, M., 7

EEC, European Economic Community, 67, 69
'enlightened national interest', 30, 40
'enlightened self-interest', 97, 100
error management theory, 203
ethical dimension (in foreign policy), 13, 23–5, 36–7, 39, 211
EU, European Union, 1, 3, 19, 36, 51–3, 111, 123–4, 125, 129, 183, 216, 219, 226
Europeanist (policy), 29, 176
Eurozone crisis, 125, 183
Evans, Alex and Steven, David, 57, 65
Evans, Gareth, 26
'extraordinary rendition', 131
Extremism, 27–8

Falkland Islands Company, 68
Falkland Islands (Malvinas), 66–82
Fallujah, 114
Fawcett Society, 91
Feldman, Noah, 116
Ferguson, N., 198, 202
financial crisis (2008), 1, 15, 49, 88, 90, 99, 206, 211, 228
  impact on foreign policy, 43
Fontaine, Richard and Burton, Brian, 147
Foot, Michael, 69
Foreign Affairs Committee, Foreign Affairs Select Committee (of the House of Commons), 29, 31, 33, 35, 37
foreign aid, *see* Department for International Development (DfID)

Foreign and Commonwealth Office (FCO), 10, 17, 25, 124, 134, 138, 153, 183, 222, 232
'foresight' methodologies, 181, 183
Forster, A. and Blair, A., 126
'fragile state stabilisation', 25, 34
and British policy, 34–6
Franks, Oliver, 46
Freedman, Lawrence, 67
Frost, Mervyn, 25
Future Force 2020, 204

'G8', 32, 58
'G20', 32
Galtieri, General Leopoldo, 67, 76–7
GCHQ, 130
General Belgrano, 66, 74, 78, 81
George, Alexander, 42
Gibson, J.J., 198
Gladstone, William, 25, 125
Global financial crisis, *see* financial crisis (2008)
Globalisation, 1, 97–9, 102–6, 200
Global Objectives (of British foreign policy), 16, 124, 127
Global Strategic Trends – Out to 2040 (MoD), 95, 181
Good, R.C., 6
Gore-Booth, Sir David, 144, 154
Gowan, P., 109, 134
Grandin, G., 108
Gray, Colin, 173, 177
Great powers, 2, 45, 62, 128
Greenstock, Sir Jeremy, 143
Guantanamo, 108, 131
Gulf Cooperation Council, 118
Gulf states
UK-Saudi relations, 112
Gulf War (1991), 62, 109

Haas, Ernst, 5
Hague, William, 29–31, 35, 37, 58, 97, 120, 219
Haig, US Secretary of State Alexander, 70–5, 80
Hall, Ian and Rengger, Nicholas, 28
'hard headed internationalism', 97
'hard headed pragmatism', 97
Hardt, M. and Negri, A., 106

Hartley, Keith, 49
Cost of wars in Iraq and Afghanistan, 49–50
Harvey, D., 103, 106–7, 109–11, 113
Hehir, A., 35
Helmand, 2
Henderson, Sir Nicholas, 77, 82
Hennessy, Peter, 95, 151, 216
Henry Jackson Society, 27
Herring, Eric, 8, 101, 113
historical materialism, 9, 116
Hobsbawm, Eric, 66, 103
Hobson, J.A., 104
Hollis, Martin and Smith, Steve, 48, 64
Hughes, Thomas, 149
Humanitarianism, 2, 113
Human rights, 4, 16, 25–6, 29–31, 35–9, 47, 51, 55, 58–60, 64, 108, 123–4
Human Rights and Democracy 2011 (FCO), 29
Human security, 34, 87, 92, 94, 96, 100–1, 228
Huntington, S.P., 5, 191
Hurd, Douglas, 60, 64

'idealist' vs. 'realist', 194
Identity, 1, 8–10, 12–14, 42–4, 47, 52–4, 58, 60–4, 66–7, 81–2, 85–6, 97, 101, 173, 188, 191–3, 198, 226, 229–30
IMF, International Monetary Fund, 55, 102, 115
Imperialism, 102–10, 114
Institute of Economic Affairs, 222
Institute for Public Policy Research, 43
Interdependence, 1, 26, 97, 171, 211
Interest, interests, 1–20
international community, 7, 10, 23, 25, 27, 31, 54–5, 57, 93, 97, 108, 127, 165
'international community' (doctrine), 23, 25, 93
International Criminal Court, 45
Internationalism, 23, 29, 97, 226
Internationalist, 26, 49–50
Interoperability, 120, 128

Intervention, interventionism, 1–3, 14, 36, 39, 48–9, 51, 54–5, 59–61, 63–5, 75, 93–9, 108–9, 117–18, 122, 126, 133, 143, 146, 151, 172–3, 176–7, 184–5, 226
   Afghanistan, 1, 2, 15, 28, 33, 39, 65, 94, 173
   and 'enlightened self-interest', 93
   'humanitarian intervention', 25, 30, 103
   impact on domestic terrorism, 28
   Iraq, 1, 2, 7, 15, 28, 39, 60, 89, 103, 126
   in Kosovo, 25, 60, 180
   Libya, 3, 33, 55, 63
   public attitudes to, 49, 60
   reactions of Brazil, India, China, 54
   Sierra Leone, 180
   sovereignty and non-intervention, 53
   Syria (rejection of intervention), 185
Iraq, 1–2, 7, 10, 15, 27–8, 32–3, 39, 49–50, 54–6, 59–60, 64, 103, 112–17, 122, 125–6, 128, 131, 134, 172–3, 180, 211, 216, 218, 233
   Iraqi Governing Council, 116
   justification for UK involvement in conflict, 55
Isolation, isolationist, isolationism, 45, 49–52, 97, 129, 131, 177, 226

Jay, Lord Michael, of Ewelme, 144
Jenkin, Bernard, 11
Jermy, Steven, 174–5
Johnson, D., 195
Johnson, D. and Thayer, B.A., 197, 203
Joint Committee on National Security Strategy (JCNSS), 172, 180, 182–4, 187, 218
Joint Intelligence Committee, 74, 133, 184
Jung, Carl, 190

Kampfner, John, 131
Kennan, George, 147, 207
Kerr, Lord (of Kinlochard), 152
Kirkpatrick, Jeanne, 69

Knorr-Cetina, Karin, 201
Kosovo, 25, 59–60, 180, 218
Krahmann, Elke, 158, 160, 162
Kratochwil, Friedrich, 7, 42
Krepinevich, A., 206

Labour Government, 1997–2010 (foreign policy during), 13, 24–8, 39, 59, 93, 217, 227
League of Nations, 121, 123
Levene Report on Defence Reform, 182
Lewis, D., 194
liberal democracy, 27, 59
Libya, 1, 3, 33, 38, 49, 55, 60–1, 117–18, 184–5, 187
Locarno Group (2011), 152, 154

McCourt, D., 54, 67
Macmillan, Harold, 138, 216
McNamara, Robert, 121
Mali, 3, 61
Mallaby, Christopher, 143
Malloch-Brown, Lord Mark, 54
Manningham-Buller, Eliza, MI5 Director General, 94
'Mansion House speech' (Tony Blair), 131
Marx, Karl, 103–4, 106–8, 110, 112–13, 117
May, Professor Ernest, 138, 153
Merkel, Chancellor Angela, 210
Military, use of, 2–3, 10, 14–15, 18, 32–3, 36–9, 47–50, 53–6, 59–64, 66–7, 69, 71–5, 77–82, 93–8, 100, 104, 108–11, 113–14, 116–18, 121–2, 124, 126, 128, 130–3, 142, 150, 159, 172–3, 175, 177, 180, 183, 185, 189, 191, 195, 202, 206–7, 209–12, 216–17, 219–24, 233
Ministry of Defence (MOD or MoD), 33–5, 50, 93–4, 96–7, 114, 142, 164, 166, 171, 216
Moore, C., 72–3, 78–9
Morgenthau, Hans, 4, 6, 42
Murray, W. and Grimsley, M., 207
Muttit, G., 113–16

National citizenry, 96
National community, 24, 85–9, 92, 96, 99–100
National Intelligence Council (US), 122
National interest, national interests, 1–20
  academic debates, 4–9
  policy debates, 9–13
National Risk Assessment, 169, 179
National Risk Register (2008), 169, 213
National security, 10–11, 19, 28, 34, 43, 50, 86–7, 92–8, 117, 140, 145–6, 148, 150–1, 153, 155–63, 165, 169, 172, 174–5, 177, 179–80, 182, 185, 187, 205–24, 230
National Security Adviser, 153, 182
National Security Council (NSC) UK, 145, 147, 152–3, 182, 184–7, 205, 216–18, 221
National Security Council (NSC) US, 148, 152, 154
National Security Risk Assessment (NSRA), 159, 179, 187, 217, 221
National Security Secretariat, 216
National security strategy, 19, 43, 168, 182, 214–18, 218–24
  National security strategy typologies, 218–24
National Security Strategy (NSS, 2008, 2010), 11, 34, 50, 86, 95, 146, 155–6, 158–62, 169, 172, 205, 214, 230
Nation state, nation-state, 87, 104, 106, 123, 228
NATO, 19, 45, 50–1, 69, 93, 111, 117, 122, 164, 166, 210–12, 214–15, 219, 224
Neo-conservatism, (US), 32
Neo-liberalism, 105, 109, 169
New Labour, 10, 13, 25–8, 59–60, 103, 215, 227
Niebuhr, Reinhold, 6, 9
Non-citizens, ethical commitments to, 13, 23–35, 39–41, 227, 233
Nott, John, 73, 79–80, 215

Nuclear security, 166–7
Nuclear weapons, 17, 156–68
Nye, Joseph, 6, 42, 101

'Occupy' movement, 102–3, 228
'offensive liberalism' (in foreign policy), 27
Oil, 108–16, 127–8
Omand, Sir David, 155–6, 160, 162
Osborne, Chancellor George, 56, 65, 89, 91
Owen, David, 25, 76
Oxburgh, Sir Ronald, 164

Palliser, Sir Michael, 141, 145, 151
Palmerston (Lord), 4, 178
Panitch, L. and Gindin, S., 106–7
Parliamentary Committee for Public Administration, *see* Public Administration Select Committee (PASC)
Parliamentary Select Committees, role of, 146
Parsons, Sir Anthony, 70, 74–5, 77, 80, 82
pax Americana, 105
pax Britannica, 105
'Peace Dividend', 211
Perez de Cuellar, UN Secretary General Javier, 77
Pew Research Center, 203–4
'pivotal power', 97
Planning, 16–17, 19, 138–54, 157, 178–9, 181, 205–11, 220, 223–4, 231–2
Plowden, Lord, 138
Polaris, 121
Policy Planning Staff (FCO), 17, 138–9, 140–6, 147, 150
Policy Unit (FCO), 140, 145
political goals (Iraq, Afghanistan), 2, 172
Porter, Patrick, 1, 29, 98, 131, 134, 159, 175–6
Posen, Barry, 209
pragmatism, pragmatic foreign policy, 23, 29, 33, 97, 140, 232
PRISM, 209
Psychology, 18–19, 194–6, 198, 203–4

Public Administration Select Committee (PASC), 42, 87, 146, 171, 233
Public interest, 7, 12, 106, 192, 233
Public opinion (British), 2–3, 29, 46, 87, 188–9, 209, 211–12
Public Service Agreements, 125
Pym, Francis, 72–3, 77–80

Rapoport, D.C., 196
Reagan, President Ronald, 69, 73, 78, 82, 166, 169
'realist' (school), 4–5, 179, 194
'recentism', 139, 232
Referendum on Scottish independence, 1, 183, 204, 226
Reicher, S.D. and Hopkins, N., 191
Resilience, 17, 155–69, 182, 227
'Resilient Nation', 87, 155, 165–6
Responsibility to Protect (R2P), 34, 126
Ricketts, Sir Peter, 185, 187
Rifkind, Malcolm, 215
Rising powers, 3, 61–2
  attitudes to sovereignty, 54
  implications for British policy, 43, 54
Risk assessment, 158–9, 169, 179–80, 187, 205–6, 213–14, 217, 220–1, 231
Robinson, Mary, 188
Robinson, Paul, 98, 106, 222
Robinson, W., 106, 113
Role theory, 9, 14, 43, 44–8, 63, 226
Rosenau, James, 6, 46
Rule of law, 14, 26, 29, 31, 48, 53–6, 57, 64, 123–5, 143

Sandys, Duncan, 215
Schelling, T.C., 168, 188, 196–7, 212
Schleifer, A.P. and Treisman, D., 194
Schweller, R., 212
Security, 2, 6, 10–12, 15, 17–19, 27–32, 34–5, 39, 42–3, 50–2, 55–6, 58, 61, 65, 70–1, 83, 86–8, 92–101, 111–12, 114, 117–18, 124, 126–7, 134, 138–9, 145–8, 150–1, 153, 155–70, 171–87, 205–25, 227–8, 230

Security Council (UN), 55–6, 65, 70, 77, 134
Security imperatives, 2
self-interest, 3, 6, 8–9, 12, 16, 39, 47, 58, 93, 97, 100, 191
Short, Claire, 10
'short-termism', 138, 182, 232
Simon, Herbert, 46, 199
Skybolt, 121
Smith, Adam, 105
Smith, Steve, 6, 48
Snowden, Edward, 145
Sovereignty, 8, 14, 28–9, 35, 54–5, 57, 60–1, 67–73, 76–7, 79, 126, 130, 132, 226
Special relationship, 16, 76, 120–2, 123, 127, 129, 131, 134, 227
State Department (US), 108, 147–51, 232
Status of Forces Agreement abandoned (US-Iraq), 116
Stokes, D., 107, 109
Strachan, H., 1, 7, 11, 50, 137, 146–7, 171–4, 178, 220
Strategic Defence Review (SDR, 1998), 48, 50, 93, 180, 215
Strategic Defence and Security Review (SDSR, 2010), 11, 18, 32, 50, 99, 155–6, 160, 165–6, 171, 205, 230
Strategy, 2, 11–14, 16–19, 33–4, 36, 38, 42–3, 50, 54, 58, 63, 78, 86, 95, 99, 107–8, 111, 133, 135–54, 156–70, 171–87, 204, 221–34
Straw, Jack, 26, 52, 64
Syria, 1, 3, 33, 56, 58, 64–5, 117–18, 122, 177, 185, 187, 189

Taylor, M. and Currie, M., 199
Territorial integrity, 4–5, 28, 35, 82, 86–7, 226
Thatcher, Prime Minister Margaret, 10, 66–82, 143–4
'thinking in time', 137–8
'Third Way', 108
Tickell, Sir Crispin, 141, 154

transparency (of decision-making process), 233
Trident Alternatives Review (2013), 156, 165
Trivers, R., 193

UAE, United Arab Emirates, 118
UK relationship with the US, 3
  see also 'special relationbship'
UK-US Joint Strategy Board, 99
Uncertainty (in international relations), 96, 146, 158, 160, 162, 165, 171, 174–7, 178, 186, 203, 207–10, 213–14, 222, 231
'universal human values', 108
UN, United Nations, 47, 51, 54–9, 61, 63, 65, 67, 69–71, 74, 77–8, 82, 96, 101, 123, 125, 126, 128, 134
USSR, Soviet Union, Russia, 5, 10, 50, 55–6, 70, 108, 111, 113, 141, 143, 164, 169, 194, 210, 226
US, USA, United States, 5–6, 11, 12, 15–17, 46–8, 52, 56, 64, 67, 70–2, 77, 82, 89, 93, 98–9, 106–1, 138, 147–54, 160, 164, 166–7, 169–70, 180, 187, 189, 207, 210–12, 216–17, 219, 224, 227, 232–3
  approach to strategy, 19, 23, 29
  Falklands War, 69–70, 76
  neo-conservatism, 32
  'pivot to Asia', 50
  'special relationship' with the UK, 3, 16, 60, 120–36

Values, 3, 6, 10, 12–13, 23, 24–36, 38, 40–2, 45, 47, 67, 86, 88, 97–8, 102, 122, 133, 137, 144–5, 173, 208, 226–7, 230, 233
Values-based approach, 18
Values-interests merger, 13, 23–5, 27, 31, 35
Versailles Peace Conference (1919), 123, 125

Wade-Gery, Sir Robert, 141–2
Wallace, Helen, 142
'wars of choice', 2
'war on terror', 15, 25, 39, 88, 93–6, 98, 102, 227–8
'Washington Consensus', 102, 108
'way of life' (preservation of), 15, 86, 91–2, 95, 129, 207
Weinburger, Caspar, 69
Weldes, Jutta, 6, 24, 42, 87, 157
Wendt, Alexander, 8, 12, 101, 209
Westphalian system, 126
Wheeler, Nicholas and Dunne, Tim, 10, 97
Williams, Michael C., 93
Williams, Paul, 25, 41
Williams, Rear Admiral Simon, 7, 12
Wish, Naomi, 44
Wolfers, Arnold, 6, 86
Wood, E.M., 106
World Bank, 35, 55, 115
WTO, World Trade Organization, 55, 102

Yarger, Harry, 175–6
YouGov, 29, 60, 65

Printed and bound by CPI Group (UK) Ltd, Croydon, CR0 4YY